HOW TO WRECK A NICE BEACH

How to Wreck a Nice Beach
The Vocoder from World War II to Hip-Hop
The Machine Speaks

© 2010 Dave Tompkins
First Melville House printing: March 2010

Melville House Publishing
145 Plymouth Street
Brooklyn, NY 11201

Stop Smiling Media
1371 N. Milwaukee Avenue
Chicago, IL 60622

www.stopsmilingbooks.com
www.mhpbooks.com

ISBN: 978-1-933633-88-6

Editor: James Hughes
Book design: Tina Ibañez, Runner Collective

Cover Photograph by Michael Waring
Illustrations by Kevin Christy

Printed in the United States of America

Library of Congress Cataloging-in-Publication Data

Tompkins, Dave.
How to wreck a nice beach :
the vocoder from World War II to hip-hop :
the machine speaks / Dave Tompkins.
p. cm.
Includes bibliographical references and index.
ISBN 978-1-933633-88-6 (alk. paper)
1.Electronic music—History and criticism. 2. Vocoder. I. Title.
ML1380.T66 2010
621.382'24—dc22

2009050617

HOW TO WRECK A NICE BEACH

THE VOCODER FROM WORLD WAR II TO HIP-HOP

THE MACHINE SPEAKS

DAVE TOMPKINS

MELVILLEHOUSE
BROOKLYN, NEW YORK

STOPSMILING *books*
CHICAGO, ILLINOIS

TABLE OF CONTENTS

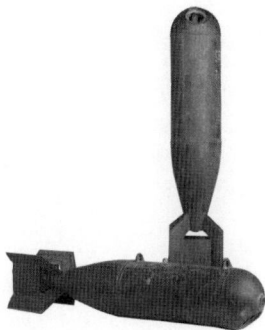

THE KORG VC-10 VOCODER came with its own ensemble switch and accent bender. It was used by the author for *How to Wreck a Nice Beach*, as well as anyone who wanted a leaf blower to sing the chorus.

IN ONE WORD, MILITARISM WAS FUNK.
— H.G. WELLS

HOW TO WRECK A NICE BEACH

AXIS OF EAVESDROPPERS

I have been bugged all my life.
— Vyacheslav "Iron Arse" Molotov, Soviet Minister of Foreign Affairs, 1955

Theoretical security was not absolute like the records.
— Ralph Miller, Bell Labs

We are clear.

It's quiet inside the Black National Theater, just above 125th Street in Harlem. Afrika Bambaataa is sitting on a defeated couch, flipping through a brochure published by the National Security Agency. He wears black sweats and fluorescent green running shoes, and there's a trainer's towel around his neck. The Thunderdome spikes, leather cape, and Martian sun dimmers have been left at home. He seems to be giving his myth the day off, looking more like a gym coach with allergies than the retired gang warlord who once borrowed his mom's records, stuck a speaker in the window and blew out the neighborhood.

Our conversation arrived at the NSA through the normal discursive channels: an old record Bam made that doesn't exist, an admiration for a British vampire soap opera, a childhood memory of sneaking to the front row to watch Sly Stone "make his instruments talk." Yet when discussing the NSA, he drops his voice into a cautious strep basso. If anything can modulate the way we speak, it's the notion of some federal protuberance listening in.

The brochure in his hands is pink and its title is not for the sore of throat. *The Start of the Digital Revolution: SIGSALY Secure Digital Voice Communications in World War II*. Bambaataa grunts and jots this down on a borrowed scrap of paper. On the cover is a dual turntable console photographed behind a nameless door in the basement of the Pentagon. Surrounding the turntables are banks of winking electronics, as if the walls are putting us on, spoofing a future that's one set of pointy ears from campy. Taken in 1944, the photo, along with the future, would not be declassified until 1976. Bambaataa is curious, having spent 1976 DJing some of the better parties in New York. By 1981, he was making people dance to German records that spoke Japanese in voices programmed by Texas Instruments.

The Pentagon turntables are now sitting at the bottom of the Chesapeake Bay. These machines were designed by Bell Labs but created by funk, back when funk meant fear, German transmitters and codebreakers under headphones. The turntables played 16-inch records of thermal noise in reverse, a randomized shush, backwards masked inside out.

Produced by the Muzak Corporation, the vinyl was deployed for the army's "Secret Telephony" voice security system, a technology that was treated with the same crypto fuss as the Manhattan Project. Installed across the globe from 1943 to 1945, these fifty-five ton phone scramblers would be used for D-Day, the Allied invasion of Germany, the bombing of Hiroshima, and the "dismemberment of the surrender instrument"—allowing Roosevelt, Truman, Churchill and Eisenhower to discuss the world's fate with voices they barely recognized, voices not human but polite artificial replicas of speech rendered from digital pulses 20 milliseconds in length.

The wall of knobs assigned this task was the vocoder, a massive walk-in closet of cryptology invented by Bell Labs in 1928. The vocoder divided the voice into its constituent frequencies, spread across ten channels, and transmitted them through band pass filters. At the receiving end, this information would be synthesized into an electronic impression of human speech: a machine's idea of the voice as imagined by phonetic engineers. Not speech, they qualified, but a "spectral description of it."

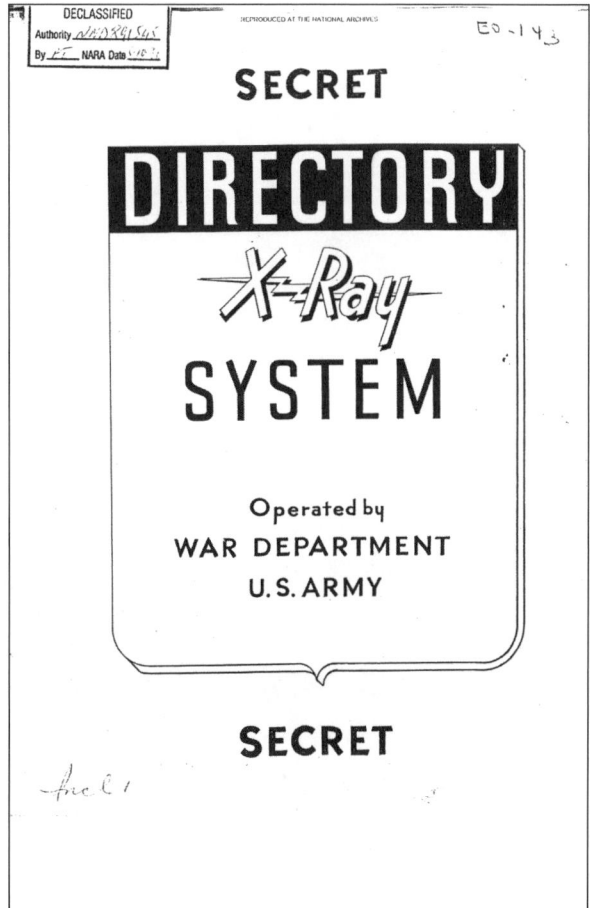

SECRET

DIRECTORY
~~X-Ray~~
SYSTEM

Operated by
**WAR DEPARTMENT
U.S. ARMY**

SECRET

The vocoder was sensitive, high maintenance and seven feet tall, an overheated room full of capacitors, vacuum tubes and transformers. Some engineers dubbed this system "the Green Hornet." Others called it "Special Customer." Bell Labs referred to it as Project X-61753, or "X-Ray," as if it was ordered from the back of a comic book with a pair of rubber Mad Doctor Hands. The U.S. Signal Corps called it SIGSALY, taken from children's "nonsense syllables" and used for strategizing Allied bombing campaigns. The *New York Times*, not knowing what to

ABOVE: Directory of personnel authorized to use SIGSALY, referred to here as X-Ray.

PAGE 16: The SIGSALY Guam Terminal, codename NEPTUNE, with vocoder walls and turntables (left), photographed in 1945. Logistics concerning the atomic bomb missions and plans for the invasion of Japan were discussed over this secret radiotelephone link. (Courtesy National Archives/ NSAz/ Mahlon Doyle)

call it, went with "Machine that Tears Speech to Pieces," and then later, like most everybody else, decided on "the robot."

To a DJ like Bambaataa, the vocoder is "deep crazy supernatural bugged-out funk stuff," perhaps the only crypto-technology to serve the Pentagon and the roller rink. What guarded Winston Churchill's phone against Teutonic math nerds would one day become the perky teabot that chimed in on Michael Jackson's "P.Y.T." During World War II, the vocoder reduced the voice to something cold and tactical, tinny and dry like soup cans in a sandbox, dehumanizing the larynx, so to speak, for some of man's more dehumanizing moments: Hiroshima, the Cuban Missile Crisis, Soviet gulags, Vietnam. Churchill had it, FDR refused it, Hitler needed it. Kennedy was frustrated by the vocoder. Mamie Eisenhower used it to tell her husband to come home. Nixon had one in his limo. Reagan, on his plane. Stalin, on his disintegrating mind.

The Seventies would finally catch the vocoder in its double life: secret masking agent for the military and studio tool for the musician. The machine that subtracted the character from the voices of Army echelons would ultimately generate characters in itself—the one-man chorus of be all you can be. Never mind the robots: what's more human than wanting to be *something else*, *altogether*? Ever since the first bored kid threw his voice into an electric fan, toked on a birthday balloon or thanked his mother in a pronounced burp, voice mutation has provided an infinite source of kicks. In 1971, that first kick was delivered to the ribs of anyone who saw Stanley Kubrick's *A Clockwork Orange*. In its big-screen debut, the vocoder sang Beethoven's Ninth to Dresden firebombings while rehabilitating a murderer who wore eyeballs for cufflinks. It was quite an association.

Soon the vocoder began showing up on records, reciting Edgar Allan Poe and making sheep bleats. If a string section could be replaced by the synthesizer, then why not the voice? The vocoder thanked you very much in Japanese. It allowed Bee Gees to be Beatles. It just called to say it loved you. It allowed people to give themselves names like Zeus B. Held, Gay Cat Park and Ramsey 2C-3D. It could sound like an articulate bag of dead leaves. A croak, a last willed gasp. A sink clog trying to find the words. Or the InSinkErator itself, with its wiggly, butterknife

CLOCKWISE FROM TOP

Brooklyn's Cut Master DC (far left), the Man Who Scratched Records With Basketballs. Photographed at the New Music Seminar, Manhattan, circa 1989, along with Just-Ice, Grandmaster Caz, King Sun, Steady B and the late Dave Funkenklein (center). (Courtesy Chris LaSalle and Dave Funkenklein)

Project Future *Ray-Gun-Omics* (released in 1984, Capitol Records)

Ramsey 2C-3D, *Fly Guy And The Unemployed* (1983, Tears Of Fire). "D.C. is into space/D.C. don't care about the human race." This disco recession 12 inch from California suggested that Reagan's policies were out to lunch.

Afrika Bambaataa on 8/17/82 in Chicago, IL. (Photo by Paul Natkin/WireImage)

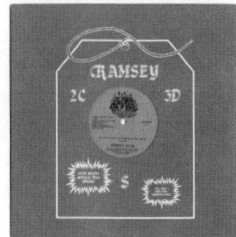

smile. In Neil Young's case, it was a father trying to empathize with his son who suffered from cerebral palsy. Or it could've just been a bad idea—as I've been told, *something that punished the atmosphere.*

Shadowing the World War II model, the vocoder would have its own Axis powers: Kraftwerk (Germany), Giorgio Moroder and Italo-Disco (Italy), and Bambaataa's Roland SVC-350 Vocoder (Made in Japan). In 1976, when SIGSALY was sufficiently dated to be declassified and allowed in public, the vocoder was already well out in the open, nodding along in Kraftwerk's daydream stretch of imagination called "Autobahn." Before the Age of Scratching Records with Basketballs, Bambaataa and his Zulu Nation DJs would use more gathered German intelligence (Kraftwerk's "Trans-Europe Express") to make people dance, buy synthesizers, steal ideas, make more records, and dress like the Count of Monte Cristo. Countless electro and disco 12-inch singles owe their dance floors to the Machine that Tore Speech to Pieces. In the early Eighties, a romance better remembered than relived, the vocoder was the main machine of electro hip-hop, the black voice removed from itself, dispossessed by Reaganomics, recession and urban renewal, and escaping to outer space where there was more room to do the Webbo, where the weight was taken but the odds of being heard were no less favorable.

As the vocoder disbanded and digitized conversations in Washington, commercially available models were all over the radio, rapping ills and blight while generating the cosmically Keytarded fantasies needed to cope with it all. The vocoder would be used in songs about safety, Raisin Bran, taxes, and black holes. Pods and poverty. A dance called "the Toilet Bowl." Christmas in Miami and deep throats in Dallas. Nuclear war, biters in the city, and the Muslim soul. Saving the children and freaking the freaks.

The ups and downs of robot relations.

Though the military had originally wanted the vocoder to sound human, the Germans didn't (calling it a "retro-transformer" as early as 1951) and somehow Afrika Bambaataa ended up with the keys to the robot. He calls the vocoder "that Joker." "I couldn't wait to get on that Joker," he says. "We used to bring it to parties and funk 'em up with it. Stop the turntables and I talk on that Joker. People were hearing the robot voice from the records, but the records weren't playing. They didn't know what was going on."

A man who wanted to use the vocoder to destroy all Pac-Man machines once said to me, "People gotta like what's going on even if they don't know what's going on." And they did and they didn't.

Of all the World War II cryptology experts I interviewed, none were aware of the vocoder's activities in the clubs, rinks and parks of New York City. ("It was just analyzing breakdowns of speech energy," said the Pentagon.) Of all the hip-hop civilians I interviewed, none was aware of the vocoder's service in any war, nor were they surprised by it.

And none were aware that vocoder technology now inhabits our cell phones as a microscopic speck of silicone, allowing our laryngeal clones to sound more human, condensing the signal for more bandwidth at the expense of intelligibility in a shrinking world. The vocoder was originally invented for speech compression, to reduce bandwidth costs on undersea phone cables—the ultimate long-distance package. Now compression is back. The voices from the tower are not our own, but digital simulacra, imperfect to be real. Conversations are minutes gobbled, and songs are ringtones chirping a T-Pain hook. Auto-Tune, the pitch-correcting software popularized by the robotox of Cher and inflicted on the twenty-first century, is often misheard as a vocoder, giving the latter currency through a revival of misunderstanding. Not as a technology, but a meme. In other words, it was what it isn't.

When I mentioned this to Bambaataa, he nodded and said, "Yeahhh." If conspiracy is your baggage, this is not unlike the way he says "Yeahhh" at the beginning of "Planet Rock," a song he recorded with the Soulsonic Force in 1982, the same year *Time* magazine replaced its Man of the Year with a computer. Stocking dance floors for the past twenty-eight years, "Planet Rock" is the first hip-hop song to say "shucks," vacuuming the sibilance, universally recognized as the white noise of secrecy. Over at Bell Labs, "shh" is called unvoiced fricatives, or "unvoiced hiss energy," pulmonary turbulence modulated by tongue, teeth and lips.

"That's bugged," says Bam, who often speaks in terms of sound effects, as if waiting for the right word to show up. It may be a while, so "bugged" will do. Though much of Bam's memory belongs to a record collection that defies mini-storage, you can always count on "bugged," a hip-hop jargonaut that has survived for over two decades, its etymology based on the act of going out of one's head through one's eyes while attended by invisible (and apparently very busy) insects under one's skin. When eyes "bug out" from their sockets, doctors call it globe luxation. Despite its provenance in pre-Industrial sanitariums, bugging out entered military argot around the time of the Korean War, referring to US soldiers in a state of bullet-hastened egress. (Retreat was less a matter of going crazy than coming to one's senses.) Yet losing one's mind never goes out of style, and hip-hop, ever reinventing the tongue, would replace "mad" with "bugged," converting the former into a quantitative adverb, as if rightfully assuming everyone is insane.

So crazy became bugged, the bugged picked up the vocoder, rappers went under surveillance, and we listened very carefully, under headphones.

+ + +

Bam continues chuckling through the NSA brochure, the towel now over his head. He hits a circuit diagram and doubles back to the Pentagon, the glowing basement and the turntables. The room looks busy yet unoccupied. He wonders where they stuck that joker. Perhaps somewhere near the world's most accurate clock. Or next to the Sumo air conditioner that kept the entire system from melting down. Or maybe behind the oven that stabilized the crystals that kept the turntables in synch 10,000 miles apart. Those capacitors have some explaining to do.

By 1943, there were two turntables and a vocoder in the Pentagon and a duplicate system in the basement of a department store in London. As the war machine kept turning, vocoders and turntables would be installed in Paris, Brisbane, Manila, Frankfurt, Berlin, Guam, Tokyo, Oakland.

Oakland?

Signal Corps officers on the turntables at the SIGSALY Paris Terminal, code name SAMPLE, circa 1944. The records played throughout vocoded conversations to ensure voice security. SIGSALY was the first transmission of digital speech. (Courtesy National Archives)

Another one, on a barge that tailed General Douglas MacArthur around the Philippines. And another, under a mountain in Hawaii. If a satellite zoomed in on the northern bump of the African Zulu medallion hanging from Bambaataa's neck, one could see General Eisenhower checking out two turntables and a vocoder in a wine cellar in Algiers.

In the fall of 1983, the Zulu Nation funk sign began appearing on my spiral notebooks, its index and pinkie horns shooting lasers at whatever subject crossed its path. "Shazulu" became the code for "Latin Vocabulary Homework" which I did for a seventh-grade classmate in exchange for vocoder record money. (He would whisper over his shoulder from the desk in front of me: "You got that shazulu?") I would then launder the cash through Shazada Records in downtown Charlotte, North Carolina.

The Pentagon vinyl was far more rare, guarded with life but destroyed by protocol once the needle lifted. Bambaataa wonders if any of it survived. This was a world where turntables were controlled by clocks, not people. Where privacy was distinct from secrecy and a digit was referred to as a "higit." Where torpedoes were equipped with 500-watt speakers and records played thermal noise backwards behind nameless doors. Where speech must be "indestructible" and the voice wouldn't recognize itself from hello. So it's not unreasonable to think that turntables and vocoders once kept the snoops out of Churchill's whiskey diction.

Bam, often just headphones away from some version of deep space, is not surprised, having once named an album *Warlocks and Witches, Computer Chips, Microchips, and You*, his old playlists being a conspiracy theory themselves. To him, it's William Burroughs, Gary Numan and Vincent Price who are the real vocoders. In a sense, everything is bugged.

Bam mutters something about "Leviathan" and scans through the NSA appendix. There's a transcript of Bell Labs President O.E. Buckley speaking through a vocoder in Pentagon Room 3D-923, July 1943, when Special Customer was first activated:

We are assembled here today to open a new service—Secret Telephony. ... Speech has been converted into low-frequency signals that are not speech but contain a description of it. ... Signals have been decoded and restored and then used to regenerate speech nearly enough like that which gave them birth. ... Speech transmitted in this matter sounds somewhat unnatural.

Bambaataa descrambles a frog in his throat, a matter of clearance in itself. *Somewhat.*

"We hope that it will be a help in the prosecution of the war," said O.E., signing off.

And so we bug.

BOOK ONE

CHAPTER ONE

NEARLY ENOUGH LIKE THAT WHICH GAVE THEM BIRTH

The time for the robots had come. So they got busy.

— Carol Greene, *The New True Book of Robots*

O MOM AND DAD

A man from AT&T has pulled Ray Bradbury's lucky ping-pong ball out of a barrel. The loudmouth in glasses just won a free long-distance call to anywhere in the United States but Queens. He'll be speaking with his parents in Los Angeles and three hundred strangers will be allowed to eavesdrop—a boast of reach and clarity, courtesy of the phone company. This deprivation of privacy doesn't concern Bradbury, the know-it-all at eighteen.

AT&T's complimentary scheme was a huge draw at the World's Fair in Flushing Meadows, New York. Free long distance was good in July of 1939. Free was good for Ray Bradbury, who had hot water and ketchup for lunch, called it tomato soup and didn't care because he'd met Isaac Asimov and a man who drew giant ants.

That summer, the World's Fair was an optimistic golly between the Great Depression and World War II. Apprehension was confused with giddiness, as Hitler had already invaded Czechoslovakia before the Czechoslovakian pavilion was even completed. By the Fair's second season, France had fallen and the queue into the Perisphere, snap-brimmed and scarved, could've been boarding the next planet out of here. When the Fair closed, in October 1940, the World of Tomorrow was dismantled and the scrap metal skipped the modern kitchen to be recycled for the war machine.

This future would be quickly assessed in "Galactic Report Card," a story in which aliens went around grading the planets. Written by Bradbury's friend Forrest J. Ackerman, the story is approximately one letter in length—Earth is handed a decisive "F." Ackerman shared Bradbury's weakness for abominable puns and paid for the bus trip from Los Angeles so the author of "Don't Get Technatal" could join him at the first annual World Science Fiction Convention in Manhattan. Afterward they would go to Flushing to see how the Fair sized up against their full-blown imaginations, less interested in the canary that tested refrigerants at the GM building than Dalí's topless squid ladies.

"Anybody out there?" People were allowed to eavesdrop on Ray Bradbury's free phone conversation at AT&T's Long Distance Exhibit at the 1939 World's Fair in New York. (Courtesy AT&T Archives and History Center)

The future would be like this: a drunk passed out in a simulated front yard. There were miniature freeways and manmade lightning. Model homes and model cities. Artifice was in. At the Firestone Farm, men in headsets triggered barnyard noises. Oinks, ribbits, lows, clucks and grunts. Yawps, quacks, chirps and peeps. Chimp hysterics. Birdtalk. The real animals weren't really into it. The real monkeys got sick and the real ducks ate most of the real frogs.

Setting new standards for nerding out, Ackerman wore a space toga and spoke Esperanto. He told people he was a time traveler from the future, a future where he would star in *Nudist Colony of the Dead*, coin the term "Sci Fi," and become L. Ron Hubbard's literary agent. Bradbury, the street corner paperboy, wandered the paved swamps of Queens hyping Fritz Lang's *Metropolis*, a film in which Germany out-futured the Fair in just under two hours, and without sound. Unlike *Metropolis*, the Fair offered no robot beauty. Just Elektro, an eight-foot clunker that could smoke cigarettes and hiccup. Canned and recorded at 78 rpm, his human voice betrayed the novelty.

"The robots weren't exciting," Bradbury told me over the phone from Los Angeles. "But the architecture was. I never much cared for robots. The robot was an idiot."

AS IF TO SAY

You flower of untimeliness, you rabbit of dark rooms! Your voice is our hereafter, and it has crowded out heaven!
— Arnolt Bronnen, addressing the telephone, 1926

My call to Ray Bradbury lasted twenty-seven minutes, cost about $10 and informed me that the eighty-five-year-old author would always take the stegosaurus over the robot. We talked about synthetic mice that cleaned houses and laughed at Albert Brock, a man driven insane by his telephone. "The phone drained your personality away until what slipped through at the other end was some cold fish of a voice, all steel, copper, plastic, no warmth, no reality." That's Brock's voice in Bradbury's words, from a 1953 story called "The Murderer." To Mr. Brock, *get the phone* meant feeding it to the InSinkErator. "It wasn't the technology," says Bradbury. "It was the voices. Albert Brock was anti-interference!"

Though the phone often gets the blame, people in the gaslight era weren't accustomed to receiving speech from inanimate objects, unless it was Edison's phonograph (billed as a talking machine itself), but certainly not a tube that originated from a vibrating pig bladder and platinum. In 1876, the pinhole gulf between voice and voice box would expand, infamously, when Brazil's Emperor Dom Pedro received his first phone call and, in a confused burst, exclaimed: "My God! It talks!"

Always in the market for a confused burst, Bell Labs would name its articulate keyboard "Pedro" when it was introduced at the World's Fair in 1939, in both New York and San Francisco. ("Facsimile

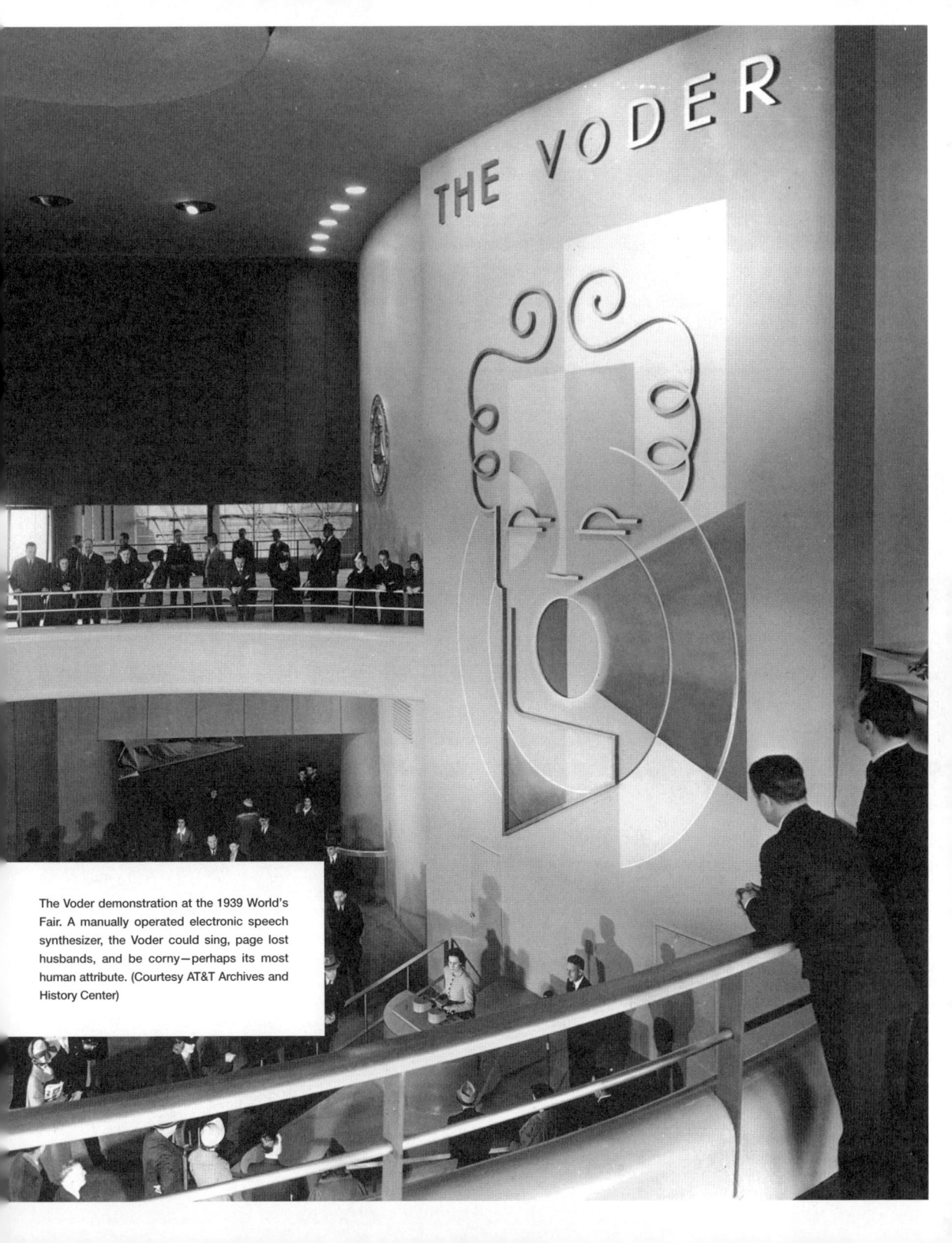

THE VODER

The Voder demonstration at the 1939 World's Fair. A manually operated electronic speech synthesizer, the Voder could sing, page lost husbands, and be corny—perhaps its most human attribute. (Courtesy AT&T Archives and History Center)

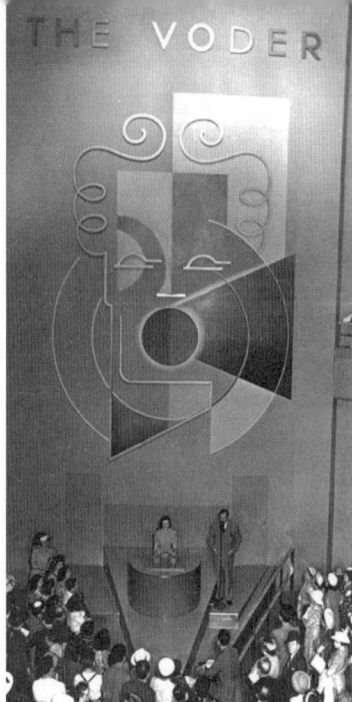

Crowd bugging out on the Voder at the 1939
World's Fair, New York. (Courtesy AT&T Archives
and History Center)

NEARLY ENOUGH LIKE THAT WHICH GAVE THEM BIRTH

Versus the Code Philosophy in the Transmission of Speech" cost too much oxygen.) Officially, Pedro was a Voice Operating DEmonstratoR, or Voder, a keyboard that simulated speech while alienating the voice from its mechanism, the human body. The Voder was a novelty outgrowth of the vocoder, then being investigated for speech privacy systems, described by the *Hopewell Herald* as "Goldarnedest… the Versatile Daddy."

Played by telephone operators, the Voder's chubby keys provided the phonetic transcription of consonants and vowels while foot pedals dictated the tonal shading and pitch. Speech was sourced from two basic oscillations: buzz and hiss. The buzz—which originated in a "relaxation oscillator"—accounted for voiced sounds (vowels and vibrations). The hiss derived from an electron free-for-all in a vacuum tube and was responsible for unvoiced sounds, breath flushed from the lungs through the teeth, lips and tongue. The air was in the electricity.

In an attempt to put a face to the voice, AT&T commissioned a painting for its awkward star, somewhere between Art Deco and Dilbert-headed, with a receding Ludwiggian brow offset by golden squiggles of phone cord (hair) and a loudspeaker stuffed in its astonished rabbit hole.

The media response to the Voder ranged from droll ("the talking wall") to freak-show hysteria ("The Terrifying Metal Man"). Its most human quality wasn't so much the ability to talk and sing but an instinct for corny banter, thus making it a huge draw at the Fair. The machine could answer simple questions and chat up the Firestone Farm. It could drawl. It could twang. It could page lost husbands. It could say "non-intercommunicability." It could mimic a woodpecker headbutting a telephone pole. It tried to put a baby to sleep but couldn't say "lullaby." (Double *l*'s were difficult and *hell* was out of the question.) When presented with larger freight like "potentiometer," the Voder stumbled groggily, like a darted bear. When one inebriated customer dared the machine to say, "Aberystwyth," the Voder seemed to mock the word, testing the bounds of elasticity. A visiting class of blind schoolchildren was utterly charmed.

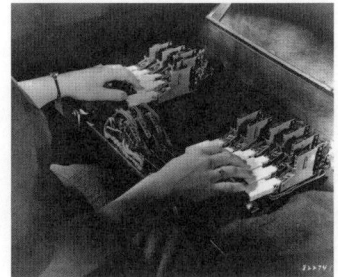

According to Bell Labs, the Voder required a "peculiar combination of particular talents which are not too common." Telephone operators trained a year to make the machine coherent and sometimes wore translucent sleeve protectors called "Cuff-Ettes." (Courtesy AT&T Archives and History Center)

(Courtesy AT&T Archives and History Center)

For all its gimmickry, the Voder was difficult to manage, a male persona played by women, whose voices were considered too high-pitched to be recognized by the vocoder itself. Only trained telephone operators, the disembodied voices of the switchboard, had the hand-ear coordination to give the machine the social skills to work the room, a sort of remedial Speak & Spell. A simple phrase ("I am not wearing a bear suit") called for deft key and foot-pedal movements. Intelligibility proved to be a challenge when machines weren't expected to speak in the first place, much less respond in Latin.

During its developmental stages at Bell Labs, the Voder would often club its syllables with an involuntary *whoomp* and *zizz*. At one point, a simple "yes" was transmuted into the word "peanuts," no less muddled than Charlie Brown's PTA.

"It's a wonder that the Voder could talk at all," wrote its inventor, Homer Dudley, in the *Bell Technical Journal*. Homer's daughter, twelve-year-old Jean, was not impressed. "Oh-ah-eh," she says, in the key of blah-blah, now living in upstate New York. "The Voder was boring." Jean and her younger sister Pat had come to the World's Fair to play in the Perisphere and eat the free cheese from Holland. "I wanted the Voder to sound like a real person. I enjoyed it the first ten times but then it got tedious. What impressed me was my father got us in for free."

FOR ILIAD D'OH

Open the door, Homer.
— Bob Dylan

Homie, please open the door!
— Marge Simpson

Homer W. Dudley invented the vocoder when he realized his mouth was a radio station while flat on his back in a Manhattan hospital bed, eyes on the ceiling, a goldfish as his witness. It was October 1928, a year before the stock market fell on its head. The end of the Era of Wonderful Nonsense. Germany had electromagnetic tape. Bell Labs, the research division of AT&T, had already broadcast Herbert Hoover's forehead on a televised signal. They had also sent a fax, invented negative feedback, and coined Quality Assurance—the nebulous back-pat of automated speech recognition menus, less assurance than a promise that someone in a building without windows was eavesdropping.

The radio inside Dudley's mouth was no whim of dental conductivity, falling for that old hygienist's tale about catching baseball games in cavity fillings. He was considering the carrier nature of speech and the frequency of muscular vibrations produced by the vocal tract. Ralph LaRue Miller, who joined Dudley in the Bell Labs Acoustics Research Department in 1929, remembers the story. "Homer was in the hospital, gazing at the ceiling and fiddling around with his mouth—that's when the real dawn came. He suddenly realized, well, I don't know if it was sudden or not, but he realized that your mouth really is a miniature radio station. The vocal cords are your transmitter and the shape of your mouth is the thing that shapes the wave. He realized that the motions of your mouth and tongue were very slow, much slower than the frequencies that came out."

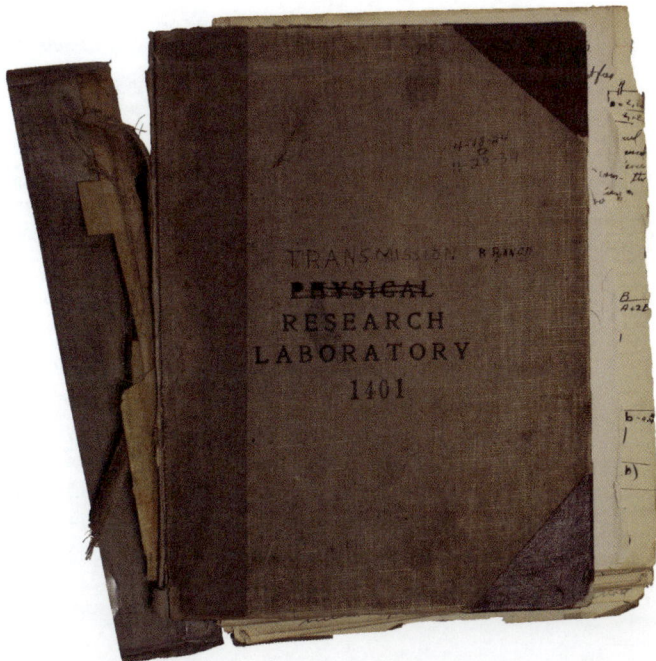

Dudley, a thirty-two-year-old speech engineer from the Shenandoah Valley, just wanted to transmit speech underwater. With new improvements on the transatlantic cable—rumored to have suffered a Kraken attack during its construction on the ocean floor in 1866—it was then possible to cram more telephone conversations within a given bandwidth. Dudley thought the articulatory motions of the tongue, lips and mouth could be electronically mimicked, being far more sluggish and lower in frequency than the speech sounds they produced. Thus a "specification" of speech—its spectral information—could be transmitted over transatlantic links, allowing ten phone channels to occupy the space of one. Though Dudley imagined his robot in every American home, the reduced bandwidth was canceled by the cost and the garble, as well as space hogged by the machine itself—as if every American home could have its own vocoder room.

THIS PAGE: Homer Dudley's lab notebook from 1928, with *Physical* replaced by *Transmission*. Includes "Results from the Artificial Head." (Courtesy AT&T Archives and History Center)

OPPOSITE PAGE: Homer Dudley plays the Voder in 1978. Dudley thought the Voder could be used to "point out a moral from a telephonic viewpoint." (Courtesy AT&T Archives and History Center)

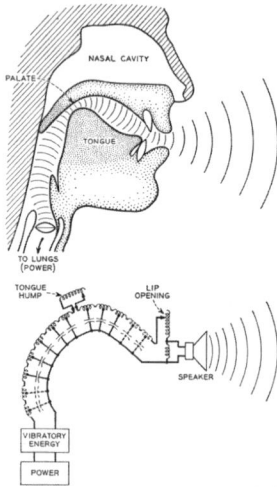

Bell Labs vocoder schematic. In his patent 2,243,089 (System for the Artificial Production of Vocal or Other Sounds), Homer Dudley described the "effect of a giant or large animal talking under control of human speech." (Courtesy AT&T Archives and History Center)

+ + +

Homer Dudley explained the vocoder to his children in terms of breakfast: scrambling eggs and then basically re-chickening them. "The vocoder took the sound and breath patterns of Pedro's technology," his daughter Jean told me by phone. "It took a coded message, broke it up like scrambled eggs and reassembled it in a different order and sent it. The vocoder on the receiving end broke them up again and reassembled [the message] in the right order, like acrostics or something."

Bell Labs described the vocoder in terms of analysis and synthesis. It divided voice frequencies into ten bands at 300 hertz each, one-tenth of the bandwidth required for phone conversations at the time. Each filter measured the voltage required for its speech frequency range. This information was low-pass filtered at 25 hertz and transmitted to the receiving end, which determined a fundamental pitch frequency (in the eleventh channel) and an unvoiced noise signal to synthesize the voice. Bell Labs favored *synthesize* over *reconstruct* because the latter implied flawless duplication.

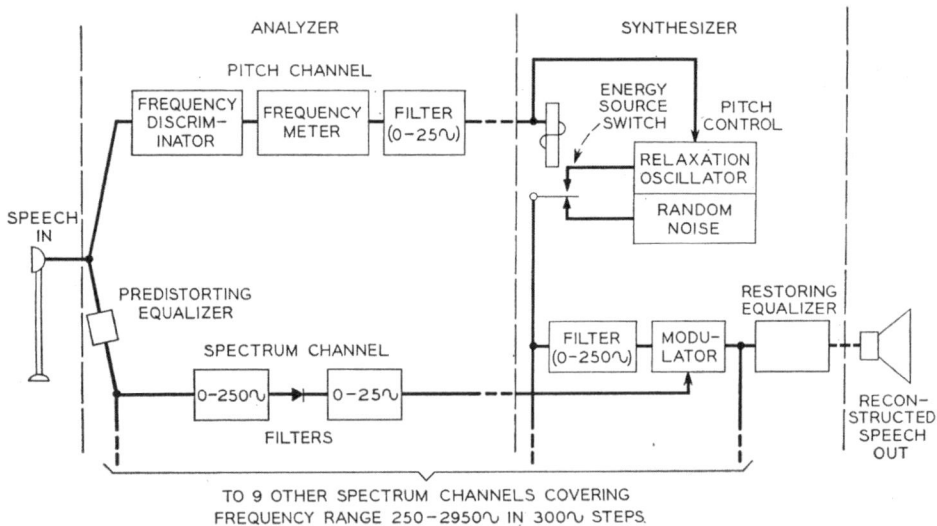

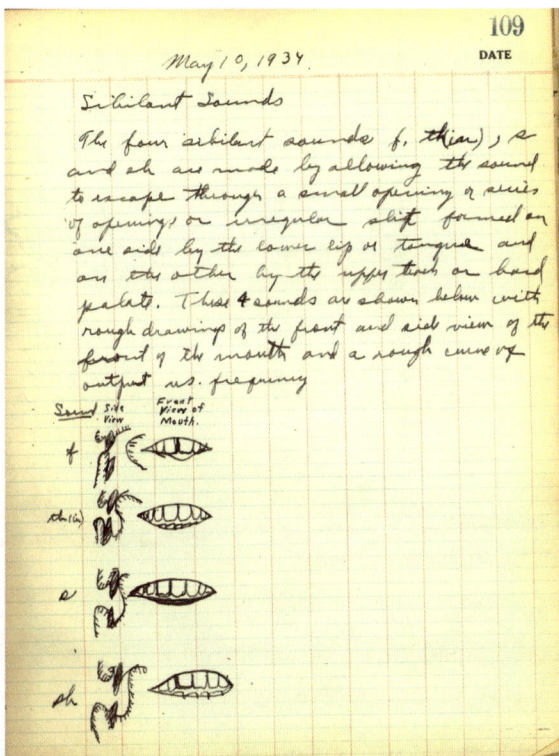

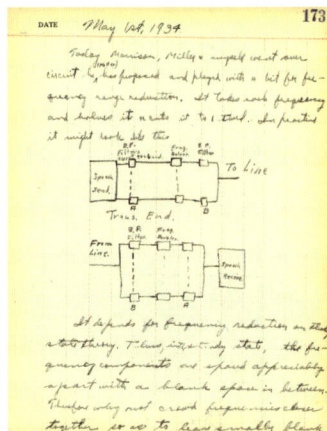

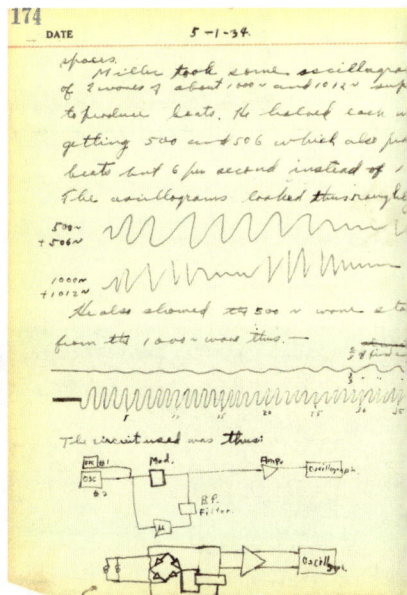

"The first telephone cable in 1956 had fourteen telephone channels," said Manfred Schroeder, hired by Bell Labs in 1953. "With the vocoder we could've made this into four hundred. That would've been wonderful. Between England and the United States, just fourteen channels wasn't enough. By the time we were ready, they had their satellites up with hundreds and thousands of channels. And by the time we had things that would've augmented the satellites, they had fiber-optic cables running through the Atlantic. So there was never much technical interest in what we did. Bandwidth was no longer a concern—this thing we had worked on for all our lives. But then came the Internet and cell phones. Now you are using compressed speech. That is Linear Prediction vocoder technology."

Teeth sibilant sketches from Homer Dudley's lab notebook. Dudley had been researching the early mechanical throats of Kratzenstein (1779, Russia), W.R. von Kempelen (Vienna) and Abbe Mical (France). (Courtesy AT&T Archives and History Center)

ES-823909-2
PER CENT ARTICULATION
EQUIVALENT SIGNAL TO NOISE RATIO
ADJACENT CHANNEL CROSS TALK

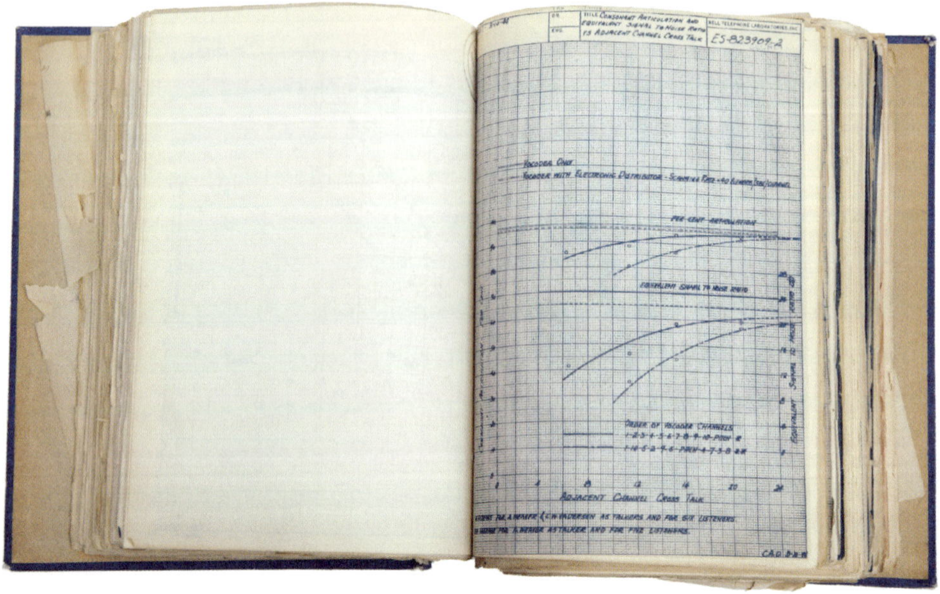

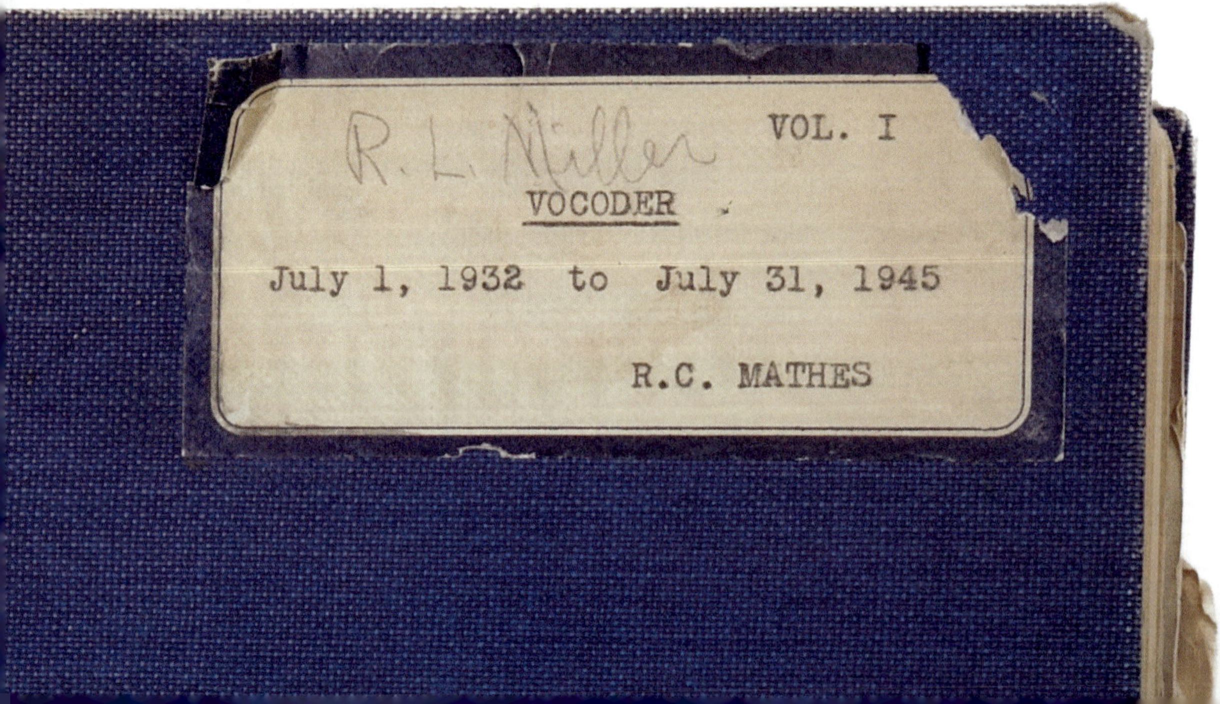

R. L. Miller
VOL. I
VOCODER
July 1, 1932 to July 31, 1945
R.C. MATHES

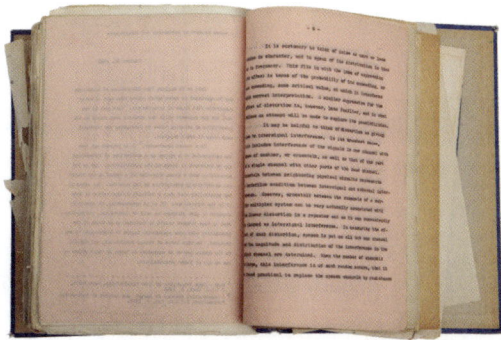

Bell Labs classified "secrecy system" vocoder bible from 1939-1945, with redactions done by razor blade. "One scarcely realizes how many sounds are of a random nature until he starts giving voice to them," wrote Homer Dudley, who spent much of the Cold War studying the speech mechanism of parrots. (Courtesy Ralph Miller)

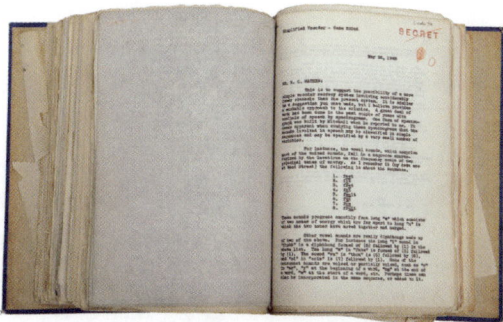

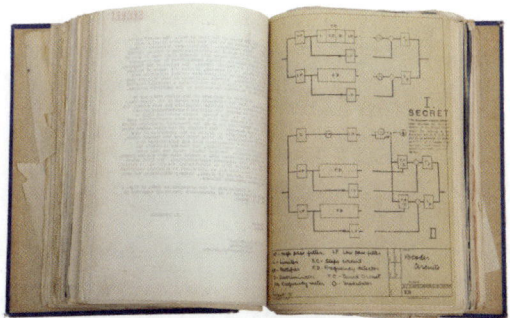

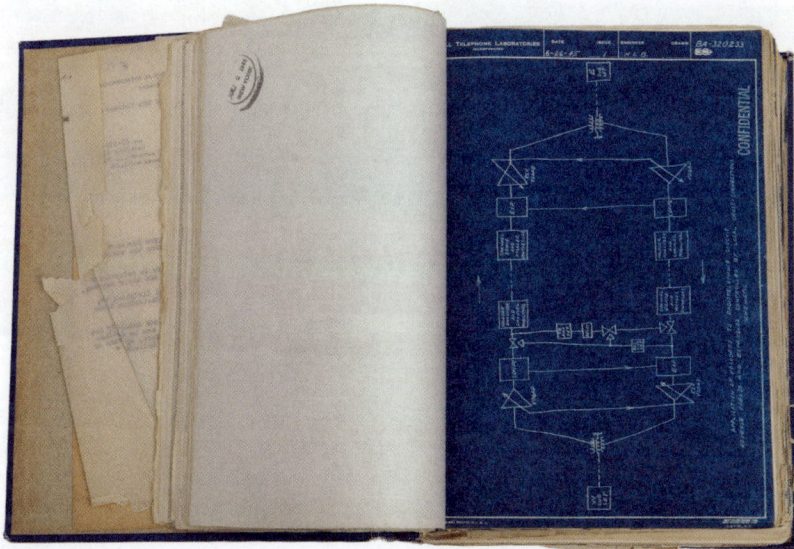

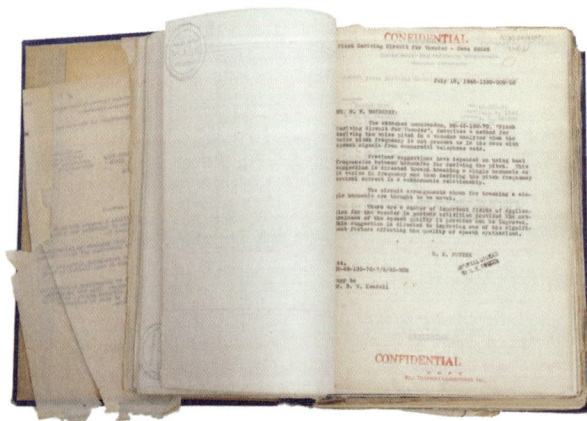

The Bell Labs vocoder bible, with memos typed on tracing paper, leaving tiny windows of "subtext." Includes testing for the Whisper Condition for SIGSALY, the first transmission of digital speech. (Courtesy Ralph Miller)

NEARLY ENOUGH LIKE THAT WHICH GAVE THEM BIRTH

Linear Predictive Coding originated as a computer model of the vocal tract shape. "Compression was the starting point of what you see in cell phones," says Bishnu Atal, an innovator of LPC who worked closely with Dudley at Bell Labs in the Fifties. "The idea [of compression] was dormant until 1980, when we started applying it to cell phones. The vocoder was a dirty narrow word because, after thirty years, it still couldn't carry a telephone conversation. But now it's all about compression—Dudley's original idea."

SHOE BENCH

Homer Dudley, a physicist who kept bees, joined Bell Labs Acoustics Research Department in 1921, the year the word "robot" was first placed in circulation by the Czechoslovakian writer Karel Capek, in his play *R.U.R.* Ralph Miller remembers Bell Labs being somewhat insulated from the Depression. "One of the things about Bell Labs in those days [was] if you had ideas about something that might help the telephone, they let you go off in the corner and work on it. When Homer got out of the hospital he started making proposals."

At Bell Labs, located at 463 West Street in Manhattan, the tongue was referred to as a lumped impedance structure and the letter k was a miniature explosive impulse. There, human speech was generated from the most inhuman of noises. Donkeys talked, storms howled sentences, and church bells scolded, "Stop! Stop! Don't do that!" The witches of Macbeth cackled "deeper than the deepest bass." The roar of the surf, Niagara Falls, submarine engines, tap dancing, birds, disturbed leaves—all had something to say. The vocoder had an anthropomorphic ball, often on reality's dime. Memos typed on tracing paper addressed problems with "buzz-saw quality" and "jars of severity." The term "shoe bench" was subjected to rigorous testing and spectral analysis, and ultimately recorded to vinyl. Other times, a simple "shh" would do, as if engineers were shushing the machine. Wrote Dudley in 1944: "One scarcely realizes how many sounds are of a random nature until he starts giving voice to them."

+ + +

SMILE, SNEEZE AND PREACH

The Euphonia was a mechanical speech keyboard invented in 1835 by Joseph Faber, a hypochondriac land-surveyor for the Emperor of Vienna. Controlled by sixteen keys and a foot pedal for its lung bellows, Faber's "verse-grinding machine" was well received in London, such that the press suggested replacing the House of Commons with Automatons. The Euphonia would later appear in the Fred Perkins story "Man-ufactory," published in 1873. Perkins' robot Patent Ministers could smile, sneeze and preach "The Discourse of Lukewarmness and Zeal." One Presbyterian android malfunctions during a sermon and explodes, causing "permanent derangement" in the congregation.

In 1933, Homer Dudley was promoted to head of the Bell Labs Acoustics Research Department. Not being a people person, he suffered a nervous breakdown and was diagnosed with acute colitis, an inflammation of the colon that triggered a near-fatal effluxion. So the beekeeper who tore speech to pieces was back in the hospital, staring at the ceiling and thinking about the vocoder, waiting for his blood to coagulate, while the goldfish twitched about in its bowl without a memory to occupy itself.

MY TEACHER'S SCREWY

According to a lab notebook entry from 1929, Dudley's vocoder was influenced by the work of Karl Willy Wagner, a German pioneer in automated speech research. Wagner developed a vowel synthesizer in 1936, a year after Dudley filed his signal transmission patent for the vocoder. In 1936, the vocoder made its public debut at Harvard University's Tercentenary Celebration in Cambridge, Massachusetts. Standing before his seven-foot tower of dials, Homer Dudley conducted paralinguistic cues, exaggerating the pitch and jumping between English and Swedish, often landing on the last syllable with both feet. He called it "The Greta Garble Effect," a joke on coherence. He then dropped into a power monk drone, as if trying to inhale the audience gasp. He harmonized with his "electrical doubles," did the Trans-Homer Express with a steam engine, and rasped an *Exorcist* version of Suzy Seashells. There were vocoder recordings of Protestant hymns, forlorn ballads, and an ad for Silly Willie Toothpaste ("You can use it to polish your car!"). For "Barnacle Bill," the pitch bottomed out like an ogre suffering from moat throat. "Happy Birthday" sounded like Mr. Bill in drag, pitched so high that the *Hopewell Herald* would later write that "a colortura soprano canary would have burst its vocal plumbing."

At another vocoder demonstration at the Franklin Institute in Philadelphia, Dudley had a power line humming as "the voice of electricity," lighting houses and claiming to be power itself, before wartime blackouts revived the candle. Thirty-six years later, Düsseldorf electronic group Kraftwerk—named after a power plant—would cover this plug tune in German, through a vocoder.

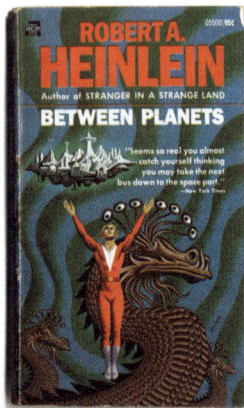

BUZZ HISS DRAGON

In Robert Heinlein's 1951 book *Between Planets*, the Voder appears strapped to the chest of a seven-eyed dragon from Venus. The dragon pounds the keyboard with his tendrils, as if to clear his throat, and thus discovers his favorite word: *Shucks*.

In 1939, while the Voder played the ham at the World's Fair, a screenwriter named Gilbert Wright discovered his electric razor could speak by essentially putting his Adam's apple on vibrate. This shaving epiphany would be patented as the Sonovox, a device that would give machines—and products—a voice. When held to the throat, the Sonovox's vibrating speaker cones could channel phonograph recordings of airplanes, engines and vacuum cleaners, allowing humans to pantomime noise into speech. Ideal for radio spots and jingles—and ultimately counting down the hits with Casey Kasem on *American Top 40*—the Sonovox's major debut would be in a wheezing steam engine in *Dumbo*.

+ + +

At the Acoustical Society of America in Manhattan, Homer Dudley would hype the vocoder's commercial appeal for cartoon voices, something beyond the helium quacks of Disney. In the summer of 1939, while the Sonovox appeared in *Time* magazine, Dudley visited MGM Studios in Hollywood, offering the vocoder as "a scientific aid to movie stars," claiming his invention could revive silent stars canned by the advent of talkies. Actors could essentially swap larynges, enunciating the pitch provided by a "surrogate throat." With its overdubbing potential, the vocoder could airbrush defective voices and create the illusion that actors could sing. This pitch-doctoring anticipated the Auto-Tune software in pop music today. Gee-whizzing in the *Los Angeles Times*, Philip Scheuer claimed the vocoder could transform any voice into The Voice True: "a squeak into an oratorio, a bumpkin into Barrymore, a hash-slinger into Lily Pons."

At the Hollywood demo, Dudley's associate Charles Vadersen sang "How Dry I Am" through the vocoder, multiplexing his voice, and then became an airplane taking a nosedive. Dudley then "fluttered" the pitch controls and triggered a domestic squabble with himself, spanning three generations. Father scolds daughter ("Nevermind that flip talk!"), daughter back-talks ("My teacher's screwy, Daddy!"), Grandpa Gizzard warbles in, and mother takes a hit of Scotch. Said the *LA Times*, "Anything so wondrous, so stupendous, so complicated and so confusing must find a place in movie-making."

WORD'S FEAR

Hollywood would have to wait. All things wondrous, stupendous, complicated and confusing must report to the army first. Though the World's Fair could make claims on the future, the military officially had dibs on tomorrow. Long before the vocoder played the voice of a missile-happy Cold War supercomputer in 1970's *Colossus: The Forbin Project*, it held an underground desk job, scrambling the phone calls of the army's triple-chinned brass. Patriotic orders to fill, eggs to scramble. Things to come, things to do.

Writing in the *New Yorker*, Martian-mongerer H.G. Wells predicted that the World's Fair would introduce teleconferencing, a snooze button of a prophecy but less dooming than the atomic conflict he foresaw in his 1914 book *The World Set Free*. Ray Bradbury, the loud blond dreamer, was terrified. No squid lady could distract him from the prospect of the sky above whistling straight to hell.

Those at the Fair who eavesdropped on Bradbury's free call to Los Angeles probably just admired the clarity, marveling at voices shooting across time zones. Perhaps they mistook his modulated quaver for homesickness, not the fear that he'd never again see his parents. *I love you. I miss you. I'm broke.*

"We were a few weeks away from World War Two," he tells me. "The sense then was that in a few months the world was going to destroy itself. The world then proceeded to kill forty million people. I thought I might be destroyed too. I looked up into the sky, smelled gun powder and saw the war coming." That night, July 4th, standing in the glow of the fireworks, the world's blindest stegosaurus fan saw the sky on fire and cried.

NEARLY ENOUGH LIKE THAT WHICH GAVE THEM BIRTH

Charles Vadersen may be the first vocoder singer. Here he demonstrates the "Greta Garble Effect," circa 1936. Vadersen would also sing vocoder versions of "Old Man River" and "Barnacle Bill." (Courtesy AT&T Archives and History Center)

CHAPTER TWO

INDESTRUCTIBLE SPEECH

It is not advisable to be without SIGSALY service.

— General Franklin E. Stoner

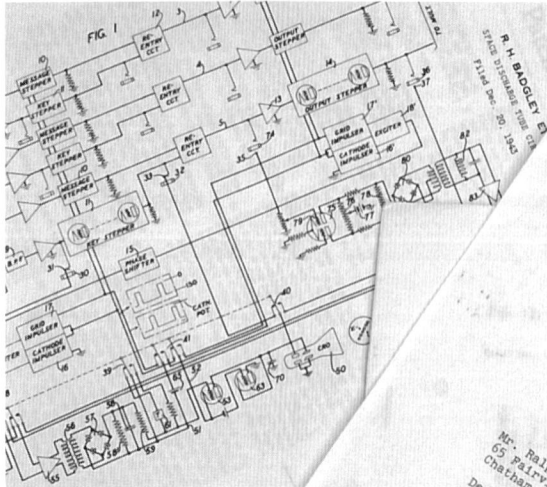
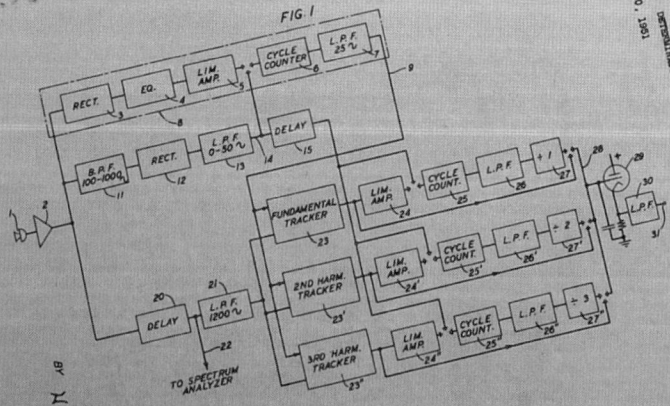
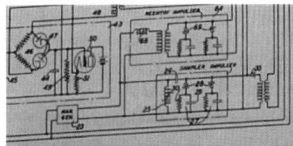

Ralph Miller's patents for artificial speech reconstruction and encoding, photographed in 2009. Miller also engineered a condensed, mobile version of SIGSALY called "Junior X," which used an eight-channel vocoder that fit in a van but was never deployed. (Courtesy Ralph Miller)

PLAYOFEEN CRINKONOPE

While Bell Labs thought the vocoder could rehabilitate shell-shocked mutes, the voice of Winston Churchill—England's prolific speech synthesizer—was caught hurtling through the ether along the coast of South Holland. In 1941, a German radio outpost near the beach in Noorwijk had been intercepting the prime minister's phone calls, unscrambling them as if they were no more than a boy scout flipping blinds. The Bell Labs scrambler of choice—the A-3—had been compromised by Hitler's post office (Forschungsstelle). "High-place people in the government had been using the Trans-Atlantic Telephone," says Ralph Miller, assigned by Bell Labs to resolve the problem. "They thought it was secret. It was secret after a fashion. You split speech up into bands and mess it all up by scrambling. But it wasn't hard to undo, either, and apparently the Germans had done just that."

I'm sitting in Ralph Miller's living room in Concord, Massachusetts, among piles of documents, many of which haven't seen daylight since the Eisenhower Administration. The floor is covered with patents. *Transmission and Reconstruction of Artificial Speech. Conference Calls Between Vocoder and Analogue Stations. Determination of Pitch Frequency*. There is a diagram for synchronizing turntables on opposite sides of the world.

Ralph glances at the vocoder scheme under his penny loafer and shakes his head. "When did I do all of *that*?"

It's been a while. At the age of 102, Ralph Miller can still tell you how to subdivide human speech. Dressed sharply in blue houndstooth pants and a putting-green cardigan, Ralph introduced himself to me as the guy who "once controlled the frequency of New York City." He doesn't own a computer, but his memory is beholden to the technology he helped innovate, including Pulse Code Modulation (PCM), a conversion of analog to digital signals now applicable to cell phones, computers and synthesizers. PCM's digitization of the voice would be key in the sampling and coding aspect of the SIGSALY system Miller helped design during World War II. Among the documents on his floor is a letter from an AT&T attorney, dated 1976, issuing Miller a SIGSALY patent, finally declassified thirty-five years after it was filed. "[Bell Labs] had found eighty patents for speech scrambling," Ralph says. "Not one of them was any good. They all could be unscrambled by scientific people." One Bell memo described a speech inverter that turned the word "telephone" into "playofeen crinkonope." Even before German spies were cracking codes like beer nuts, rumors circulated about people eavesdropping on London stockbrokers and calling New York before breakfast to score on a hot tip when the market opened.

On September 30, 1941, US Army Chief of Staff General George Marshall wrote Bell Labs requesting help with the military's "communications problems." Three months later, on the morning of December 7, after Marshall had received an intercept of a Japanese ultimatum, he notified Pearl Harbor by Western Union, due to his distrust of the phone. His warning would spend its day of infamy in transit. By the time the teletype message finally arrived in Honolulu, Pearl Harbor had been transformed from a base to a motive. As the US publicly entered the war, there was a cry for "Indestructible Speech," illocution that could withstand the codebreaker.

Ralph Miller (on phone) talks seashells through the vocoder, circa 1953. (Courtesy AT&T Archives and History Center)

During that first week of December in 1941, an article titled "Methods for the Automatic Scrambling of Speech" appeared in the Swiss journal *Brown Boveri Review*, describing a device that was a vocoder in all but name. The National Defense Research Commission (NDRC), then co-chaired by Bell Labs president O.E. Buckley, took note, and a test unit designed by Ralph Miller, O.O. Gruenz and others, was ready by March 1942.

In the spring of 1942, the crowd at the New York Yankees season opener heard a dive bomber growling "Remember Pearl Harbor!" and "Slap a Jap" over the PA system. It was the Sonovox, the vocoder's Hollywood rival. That year, General Electric's WGEO had

Signal Corp. officers at the SIGSALY SAMPLE terminal in Paris, 1944. (Courtesy National Archives/NSA)

been broadcasting Sonovox messages to Allied forces over shortwave radio. The wind whispered, "Give us revenge" and a bomb screamed, "Kill, kill, kill!" Back home, NBC's signature doorbell chimed, "Buy war bonds!" while the naval air school used Gilbert Wright's invention to teach Morse Code by enunciating signals into their corresponding letters.

By November 1942, the NDRC had commissioned Bell Labs and its manufacturing contractor Westinghouse to begin work on an unbreakable phone system under the supervision of Ralph K. Potter and Robert Mathes. Construction took place on the twelfth floor of the Graybar Building at 180 Varick Street in Manhattan and at West Street, where the windows were painted black. At the time, 80 percent of the Bell Labs budget was funding military research, "new instrumentalities for warfare," including radars, sonic deception research, missile guidance systems, ghost armies on vinyl, bazookas, magnetic mines, cameras that photographed bullets in mid-flight, and the "Water Heater"—a twenty-one-foot acoustic torpedo equipped with a 500-watt sound system. At a preordained moment, the speaker would pop out of the torpedo's nose and play tape recordings of "tactical sounds" to distract enemy ships before self-destructing. A more practical acoustic device was the Laryngophone, a sensory receiver that attached to the throat and transmitted laryngeal vibrations directly into the radio, allowing pilots and tank commanders to be heard over "noisy mechanized forces."

The vocoder, on the other hand, conveyed intelligence as deformation. As Ralph Miller had reported in Bell's preliminary testing, the machine committed various atrocities on the voice, reducing speech to a "series of miserable grunts." "Badly mutilated," he wrote in the *Bell Technical Journal*. A clumsy homily soon began making the rounds: "Thirty kilowatts of power for one milliwatt of poor quality speech."

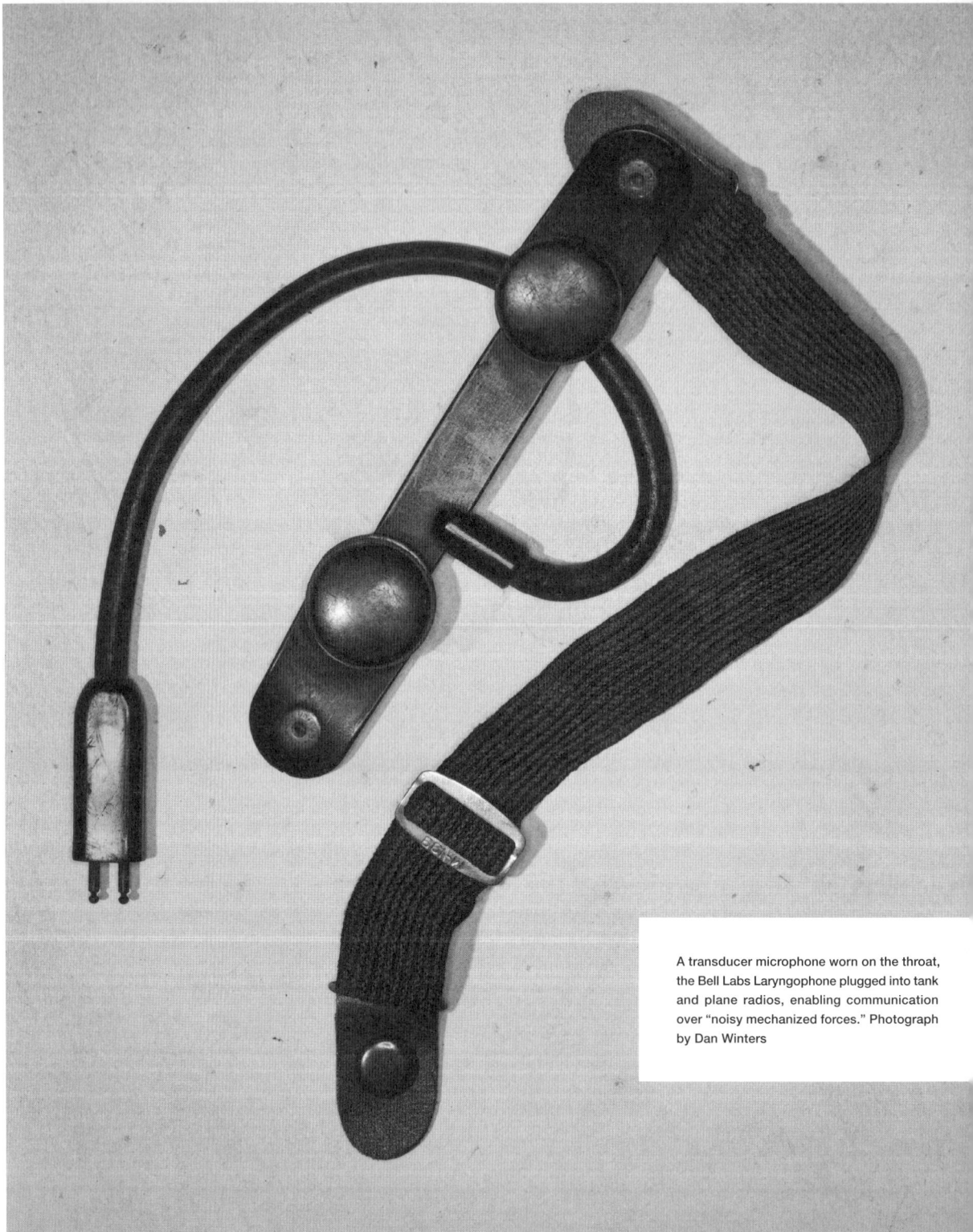

A transducer microphone worn on the throat, the Bell Labs Laryngophone plugged into tank and plane radios, enabling communication over "noisy mechanized forces." Photograph by Dan Winters

HOW TO RECOGNIZE BREACH

On February 15, 1941, W.G. Radley of the Dollis Hill Research Station in London wrote to Bell Labs requesting information on the vocoder: "This is of particular interest to us, not less so on account of present war conditions." Bell Labs agreed to send the specs by courier but withheld any details concerning any speech privacy. Three months later, on May 15, 1941, the ship delivering the documents to Britain was torpedoed and sunk.

The U-boat control of FDR's Lend-Lease supply corridor in the Atlantic would be broken when England's chief cryptanalyst, Alan Turing, who had solved the German ENIGMA cipher by 1942. In January 1943, Turing visited Bell Labs to vet the vocoder but was initially denied admittance. (Despite the importance of the ENIGMA breakthrough, history has been reluctant to acknowledge Turing's war hero status because he was gay.) As the only British officer permitted to evaluate the X-System, Turing would generate enough Bell Labs and Pentagon memoranda to choke a file cabinet. He would ultimately receive clearance from the White House and enemy of the telephone George Marshall.

In 1936, the year the vocoder sang "Barnacle Bill" at Harvard, Turing published "Computable Numbers," an essay proposing that a machine could mimic the human brain. (Turing once dreamt of engaging a supermachine in chess and outsmarting it by playing so dumb that the machine was depressed by the ignorance of its creator and committed suicide.) At 463 West Street, Turing met Claude Shannon, author of "Communication in the Presence of Noise," which defined noise as a precise measure of compressed intelligence that could "wiggle." Though discussing the military's artificial speech analyzer was prohibited, artificial intelligence was another story. Over lunch in the Bell Labs cafeteria, Turing and Shannon decided that the brain was no longer sacred and called for an assault on inner space. It was time to feed "cultural things" to machines, including music. Turing held forth in a voice that his biographer Andrew Hodges likened to a vocoder. He declared that Bell Labs president O.E. Buckley had a mediocre brain and that he could build a better one. Tables rattled, faces fell, phones rang, and coffee flew from noses.

Chief British cryptanalyst Alan Turing was the only British officer cleared to evaluate the SIGSALY vocoder at Bell Labs. When testing his own scrambler Delilah (which was not a vocoder), Turing sampled chopped up recordings of Churchill speeches. In 1945, Turing made a secret trip to Feuerstein, a German vocoder lab in upper Franconia, to investigate encoded transmissions intercepted over Hanover.

SIGSALY vocoder photographed in Guam, circa 1944. Each seven-foot "cabinet" of transformers and vacuum tubes served as a vocoder channel. At one point, Bell Labs had designed a 30-channel model that occupied two floors. This would be the first articulate modular synthesizer. (Courtesy National Archives/NSA)

The vocoder would pass Turing's inspection, and on July 15, 1943, the inaugural link was established between the Pentagon and the basement of Selfridges, a London department store connected to Churchill's bunker. The 805th division of the Signal Corps was charged with overseeing maintenance and operation. The Signal Corps named the system SIGSALY, which stood for nothing, while Bell Labs called it Project X, as if choosing the most obvious mysterious alias. In the official SIGSALY user manual, its main component, the vocoder, is never mentioned by name. Nor does the word appear in the SIGSALY "Secret Telephony" patent, ultimately awarded on June 29, 1976.

Two weeks after SIGSALY's debut, the German Research Bureau picked up yet another call between Roosevelt and Churchill. Mussolini, prime minister of Italy, aka Il Duce, had resigned. The boot was open. Using the A-3, Churchill and Roosevelt's conversation was decoded virtually in real time, and Hitler knew to bolster his forces in Italy. Still Roosevelt refused to have a vocoder in the White House, perhaps due to Churchill's inobservance of time zones—a fear of being drunk-dialed at any hour of the night. The prime minister, however, accumulated hundreds of SIGSALY calls in one year. Roughly a year after the German intercept, FDR and Churchill were on the vocoder, joking about the clout of the presidential dog while planning a surprise landing on the beaches of Normandy in early June.

SHIPPING AND HANDLING

During the war, a network of twelve SIGSALY terminals would be installed worldwide, including an OL-31 barge that ended up in Tokyo Bay, with vocoder and non-skipping turntables operating in the hold.

"It was a major technological weapon with human appeal," said Dr. Robert Price, a SIGSALY historian who estimated that the system trafficked millions of words through the ether in 1945 alone.

Though General Douglas MacArthur didn't trust SIGSALY, brass like Chester Nimitz, Hap Arnold, and Manhattan project foreman Leslie Groves all frequented the secret channel. Ralph Miller still can't believe it worked. "They actually transmitted speech from North Africa to the US, across the US to Australia. On the vocoder. On that system. It actually worked, clear down around that loop."

The last SIGSALY oscillator, photographed in an NSA storage room, 2009.

With forty rack-mounts of gear, SIGSALY averaged fifty-five tons and occupied 2,500 square feet, essentially a three-bedroom home and a garage. "A couple pounds less than a sawmill," cracked General Dayton Eddy, who claimed to have "nursemaided" the vocoder. The vocoder itself was a dainty forty tons, with one rack tower assigned to each of its ten voice channels. "The size of the X-System is not an accomplishment to be very happy about," wrote Ralph Miller in *A History of Engineering & Science in the Bell System*. Despite this, the army believed that its 850 boxes of equipment could be air-dropped into Berlin. With production costs topping a million dollars per terminal, Project X was billed in the ledger, somewhat innocently, as "Overseas Telephone Service." When General Eisenhower saw these walls of relays, transformers and vacuum tubes, he was believed to have grunted, "You can make a whole lotta bullets with all that copper."

SIGSALY was the fat kid in the wagon, requiring a barge and an aircraft carrier to tow the terminal to its designated theater. Shipping and handling in a U-boat world was not easy. According to Miller, one vocoder fell off a barge in the Philippines and had to be rescued by frogmen. Another, intended for New Guinea, contracted a fungal infection and had to be de-spored on a beach in Hollandia. Humidity was to blame.

Bell Labs' first vocoder singer, Charles Vadersen, would find himself deposited on a beach near Townsville, undercover and 800 miles from the terminal in Brisbane. Most of the 805th Signal Corps had been recruited from the Bell System. Eggheads who had been splitting speech in New York found themselves packing service revolvers in New Guinea. Fresh out of the Bell Labs School of War Training, one officer was photographed in a Manhattan hotel room posing in a gas mask, while another brandished a pair of pliers. Another identified himself as a "X-Toll Test Board Repeater Man." Another would accidentally overhear the date of the D-Day invasion over a SIGSALY line and immediately destroy the recording. The detachment in Algiers would receive bronze stars for service in the North African campaign. A detachment in the Mediterranean was commended for reporting approximately zero cases of venereal disease. Their mascot: a thyratron tube.

THE WHISPER CONDITION

During World War II, artifice—the illusion of conflict—was a weapon in itself. There were wooden bombs, fake factories, inflatable tanks, synthetic fogs, electronically generated ghost armies, psychoacoustic ventriloquists, and magicians hired to make the coastline disappear. A synthetic reenactment of the voice was just another Decepticon. Even without the vocoder, speech sent across the globe over radio channels often arrived in pieces. A relatively new technology, long distance may as well have been outer space. "The SIGSALY voice was artificial, sure," says Lieutenant Donald E. Mehl, who supervised terminals at the Pentagon and then later in Manila. According to Mehl, callers often had to become "psychologically adjusted to reaction time," if not be outright told who was on the other end. "It made a curious kind of robot voice," said Henry Stimson, the newly appointed secretary of war. William Bennett, a Bell Labs engineer who worked on SIGSALY, had his own motto: "Accept distortion for security."

The Signal Corps was more concerned with the vocoder's ungovernable pitch than a failure to recognize. Occasionally, Ralph Miller reported to the Pentagon for tech support. "I was working on extracting the pitch. They were trying to get Eisenhower to use it in North Africa. So

805th Signal Corps graduates of the Bell Labs School of War Training, one brandishing pliers, the other in a gas mask, circa 1943. Members of the 805th weren't allowed to discuss SIGSALY, not even among themselves, until it was declassified in 1976. (Courtesy National Archives/NSA)

they got Mamie, his wife, to go into [the Pentagon terminal] and get on the phone. I was scared to death because the pitch channel wasn't designed around women's voices. But apparently her voice was low enough." Ike thought the vocoder turned his wife into an old woman. Mamie told him to come home.

Ralph grins. "We had a saying back then: 'Pitch is a bitch.' It was crazy. With your pitch jerking around at five levels, it would make your speech jump all over the place." Ralph would issue a memo concerning the "Whisper Condition," toying with the unvoiced circuit. "We even tried cutting out the pitch altogether," he continues. "Then you get whispered speech. Well, this is supposed to be a secret system, so why not whisper it? This didn't go over with the people who wanted to use it. Churchill did not want to whisper."

SOMETHING TO THAT EFFECT

In 1940, Royal Air Force pilot Roald Dahl awoke in a flying hospital bed, losing altitude somewhere over Libya. He smelled oranges, lemons and melting steel. There was singing. He recognized the melody as "Bells of St. Clement's," a seventeenth-century nursery rhyme about a group of church bells who haggle over fruit prices until someone gets beheaded. Dahl's brain telegraphed him. *Down here there is a great hotness. What shall we do?* He noticed the rhymes weren't coming from bells but planes, circling him from above. The black crosses painted under their wings had joined hands, their engines chanting, "Here comes a chopper to chop off your head!" Dahl cried out for the nurse. He was being taunted by the German Messerschmitts that he believed had blown him out of the sky. The morphine seemed to be working.

VARIATIONS IN TIMBRE AND ATTACK

Brigadier Fitzroy Maclean just put his foot through a cloud. He has jumped out of a plane over Yugoslavia with an autographed glossy of Winston Churchill in his rucksack. The sky is quickly upon him, snatching at his ears, chasing him into darkness. It is the fall of 1943, possibly the worst time to be dropping into Eastern Europe. Yugoslavia is under German occupation and the airwaves hiss with radio spooks who have

Ralph Miller on the vocoder at Bell Labs, 1954. In addition to helping design the Voder and SIGSALY, Miller was a pioneer in Pulse Code Modulation. (Courtesy *Scientific American*)

taken an interest in Maclean's whereabouts. He pulls the ripcord. If things go as planned, he will bloom into a nylon jellyfish and float into the mountains of Bosnia.

As Churchill's personal emissary, Maclean, a Scottish-born "correspondent," has been dispatched to meet with Josip Tito, rebel leader of the Yugoslav Communist Party. For the past two years, Tito's guerrillas have defied Hitler's invasion of Yugoslavia, but at great cost. They wear the uniforms of dead German soldiers while fighting for an independent communist state. Churchill wants to back Tito despite worries that Yugoslavia could become another satellite for Josef Stalin, once an amateur meteorologist, now dictator of one-sixth of Earth. Stalin can't be trusted any farther than you could throw Churchill. Churchill can't be trusted any farther than you could throw the Politburo. Stalin once trusted Hitler but now only trusts the weather. Russia's ice-pick winter has been a dependable ally during the German invasion and, better yet, when terrorizing one's own people and cultivating loyalty in the Arctic Circle. Nor does Stalin trust Josip Tito, a man who once barfed at a Kremlin banquet.

"We shall fight on the beaches," said Winston Churchill to Parliament in 1940.

Tito's desire to be Moscow-free is encouraging to Churchill. In the spring of 1943, he invites Fitzroy Maclean over to his bomb shelter at 10 Downing for a final briefing on the Tito mission. There will be whiskey and Disney cartoons. Dumbo's talking steam engine and the helium sailor duck without pants were good for laughs at a time when machines spoke death and ducks sat in their shadows. That spring, a German V-2 rocket exploded thirty feet from Churchill's subterranean vocoder booth in London.

+ + +

The next time Fitzroy Maclean heard from Churchill, it was over the phone, through the vocoder, and it was unpleasant. In April 1944, after spending nearly a year with Tito's rebels, Maclean reported to a SIGSALY terminal in the wine cellar of the St. George's Hotel in Algiers, wearing a highland kilt. Allied forces had been using St. George's as a communications center since the defeat of Rommel's Afrika Korps in 1943. The British Eighth Army would recover a variety of sophisticated voice gadgets from captured Panzer tanks, including a "Photophone" (or "Optiphone"), a device that transmitted radio conversations over a primitive laser beam. The Photophone was invented by Telefunken engineer Paul Kotowski, godfather of the German vocoder who was interned in the United States at the time.

The telephone is alien enough for Fitzroy Maclean, sitting in a rigged conference room under the desert, waiting to have his voice launched across the ionosphere to Churchill's bunker. He is handed a phone with a gouted mouthpiece, called the "Mysterious Microphone," and the link with Churchill is consummated. The Scot identifies himself. Thinking their voices aren't scrambled, Churchill's robot tells him to shut up. Maclean drops his stomach. The prime minister can be a tough read at times—a split-fingered peace sign could easily break into a fuck-you at the last second. But hadn't they recently shared Disney cartoons back in Churchill's bunker in London? Hadn't the prime minister fogged him in second-hand cigar smoke?

On the other side of the conference room wall, the vocoder ensures that Churchill's two-syllable gag order has arrived in Algiers, undetected though somewhat bent out of shape. Maclean stares at the receiver in his hand, thinking the boss has chosen an inconvenient time to lose his mind. He hears an "inhuman wailing" noise, some banshee interference, and then Churchill yelling for Pippin and Pumpkin. Maclean looks at the stenographer for help. Churchill cries, "Good god! They haven't got the code!" A Signal Corps officer intervenes, assuring both parties that the line is secure, and that the callers are indeed who they claim to be.

The first two words Churchill's spy Fitzroy Maclean, pictured above, heard on the vocoder were "shut up." Undercover in the mountains of Bosnia, Maclean was a key liaison between Churchill and rebel communist leader Josip Tito when Tito's guerrilla forces drove the German Army out of Yugoslavia.

Churchill liberates something mucosal from his throat. "Shall we scramble?" Maclean provides the Tito intel and receives orders to return to London with Tito's major, Vlatko Velebit in tow, a sign of Britain's commitment to the Yugoslav rebels. Pleased with the call, Churchill has a bottle of scotch sent to Algiers. Maclean, who is thrilled to be done with the phone, sneaks a glance at the stenographer, who listens to a recording of the conversation, perhaps wondering what the vocoder had done to his sexy Gaelic accent. He shakes his head, in need of a Bromo Seltzer. In the SIGSALY engine room, the vocoder runs hot. An officer in starched khaki sweatstains douses a stack of vinyl records with gasoline and sets them on fire.

BEES TO MEN

What do you mean random? You can't control anything with random noise!
— Theodore Sturgeon, *The Pod in the Barrier*, 1957

It was not good to listen to what they whispered at night in the forest with voices of bees that tried to be like the voices of men.
— H.P. Lovecraft, *The Whisperer in the Darkness*, Special Armed Forces GI Edition, 1943

It was never confirmed whether Churchill's bottle of scotch made it to Algiers, or if the 805th drank it. Perhaps they expected cigars. In the basement at St. George's, on the table across from the phone, sat a special SIGSALY ashtray. This lump of melted copper tubing—maybe five bullets' worth—had been converted from the air conditioner, perhaps the unsung hero of Project X. Engineered to cool off an airplane hangar, this overstated metal box weighed five tons and stood nine feet tall.

In basements without ventilation (since voices tend to carry), the vinyl records were dependent on AC. Called SIGGRUV, these random noise disks were the most classified sensitive component of SIGSALY (despite advertising "groove" in the code name). As the code key, the records had to be playing at all times during vocoded conversations. "Records don't play, they transmit," says Lieutenant Donald E. Mehl. "These turntables were not for entertainment. They were the security for vital communications in a deadly war. Two turntables at the transmitting end

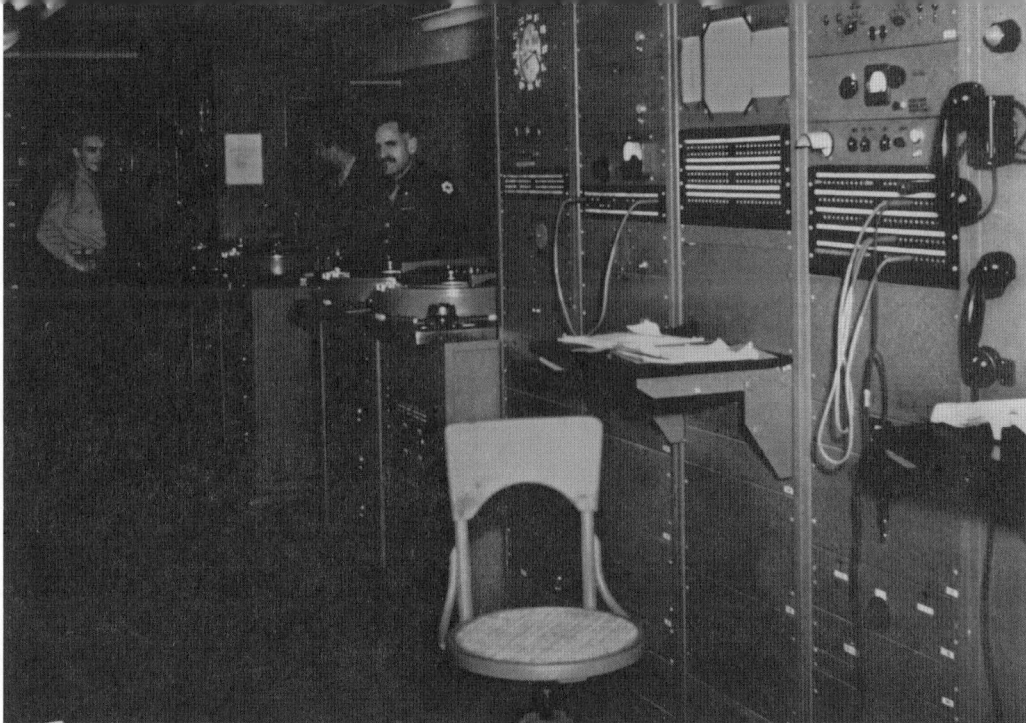

and two turntables at the receiving end—so we could operate continuously. After twelve minutes, it would automatically switch over to the other turntable. When we started a turntable in Manila, it had to be synchronized with the one in Washington, DC—ten thousand miles away."

Duplicate records, or "doubles," had to be synchronized at each end of the conversation. Guarded with a collector's zeal, these "one-time records" enjoyed but a twelve-minute life span. When talks dragged on in a Churchillian fashion, another record was cued to play backwards, its needle indexed at the center. The mix was automatic. "We had to be on point," says Mehl. "If the needle jumped the groove, you hear garble because you no longer had the key in synchronization. When you're out of synch, you just hear babble. We had to fix that."

Activated by crystal-controlled railroad clocks, the turntable motors remained synchronized despite time-zone hiccups and fading. A

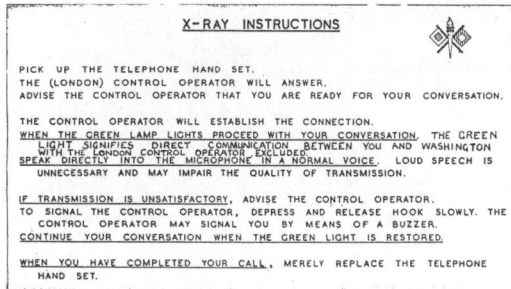

ABOVE: SIGSALY SAMPLE terminal, Paris. (Courtesy National Archives/NSA)

BELOW: "Speak directly into the microphone in a normal voice." SIGSALY user's instruction card. (Courtesy NSA)

Westinghouse oven was retained at each SIGSALY terminal to keep the crystals stabilized. Bell Labs followed its own time standard, reportedly "several orders of magnitude better" than whatever ruled the rest of the world. The future was quantified to the millisecond, just so the record could stay on beat, randomly. For the recording of SIGGRUV, the Signal Corps hired the Muzak Corporation, located at 46th Street in Times Square. Randomized covert noise was a considerable leap for a company that transmitted crooners and waltzes over phone lines. Intended for depressed office geraniums, Muzak was invented by George Owen Squier, a Signal Corps officer who spent World War I designing remote-control mine detonators. The company's deceptive lull of a motto—"Muzak fills the deadly silences"—in a sense abided by SIGSALY's strict policy of constant noise, though instead of Guy Lombardo, it was a concentration of millions of panicked electrons banging around inside fourteen-inch glass vacuum tubes. Ralph Miller says the records sounded like "TV noise," a thing of snow-blind reception. Disruptive yet no less disturbing than Muzak, SIGGRUV seemed to skip the dentist's waiting room and get right to the ultrasonic drilling, the "shhh" of unvoiced fricatives.

805th Signal Corps Lt. Don Mehl helped monitor vocoder operations in the Pentagon and MacArthur's base of operations in Manila, where he was photographed here in 1945. According to Mehl, preparations for the Surrender Conference took place at the Manila terminal, the last building standing with air conditioning. (Courtesy Don Mehl and NSA)

"They kept Muzak tied up all during the war making records of these random signals," says Miller. More than 1,500 gold-splattered records were initially pressed and duplicated for synchronization on both ends of the conversation. Each record was one-sided as a safeguard against B-side confusion and assigned CB-trucker code names like Red Strawberry, Wild Dog and Circus Clown. As the war spread, the Pentagon began pressing up cheaper acetates in-house rather than risk shuttling them throughout Manhattan by limousine. Upon completion, the records were transported via armored truck to a former girls' school in Arlington, Virginia, and kept in a safe with the combination entrusted to three officers who were then blindfolded and turned around twenty-five times, thrown in the back of a white van, driven to the next county and dropped off in their underwear with a bag of peanuts and some kite string.

SIGSALY Guam terminal, code name NEPTUNE, photographed from the rafters. (Courtesy National Archives/NSA)

"Very little about the coding part was allowed to be printed," says Ralph Miller. "They had a way of taking the sample and randomizing it. The noise power was sampled every twenty milliseconds." The math itself was driven insane—the vocoder signals were "sampled and quantized to base six." At the transmission end, the vocoder divided analog frequencies across ten spectral channels, sampling each at fifty times per second. The record noise would be subtracted at the receiving terminal while the vocoder measured the pitch energy (Channel 11) and tried to make sense out of it. "The vocoder added intelligence to pulses," says Lieutenant Mehl. "The pulses were twenty milliseconds long."

The records had to be random. Had a pattern been detected, the code could've been broken and small talk about the president's Scottish Terrier could've been mistaken for a full-scale invasion. Though the randomness of SIGGRUV opposed the nature of Muzak's ambience and repetition, it assured the codebreaker, that random freak of probability, that noise was noise, just another jamming frequency. "German decoders noticed this strange sound over the radio," says William Bennett, Jr., whose father worked on SIGSALY. "They were hearing a buzz. But it was really SIGSALY. All the time it was random key noise over a normal shortwave receiver. But they didn't know what it was. Even if the equipment had been duplicated, the code could not be compromised without SIGGRUV. The only practical vulnerabilities were disloyalty, indiscretion and incompetence." According to Bennett, another unintended safety feature was that SIGSALY "was so damn complicated nobody else could make it work."

BELOW: A test dummy of the last remaining SIGGRUV, photographed at the NSA in 2009. "The acetate records had an aluminum base that could be converted into airplanes," said Don Mehl of the 805th Signal Corps. The pressings were one-sided as an idiot-proof precaution against "replaying" the code.

To the codebreaker, the encrypted signal could've been the migraine Moog synth played by James Brown in 1973's "Blow Your Head," somewhere between a B-29 with nose plugs and a bee with a sinus infection. Since no one at Bell Labs listened to James Brown in 1944 (the Godfather of Soul was just eleven then, dancing for troops at a Signal Corps base in Fort Gordon, Georgia), SIGSALY was nicknamed the "Green Hornet," after the popular radio serial that used "Flight of the Bumblebee" as its theme, swapping masked man for masked voice. (A Tsarist violin freakout, "Flight of the Bumblebee" was composed by Nicolai Rimsky-Korsakov, who did codework with player-piano sheets.) The radio show's signature buzz came from the theremin (termenvox), invented by Leon Theremin, a master eavesdropper who would later be forced by the KGB to microwave-bug the US embassy in Moscow. Yet while his instrument brought the Green Hornet to the rescue in America, Leon Theremin himself couldn't hear it, having been imprisoned in Siberia for espionage.

The Green Hornet code name was actually a vocoder being called a theremin, unbeknownst to everybody involved—the first and only double-crossing of the two devices. To the operator ferrying the SIGSALY buzz, it could have been the mechanical bees of Dr. Zapparoni, described by the German writer Ernst Juenger as being plugged into their hive like a phone switchboard in his 1960 novel *The Glass Bees*.

✤ ✤ ✤

In a Signal Corps log for the Algiers terminal, somewhere between "Request to marry local French girl" and "An epidemic of bubonic plague has broken out," it was reported that the Destruction Machine was yet to arrive. The Destruction Machine ensured that the SIGGRUV would never be played again. Some called it the "Record Chopper."

SIGSALY modular speech synth cabinets in Guam, circa 1945. (Courtesy National Archives/NSA)

The Pentagon originally tried using a furnace, but the vinyl released gasses that attacked the SIGSALY equipment. When the chopper jammed, officers resorted to gasoline or an oven. The SIGGRUV instructions read: "The used project record should be cut up and placed in an oven and reduced to a plastic 'biscuit' of Vinylite." If none of these methods was available, they simply gouged the world's rarest records with a screwdriver and "scratched all over them." As a final precaution, the turntables were equipped with a self-destruct mechanism, a thermite process used in bomb design. Activated by the last man out, it essentially melted the turntables into an abstract blob. Officers grabbed whatever records they could, or just threw them in the oven with the crystals, leaving the world's most accurate clock to fend for itself.

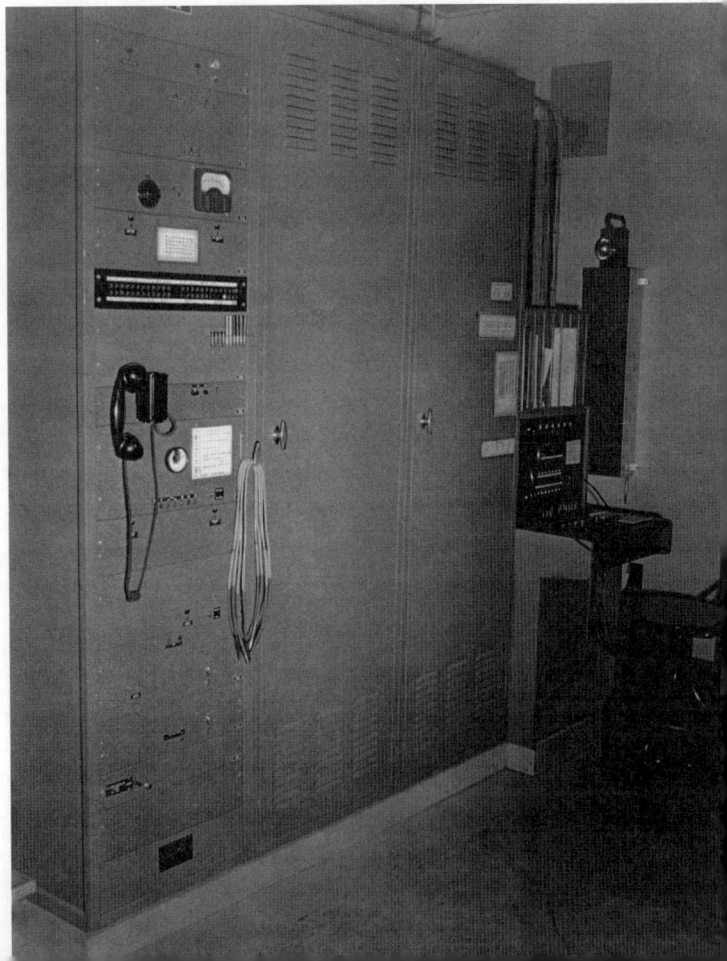

CHAPTER THREE

VOCODER KOMMISSAR

Have you said anything to the Russians yet?

— Churchill to Truman, on the vocoder, April 25, 1945

COLD WIND MADNESS

The Destruction Machine ate well in 1945. On April 25, the day after a SIGSALY terminal was installed in a seized Luftwaffe base in Frankfurt, Churchill phoned Harry Truman at the Pentagon.

"How glad I am to hear your voice," said the prime minister, not hearing Truman's voice, but a mechanical simulacra.

Standing in for the incapacitated Hitler, SS captain Heinrich Himmler had offered a surrender proposal. Would it be possible for Germany to capitulate to the United States and Great Britain in the West, yet still continue fighting the Russians in the East? Churchill said no, three times. Truman agreed. Himmler would excuse himself from further negotiations by taking a cyanide pill while Stalin began dismantling Berlin and freighting it back to the Soviet Union.

On May 4, British ambassador John G. Winant and the director of European Affairs in Washington used SIGSALY to parse the language of surrender as defined by the Dismemberment Committee. "I thought the amendment to the Surrender Instrument contained the word 'dismemberment'?"

"We cannot keep it silent any longer," said a vocoderized Churchill on May 7, before V-E Day. "We must go off!"

Speaking over SIGSALY with Truman's chief of staff, Admiral William Leahy, Churchill hesitated to include Stalin on the news of surrender. "My chief tells me I cannot act without the approval of Uncle Joe," Leahy said. "Do you understand, sir?" As if feigning a bad connection, Churchill responded, "My ears are a bit deaf." The only officer authorized to eavesdrop on the Truman-Churchill call was Dorothy Madsen, a lieutenant who often edited out SIGSALY profanities and transcribed vocoder garbles. According to Madsen, the only words she wrote that day were "cerebral hemorrhage," referring to Hitler's health.

Logistics concerning "transmission of bomb programs" had already been discussed over SIGSALY links in Paris, Manila and Guam. As the SIGSALY phones crackled with V-E Day activity on May 8, 1945, the true surrender instrument was nearing completion. That July at the Potsdam Conference, Truman was informed, by whisper, of the atomic bomb test at the Trinity proving grounds in Alamogordo, New Mexico. Over the Washington-Paris link, Manhattan Project Foreman Leslie Groves talked about the detonation of nuclear weapons over Japan, hoping to end the war before it ended without him. According to General Barney M. Giles, SIGSALY was used in discussing the logistics of payload to Hiroshima and Nagasaki. On August 6, 1945, a drop of 20,000 tons of TNT was compressed into twenty-millisecond pulses of tactical conversation: "If the second bomb doesn't work, we're out of business, because we have no more bombs"—this from a SIGSALY transcript, speaker unknown.

During the Red Army's pillage of Berlin, Stalin's NKVD (later the KGB) used a scrambler phone to relay intelligence concerning Hitler's dental forensics to Moscow, confirming the Führer's suicide. Evidence of the first Russian vocoder—invented by sampling theorist/radio-engineer Vladimir Kotelnikov in June 1941, two weeks before Russia entered the war—would not be declassified until 1999. Compressing ten speech channels into one, the Kotelnikov Vocoder was devised in a lab in the West Urals, under extreme evacuation conditions, and ultimately constructed in Factory #209 in Leningrad in 1942. During the war, Kotelnikov's scrambler encrypted radiotelephone connections across Transcaucasia from the front lines to Moscow. In spring 1945, the conditions of Germany's surrender, from reparations to looting, would be discussed over a NKVD vocoder radio post in Berlin.

Artificial intelligence and misinformation often ruled in the Soviet Union. Josef Stalin's head of the NKVD, the backstabbing Lavrenti Beria, oversaw the atomic bomb project and the development of a vocoder for secret telephony.

The Soviet postwar take-home included Goebbels' private film collection, women's lingerie, 250 kilograms of confiscated uranium and the scientists needed to convert the uranium into a fissile isotope. These white-collar POWs would be consigned to gulags called *sharashkas*, prisons established to help industrialize Russia out of postwar starvation. Physicists and engineers could not be wasted in Siberia, not with the arms race underway.

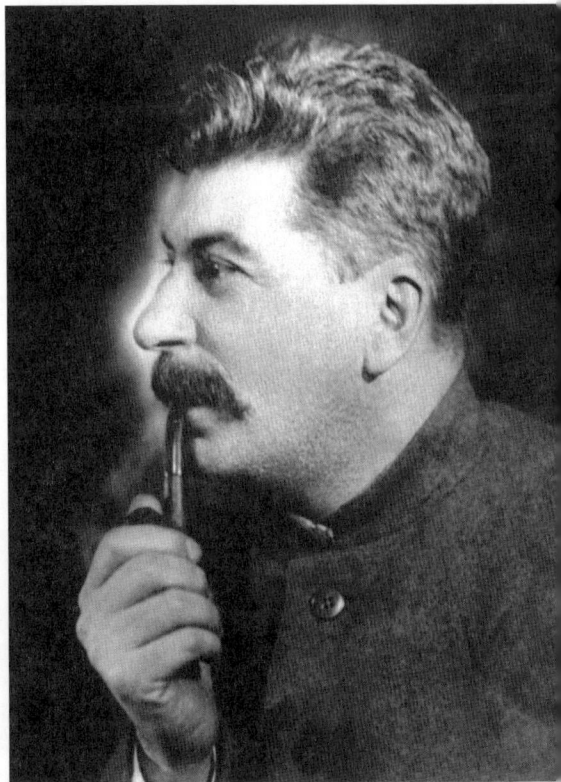

Of particular interest to Moscow was "a US technical journal containing a broad and detailed description of the American vocoder project." Published by Bell Labs, the journal was filed at the Church of Assuage My Sorrows, a seminary in Marfino, just north of Moscow. Marfino had been converted into a prison acoustics lab in 1947 so that inmates (*zeks*) could research Secret Telephony. The order from Moscow was clear. Having filled the Kremlin with backstabbers, Stalin, the two-faced dictator, needed a vocoder to guard his phone.

BURNT BY THE SPECS

That guy is the writer of a few banned books.
— Test sentence for vocoder intelligibility, Ft. Huachuca, Arizona, 1971

The vocoder? Ready? Ha! Ha!
— Alexander Solzhenitsyn, *The First Circle*

Assuage My Sorrows is now Special Prison No. 1. Alexander Solzhenitsyn stands in the prison yard holding a frozen axe, wearing overalls and a druid's tree-beard, unaware of the tumor in his stomach. He has spent the day under headphones, breaking the Russian dictionary down into syllables. Some frequencies can be encrypted over the phone, while others are discarded phlegm. This migraine of phonetics and math cannot distract Solzhenitsyn from the fact that he's designing a vocoder for the Kremlin. At thirty-two years of age, he hopes to be pardoned before the guilt kills him. For now, the best recourse is to rub snow in his face, anoint himself "Director of Articulation," and start wailing on a woodpile like it said the wrong thing. In these parts, in this forever of terms, this could be just about anything.

Solzhenitsyn's fellow inmate Dimitri Panin would describe the semantic perils of the Russian language as a "garbled telegraph signal … a fruitful source of confusion facilitating distortion." Deciphering double-talk was a survival tool in the Soviet Union, where one's belief could mean both conviction and indictment. In 1945, Solzhenitsyn was arrested for criticizing Stalin, "Leader of All Progressive Humanity," in a letter to a friend. As it was learned during Stalin's interoffice purgings in the late Thirties, "comrade" and "friend" had acquired a conflicting

Alexander Solzhenitsyn, Director of Articulation and author of *The First Circle*, worked on a vocoder for the Kremlin while imprisoned in a former seminary outside Moscow in 1949.

list of new definitions, none of which could be trusted, and many of which the Soviet public has not been informed. It's not that the word hadn't been getting around; people just never knew when it would get them next. Understanding was in the apprehension, never beyond grasp.

Once a decorated artillery commander for the Red Army, Solzhenitsyn suffered nine years in the gulags before publicly criticizing Stalin's regime in *One Day in the Life of Ivan Denisovich* and *The First Circle*, both making the author an international hero and a fugitive in his own country. Published, seized and denounced in 1968, fifteen years after Stalin's death, *The First Circle* is based on Solzhenitsyn's experiences as a zek at Marfino, after Stalin made the vocoder a priority. At one point, Solzhenitsyn slips inside Stalin's senile brain on his seventieth birthday as the Premo tries to remember two words: "secret telephony."

Originally assigned to the prison library, Solzhenitsyn, aka The Walrus, would sit in the church's hexagonal tower under a blue lightbulb, sorting through postwar loot, keeping the confiscated tech manuals separate from the prison's generous collection of banned Soviet literature. Compared to the conditions at labor camps up north, those at Marfino were relatively humane. There was white bread, BBC radio and volleyball. An intellectual refuge, Marfino was the one place in the Soviet Union where lonely geniuses could safely commit treason, debating politics and religion, while developing technologies to be used against their own people. With this absurd association with freedom of speech, the sharashka's provenance in Soviet slang was "a sinister enterprise based on bluff and deceit."

+ + +

According to *The First Circle*, Stalin wanted a vocoder for his phone almost as badly as he wanted the Bomb for his country. One dehumanizing machine deserved the other, and the vocoder would have suited the dictator who growled in monotone and eavesdropped on the voices in his head, in a country ruled by misinformation, artificial intelligence and denouncements. Paranoia invoked among millions originated with the megalomaniac in charge—if you think everyone's out to get you, maybe they should be. Something had to protect Stalin's busy imagination from itself. If anyone needed an artificial speech analyzer, it was this control freak who scrambled reality, whose throat was often robotized by streptococcus, a shrewd neurotic who wanted conversations scrutinized on all levels of the spectrum, in a place where shrill hysteria could be detected in the scratch of a whisper. In Russia, the fundamental pitch was fear.

If fear could be read in the spectral analysis of the voice, composer Boris Yankovsky might've been able to isolate its frequency. During the Great Terror of the Thirties, when Stalin was busy eliminating his enemies through forced confessions, Yankovsky achieved breakthroughs in speech decomposition and "re-synthesis." Close to building his own vocoder, Yankovsky had to abandon his research when the avant-garde was denounced as radical. All it took was a voice over the phone, a useful instrument of dread ever since Stalin took power in 1929.

Appropriately, *The First Circle* began with a wiretap. A recording of the conversation is sent to the Marfino prison, where the suspect is to be identified through a voiceprint "phonoscopy." While fellow inmates raced to decode the voiceprint, Solzhenitsyn would spend much of his zek time deconstructing three volumes of *Dahl's Russian Dictionary*. This research, which he called "Relative Frequency Speech Analysis," would get him transferred to a special Acoustics Brigade with his friend Lev Kopelev, a Marxist polyglot and fan of the Mayakovsky poem "A Cloud in Trousers."

The Marfino vocoder was cribbed from Bell Labs, using laboratory equipment that had been looted from German companies like Philips and Lorenz. Analyzing the fidelity and clarity of raw syllables, Solzhenitsyn and Kopelev listened to recordings of zeks reading *Pravda* articles, some of which slandered the Yugoslav rebel Josip Tito, informants and formants alike. These were combined into test phrases for clarity: "He looked, he leapt, he conquered."

Over in Laboratory No. 7, Solzhenitsyn's friend Dimitri Panin went nuts over the fusion of dialect and thermodynamics. While trying to create his own "Language of Maximum Clarity," Panin earned himself a solitary year in vocoder production, to his satisfaction. Marfino's cryptography guru, Professor Timofeyev, would urge Panin to give his vocoder specs to the Kremlin, assuring his freedom. Panin responded by setting his work on fire. The vocoder was Panin's "engineering triumph," a tribute to mental stamina after he had survived more than a decade in the gulag system, mostly in the labor camps near the Arctic.

In the spring of 1950, the chief of Special Prison No. 1 designed a vocoder prototype and asked Solzhenitsyn for an evaluation. Solzhenitsyn panned the chief's design, calling it weak, and was expelled from Marfino, but not before torching his own vocoder diagrams. Transferred yet again, the Walrus ended up in a red cattle car with Panin, en route to more labor camps, stomach cancer, exile, reinstatement, literary fame, more exile, and Vermont. The dictionary went with him.

THE LAST RESORT

In 1984, while Solzhenitsyn was living in the US, Stevie Wonder's keyboard tech Gordon Bahary released the 12 inch "Siberian Nights," under the alias Twilight 22. Issued on Vanguard Records, it was a mediocre electro song about deportation in darkness. At one point, "work" is chanted no fewer than eighteen times. That same year, Bahary recorded a virtually unknown single called "The Dark Side" under the alias Zero Hour. It ends with the vocoder channeling the Russian dirge "Song of the Volga Boatman." As a teenager, Solzhenitsyn had traveled the Volga in a canoe, witnessing famine and blight, Stalin's policies at work.

During the Big Bug Fifties, when movies depicted Communists as giant ants, the Kremlin denounced any Soviet praise of American *teknik*. By then the United States had fallen suspect to another paranoid Joe, this one a senator from Wisconsin. One of Senator McCarthy's more ardent subscribers was Homer Dudley, inventor of the vocoder. Dudley's protégé, Manfred Schroeder, learned this when he was hired by Bell Labs after immigrating to New York from Germany in 1952. "There were two things Homer Dudley liked to talk about," says Schroeder. "The Communists and the vocoder. I didn't have the words at my fingertips in those days, but today I would call him a right-wing nut. He thought the State Department was infested by Communists."

Manfred Schroeder served on a German artillery target acquisition unit during the war, identifying blips in the fog. At times, Russian POWs manned the guns in exchange for food. "They were Communists; they were nice people," he says. "When Sputnik went up in 1958, Dudley came to my desk with the following idea. He said the Russians could not put up a satellite like that and the beep-beep-beep that people heard around the world, coming from Sputnik, was just an electronic fakery."

Working with Dudley in the acoustics department, Schroeder would consult *The First Circle* while developing his own voice-excited vocoder—the first of these machines to actually sound human. Demonstrating for his associates, Schroeder assumed that his vocoder could be understood, only because he'd been listening to it all day, the same pratfall that occurs in *The First Circle*. Struggling between intelligibility and just hearing things, he noted its annoying habit of turning a phrase. "How to recognize speech" sounded like "How to wreck a nice beach."

"People will go to any length (and width) to be unintelligible," wrote Schroeder in his book *Computer Speech: Recognition, Compression, and Synthesis*. So much for the Language of Maximum Clarity.

In *The First Circle*, Solzhenitsyn compared speech encoding to disassembling a beach and then re-synthesizing it at another location—essentially transposing a summer getaway as if it were a Soviet munitions factory on the run. He called it "an engineering desecration," the equivalent of pulverizing a southern resort into grits, sticking them into a billion matchboxes, shaking them up and then flying them to a different sector for reconstruction. "A re-creation of the subtropics, the sound of the waves on the shore, the southern air and moonlight."

The sand in your shorts, the bad radio reception, the copper tonality, the jellyfish parachute squishing between your toes, the effervescent fizz of unvoiced surf. The burning red sun. For the zeks at Marfino the vocoder could make getaways out of sentences, if only inside their heads. A gulag prison term, an imagined escape. The last re-sort, a desperate scramble. As if Solzhenitsyn had burst from his lab table in a flock of schemata, his beard tangled with headphones, denouncing the artificial beach. Somebody had to say something.

Bell Labs' Manfred Schroeder, inventor of the Voice-Excited Vocoder, photographed in his New Jersey home with Jonzun Crew's *Lost In Space* LP. When conducting intelligibility tests with the vocoder, Schroeder liked to use the word *Aztekenexpresszuggesellschaft* (Aztec Indian Tribe).

CHAPTER FOUR

AS IT IS, ON MARS'

We are but the shadows of still more shadowy things.

— Kenneth Patchen

THE BEAST FROM 20,000 TONS OF TNT

In the summer of 1949, it appeared that an amusement park had crashed into Venice Beach. Construction for new attractions was underway. On an ice cream stroll with his wife Maggie, twenty-nine-year-old Ray Bradbury saw the coils of an extinct rollercoaster, sad with rust and seaweed, and called it a washed-up dinosaur. Having married someone who believed dinosaurs still ruled, Bradbury's wife went with it. In the distance, a lighthouse belched.

Two years later, the *Saturday Evening Post* published "The Fog Horn," Bradbury's story of a hard-up Rhedosaurus who mistakes a fog horn moan for romantic interest and clobbers a lighthouse in frustration. At the time, a commercial for Lifebuoy soap used a Sonovox and a foghorn for a sustained "B.O." signal. (Homer Dudley had already dedicated a paragraph to fog horn articulation in vocoder patent 2,339,465, filed in 1944.) This blast from a docker's armpit made gulls plunk dead from the sky and so became one of radio advertising's most memorable hooks.

In 1953, "The Fog Horn" was adapted for the screen as *The Beast From 20,000 Fathoms*. Bombed out of bed by the Cold War—and not having had sex for a million years—the creature went to New York and adjusted Manhattan's Kong insurance and then lumbered over to Coney Island, only to be shot with a nuclear isotope and "die like an opera singer" in front of the Cyclone. The Beast had been brought to life by incredibly patient stop-motion animator Ray Harryhausen, a close friend of Bradbury's who blew up model U-boats for Navy training films while serving in the US Signal Corps. During the war, Bradbury had happily failed his Army physical after being diagnosed as too blind for combat, leaving him free to squint at the future from the safety of his typewriter. "I went into the future and never came back," he tells me. "I started out in the center of the earth. Then I went to Mars."

Unfortunately for Mars, Bradbury brought some Earth baggage along with him. His nuclear fears would manifest on a Godzilla scale of destruction while inside the quiet comfort of the last house standing on

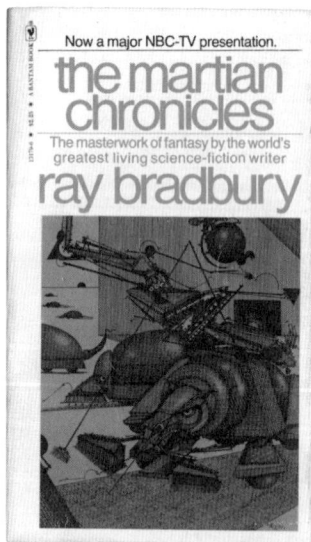

Robot-mouse cleaning as pictured on the cover of Ray Bradbury's *The Martian Chronicles*, adapted with vocoder for a BBC Radiophonic Workshop radio play in 1977.

the red planet—empty, automated and in complete denial. In 1950, while America habituated to postwar convenience and *Popular Science* celebrated robot servitude, Bradbury published *The Martian Chronicles*, which included "August 2026," a story where the ultimate efficiency home meets the ultimate efficiency weapon. Like those who live alone, the house talks to itself while conducting the day's business, preparing an Olympian's breakfast as synthetic voices chirp about overdue bills and the weather forecast: "Galoshes and raincoats today!"

After the robot cleaning mice complete their chores, the house lights a cigar and asks for any poetry requests. Room cleared, it defaults to "There Will Come Soft Rains" by the poet Sara Teasdale, reciting it down to the last singing frog. It posed a rhetorical question: Would Nature care if man ceased to exist, with technology subbing in for Nature, as if man couldn't help himself? The frogs answer no.

"My wife had read me that poem. I was so touched that I ran home and wrote the short story. During that time, they reproduced photographs of buildings in Hiroshima. People were photographed against the walls of their houses. All that was left was the shadow where they'd been standing." Accordingly, the eastern flank of Bradbury's Martian house bore the silhouettes of its occupants, along with the shadow of a child's ball, fried in mid-arc.

+ + +

In August 1945, the vocoder continued to play the dehumanizer—in SIGSALY's voice timbre (the laryngectomee's monotone) and with the casualties themselves, the subtraction of a population. Earlier that summer, at the Trinity test site, Manhattan Project physicist Robert Oppenheimer was in the process of chain-smoking himself to cancer, the lump in his throat malignant, his voice box in no better condition than his conscience. Though General Stoner had ordered the SIGSALY transcripts from Hiroshima to be immediately destroyed, one anonymous Signal Corps officer recalled hearing two words through the vocoder. "Hell-Bomb." The spectral description of speech had described what could not be imagined, a carbonized human outline in a ghost town. The shape of things to come.

According to Malcolm Clarke, he was hired by the BBC for his pronounced two-minute burps. Clarke's award-winning vocoder adaptation of Ray Bradbury's "August 2026" originally aired in 1977.

KEEP ME WELL AWAY FROM THE NAKED LIGHT

In 1977, the British Society of Authors awarded Best Drama to the BBC Radio adaptation of Bradbury's "August 2026." In the credits, top billing went to the vocoder and the show's producer, Malcolm Clarke, a man believed to have "cornered the market in deteriorating states of mind." Clarke was employed by the BBC Radiophonic Workshop, established in 1958 to provide customized sound effects for radio and television shows like *Doctor Who*, *Dr. Quatermass* and *The Goon Show*. The Workshop was stashed in a skating rink near a zoo in Westminster, in a building said to have looked like a mildewed wedding cake. "I always heard of the Radiophonic Workshop, but I never knew it was anywhere you could go," says Peter Howell, a composer who used the vocoder for *Doctor Who* as well as a gurgling trip inside the body. "I thought it was something that just existed." Less a studio and more of a foxhole, the Workshop was known for innovation that transcended its peanut-butter-and-jelly budget. Personnel constantly raided redundant shops for equipment, improvising and embellishing their Philips tape machines and turntables. "It was always on 'beg, borrow and steal,'" continues Howell. "The stuff nobody wanted."

Annoying parents and frightening children within the same cosmic scream, the Workshop would fill orders for an oscillation for the end of the world, "a high hum of pure agony," the rustle of man-eating plants, Daleks exploding into "screaming jelly," and the sound of an office building flying through space in the grip of seven powerful tractor beams. The BBC switchboard was jammed with curiosity. "People were genuinely open-mouthed about this stuff when it came out," says Howell. "It's difficult to believe, but it was something they'd never heard before. It was an interesting time because we were just as wide-eyed about it as the public was, really. It's just we were privileged enough to get our hands on the [equipment] and fiddle around with it."

In 1969, the Workshop hired Malcolm Clarke based on his ability to burp for the better part of two minutes. He would be immortalized in Radiophonic lore when recruited by Workshop head Delia Derbyshire for a radioplay of Aristophanes' *The Clouds*. (A gastronomer himself, Aristophanes once punctuated speeches with hiccups.) "She needed a stomach-rumbling mating-fart ritual dance," says Clarke over the phone from his London home. "So I spent a half-hour swallowing air. I did one out right on the green cue light. It went on for nearly a minute. It was a beauty."

Derbyshire, the tape loop genius, was impressed. Clarke had outdone himself. "I hope my burp is still in the library, because I made myself feel quite ill doing it," he told me. "It had nothing to do with diet. It's entirely done by skill and virtuosity. Keep me well away from the naked light, I'll tell you that!"

Malcolm Clarke had learned to convert his stomach into a studio via an esophageal speech technique used by throat cancer patients. "I was interested in how they'd teach laryngectomy patients to swallow air and bring it up. Once they brought up the air, they use the burping sound to articulate words. When you burp your vocal cords don't play any part in it. It sounded quite vulgar, but at least people could speak."

Clarke was first introduced to his gift at the age of six while growing up in Leicester, England, city of vice, bingo and great potato chips. To treat his whooping cough, Clarke's parents would wheel him down to the gas works, where he'd sit in his push-chair and inhale. "Gas is a rich source of harmonics. When you're first faced with a vocoder, it's kind of a reverse-synthesis thing. You've got to put in more than you need in order to get intelligibility out. You need something that's got lots of harmonics in it in order that the rest of the gubbins that comes in after the sound can modulate it. The richer the sound, the more intelligibility comes out of the vocoder. There are a lot of low harmonics in the burp, which might be a nuisance. Your imagination is much more talented than the reality because once you get some stomach rumbles together, they're not as exciting as you think."

MAJESTIC HORRIBLE NOISES

In 1976, a massive piece of electronic furniture appeared at the Workshop, with "cheeks of teak" and armrests. This was the EMS 5000 Vocoder, a £10,500 machine that could detect the difference between a noise and a sound. "You couldn't avoid it," recalls Peter Howell. "It was a very unusual shape—higher at the back and all the controls were tipped toward you. When you first came to it, it certainly looked weird and wonderful because it just had interesting labels on it, like Frequency Shifter and Pitch Extractor."

According to Howell, the EMS vocoder allowed them to control the consonants separate from the vowels. ("You could turn down the consonants and they sound as if their teeth had dropped out.") While trees were "too polite," Clarke would often rile up the vocoder using external noise recordings of steam trains and roadwork. "A talking concrete mixer is very rich. You can filter it and make it talk. It's a horrible noise but very interesting. Loud mechanical things were ideal. I don't think there's anything purely electronic that hasn't owed itself to nature and nature usually does it better. [Nature] has more imperfections in it. As humans, we like the imperfections. You'll always have a reference to what happens in nature. Even if it's completely outlandish, it has to relate somehow." While suffering through a management training course, Malcolm Clarke daydreamed about vocoders ("I was desperate to get back to it") and read Bradbury's *Martian Chronicles* to cope with the separation. "'August 2026' is about the death of a house. I thought we could do the whole bloomin' lot electronically." However, it was hard to keep actors from scrunching their noses when speaking through the vocoder. "Actors are lovely people, but when it came to using the vocoder, they are suspicious animals. They think their performance is going to be destroyed. They were determined to behave like robots and I couldn't stop them. I said, 'Look, this is in the year 2026, *we don't sound like Daleks*!" Just because there would be electronic voices in the future doesn't mean that humans wouldn't make sense."

This EMS Synthi 100 Vocoder went to the WDR in Cologne while the BBC tackeled the 5000. In a letter to Malcolm Clarke, Ray Bradbury wrote, "The sound you imagined and the quality you gave my robots was truly amazing." Bradbury asked if the BBC would release it on LP, along with another vocoder story for the B-side. The Dust Witch balloon attack from *Something Wicked This Way Comes* would've been ideal for unvoiced hiss energy.

"The vocoder is not man's best friend," adds Peter Howell.

Clarke remembers the vocoder being unforgiving when it came to artifacts between speech sounds. "When people speak they tend to generate sounds, which are not going to be helpful. The vocoder assumes that every sound that goes in there is speech—be it a splutter, plosive, script rustle, studio atmosphere, unwanted mouth noise or fart. It will translate in its own terms. Any extraneous sounds were translated by the vocoder into speech-like sounds, which became very confusing."

Through tape edits, Clarke removed any sounds that weren't part of the voice information, including any gasps and heaves between the lines, leaving him with a cachet of random noises. "I remember joining the fricatives and plosives all together and playing them back. It went *skhlrrp-sklurp*. I played those majestic horrible noises backwards through the vocoder, and I thought, 'A clock!' You should never turn your back on a good accident."

The cleaning mice with vibrato mustaches were personal favorites of Bradbury's. "I got to thinking about mice and how they occupy a house," he says. "You don't know that they're there. I thought it would be wonderful if you had mice that ran around the house and cleaned it for you but you never saw them. They came from the warrens in the wall." Inspired by an electric toothbrush, Clarke gave the mice a fussy pitch for the clean-up scene when the family dog comes home covered in radiation sores. Overwhelmed by the smell of automated pancakes, the dog goes berserk, chasing his tail in circles until Clarke makes him "disappear up his own asshole."

ANSWER ECHOES DYING

In May of 2003, I received a package from Malcolm Clarke of Everlasting Lane in Herts, England. Included was a CD of preliminary vocoder tests for the Bradbury play and a brief letter. Apparently, Clarke couldn't find the recording of the original broadcast but here was "some vocoder stuff." The letter parted with an Irish beer salute and a drawing of a chubby spider with nostrils, smiling. The CD began with sustained noise at various pitches, from snub-nosed power drills to proboscis whining, as if the Green Hornet had donned a mosquito mask. This was followed by a cringing version of a HAL standard, "Daisy Bell," pitched into the nosebleeds.

Two months later, I called Clarke to thank him, only to sadly learn that he had died of a heart attack at the age of sixty-four. I then returned to his test demo, focusing on the incontinent white noise. The signal appeared to be in pain, struggling to birth speech, but something was there—the voice of a day, repeating itself mindless. Clarke had explained this during our last phone conversation, playing a game with intelligibility and intelligence. "Some people hear [the voice] very early on in the transition from pure chaos and noise into perfect speech. I took the voice of the calendar ("Today is August the fourth 2026") but I started with the raw ingredients, filtered white noise, which gradually begins to pulse and shape. The beginning is a barren landscape out of which emerges intelligence—the house. The discovery of intelligence."

The process was reversed for the end of "August 4th," when the house catches fire and dies. "In the beginning, the barometer has a very low voice," said Clarke. "Towards the end, the quality of his voice catches fire. The barometer turns from flames into steam and evaporates."

"They did a fine job when the house catches fire," adds Bradbury. The mice whiz about spewing water and the house is frantic, caught between survival and loops of habit, "making breakfast at a psychopathic rate," mowing the lawn, slamming doors, chucking umbrellas out the door. Several vocoded voices scream all at once, pitching fits, a crying of lot 451, one singing "Daisy," another reading a Tennyson poem in the burning den. "Blow bugle blow answer echoes dying, dying, dying..." Then smoke. Then silence.

One wall stands among the ruins and inside it, the last vocoder, the daily minder repeating the day after, "Today is August the Fifth," the voice disintegrating into the white noise landscape, what Malcolm Clarke called "the demise of intelligence," information itself. The repetition seems to be nagging, as if mocking an attempt to perpetuate ourselves, in the event—a flashing instant—that we forget.

CHAPTER FIVE

COLOR OUT OF SPACE

Spectrum Spreading was a natural result of the Second World War battle for electronic supremacy, a war waged with jamming.

— Robert Price, *A History of Spread Spectrum Communications*

ON THE BEACH

Sky's afummadiddled!
— Richard Matheson, "Tis the Season to Be Jelly"

It's not easy being obsessed.
— Nils Hellstrom, entomologist

Fuck that shit, let's go to Pac Jam.
— Poison Clan, "Shake What Ya Mama Gave Ya"

Today is August 25, 1983.

The barometer screams for intelligence. Miami Beach screams back with the wrong answer, and in neon. The wavelengths have changed. Spectrum communications is now spread across beach towels, its frequency bands blaring in stripes: sunburnt Swatches, ultraviolet bikinis, flip-flop drunks. A small plane drags an announcement across the sky: The Coca Cola Y100 Amazing Fun End of Summer Marathon of Music. At this altitude, the crowd noise is but a hum, sucked into the plane's nose, the vortical shredder. Down below, in the shadow of a giant inflatable beer can, the vocoder is tended by a man dressed like an eighteenth-century French aristocrat. His name is Michael Jonzun, and his powdered wig is itchy.

The throng glows. They came to hear Jonzun perform "Pack Jam," an electro-funk 12 inch released on Tommy Boy Records, a song that wanted to exterminate all Pac-Man machines but couldn't, and settled for transforming Jonzun's voice into the spectral description of all hell else. Off to the side of the stage is Weird Al Yankovic, a frizzy accordion player in a cheerleading uniform and sweaty glasses. Next to Weird Al is a tiny R&B singer named Stacy Lattisaw and behind her is Sylvester Stallone's brother Frank. Frank is juiced from performing "Far from Over," a push-up jam that inspired John Travolta to tighten a piece of string around his head in *Staying Alive*. Weird Al is juiced because he's Weird Al. The humidity has introduced his hair, a spoof of hair, to moisture retention—an asset for one in the business of being zany and imitating Michael Jackson. Lattisaw is juiced because she's seventeen

Freestyle "Don't Stop the Rock" (1985, Music Specialist). Produced by Pretty Tony Butler, "Don't Stop the Rock" is the first vocoder song to use the word "Freakathon." Pretty Tony wore a pilot's hat like Rocky the Squirrel and created at least three incarnations of Freestyle, each masked by vocoder, and no less than five Debbie Debs.

and just sang "Let Me Be Your Angel" on Miami Beach. Her earrings are bright and her collar could poke out the sun. Though attendant to their own planets, they can't help but stare at Jonzun, who seems to be dressed for the headless side of the French Revolution, an unporous move in this climate. His band, the Jonzun Crew—Gordon Worthy, Steve Thorpe and Jonzun's brother Soni—are three sparkly musketeers in fringes. It's too hot for hair, much less a powdered wig. The only powder going around Miami in 1983 was the coke that paid for Italian sports cars in cash, embarrassed the Federal Reserve, and funded The Music Specialist, Miami's first successful electro hip-hop label and home to vocoder producer Pretty Tony Butler, the first man in Dade County to have Space Invaders hooked up in the glove compartment of his Delta 88.

Michael Jonzun never touched the stuff. Born Johnson, he is the youngest of six Johnson brothers who as a band could mimic the Jacksons and the Brothers Johnson. Something of a literalist, Jonzun had to make a name for himself and consulted the phone book first, no Jonzuns there, and so changed his signature. "Jonzun" had a French zing, kind of.

The Amazing End of Summer Jam took place on Miami Beach in 1983 and featured Jonzun Crew, Weird Al Yankovic, Frank Stallone, Stacy Lattisaw, and Champaign.

COZELL MCQUEEN

After North Carolina State upset Houston in the 1983 NCAA basketball championship, fans and students burned couches to "Pack Jam." (The man behind "Pack Jam," Michael Jonzun, is pictured above.) According to Wolfpack guard Derek Wittenberg, "Pack Jam" was the soundtrack to their impossible tournament run, a 35-foot air-ball rescued from prayer and dunked when the buzzer screamed red—an entire season, compressed into a final second. That spring, Jonzun Crew and New Edition played at Reynolds Coliseum on NCSU's campus in Raleigh.

Officially, his hit song is "Pack Jam (Look Out for the OVC)," though nobody seemed to know what the OVC was, nor why they should be looking out for it. The first to bring "Pack Jam" down to Florida was Allen Johnston, a record hustler for Tommy Boy who'd been thawing out in Miami after spending the Vietnam War doing glacier search-and-rescue in Alaska. Allen first tested "Pack Jam" on his kids (they freaked) and then pushed the song on the radio, clubs and record stores. You could soon hear "Pack Jam" in Woolworth's, piped in over the impulse-buy Venus flytraps. Over at Superstar Rollerteque, North Miami's first all-black rink, kids took off their skates in the middle of the floor and danced to "Pack Jam." At a synagogue down in Coral Gables, kids did jumping jacks to "Pack Jam."

The Jonzun's Prophet-5 synthesizer played a frowning metal sky. The song's only words, "Pack Jam look out," were a warning, maybe a threat. Maybe prepare for lunch. The vocoder's throat seemed to be dislodging something, namely darkness, less night than deep space. And it actually *cackled*, like it was onto something, maybe your sandwich, a greedy fly rubbing its hands together.

Whatever "Pack Jam look out" meant, at least Miami could say they had been warned and that they had been warned by the only black guy in a Bastille wig to use a vocoder to control a crowd in South Florida—not exactly the most evolved slap of real estate in the gun handle. Last out of the water, one of the last to desegregate. The fact that Jonzun was causing such a racket must have been unsettling to some of Miami's older, leatherier resident tourists, sitting inside mumbling into their air conditioners. That is if they could even hear it, old folks being old folks, searching the radio for something quiet. (Pack Jam! Heavy rotation!) And if they could, they wouldn't believe it, staring through tight-lipped windows.

Historically, Miami itself was very familiar with pack jam, an exchange of fat suitcases in the restless heat, where the ground itself never settled. In the Eighties, Miami enjoyed a growth boom unheard, paying for its new skyline through the nose, oblivious to the decade's violent birth, back when five white Dade County police officers were acquitted after fatally beating a black insurance agent for flipping off a squad car at a stoplight. The ensuing riots in Liberty City on May 17, 1980, left eighteen dead and $80 million in damages. That day, Bell Telephone operator James McCauley returned from his lunch break to a panicked switchboard, thinking it might be the usual wiretap paranoia (a common occurrence in Miami). Instead, it was the tremulous elderly, reporting the end of civilization. "Back then, 9-1-1 was in its infancy," says McCauley, who went on to become the most vocodered voice in Miami, recording under aliases like Maggotron and DXJ. "People think the operator knows everything, especially the older generation. They figure the operator knows who you are. They'd call up, '*Operator, I need to tell you! They're breaking into the Winn Dixie!*' And hang up."

The following October, when the Mariel Boatlift brought 125,000 Cuban refugees to town, McCauley's switchboard lit up with more hysterics, this time in Spanish. Named after its port of flight, the Mariel Boatlift began with a siege at Cuba's Peruvian embassy and ended with

The Jonzun Crew, "Pak Man (Look Out for the OVC)" (Boston International Records)

Fidel Castro cleverly exporting his dissident problem to South Florida, essentially calling the White House bluff of providing amnesty from communist dictators. In a matter of weeks, the city's population increased by an Orange Bowl and a half. Miami had, in its many selves, become pack jam.

Willie Perez, now regarded as the best poplocker in Miami, was an eight-year-old *Marielito* when his parents fled Cuba in 1980. He remembers it as a "long-ass boat ride." Three years later, Perez saw a blind DJ named Mickey C playing "Pack Jam" and danced like an escapist with syrup for bones, less an elusion and more a way of getting into something, playing the Martian card, something from a place where

A former telephone operator in Miami, James "Maggotron" McCauley's electro-bass music drew inspiration from nematodes, boating instructional records, his garden, Nikita Khrushchev, skating backwards to "Rock Lobster," bacon, Nazi propaganda, plastic furniture covers, and a Funkadelic song called "March to the Witch's Castle."

kids didn't make fun of his English and his light skin, calling him "white boy." For Willie Perez, "Pack Jam" wasn't a capacity for understanding. It was a matter of space. So he started calling himself "Chillski" and danced at a teeny hip-hop club called Pac Jam, located in Liberty City in North Miami. Perez said he'd go there, look good and get the hell out.

Pac Jam was all things Miami: a party, a place, a pirate radio station, a handy buzzword for overstating the room, another dimension in itself. But for Willie Perez, "get in where you fit in" was a shrinking elastic contradiction in the club, in a world crammed into a city, where spread spectrum was in itself compression. At Pac Jam, the bass was as purple as a heart attack. Cuban was white, white was lines and black was Dominican, Haitian, Jamaican, Creole, Georgian. Whatever fit the Dade County police's idea of spectral description.

Pac Jam Teen Disco had dropped its "k" in deference to Pac-Man, a dot-gobbling arcade game that Michael Jonzun avoided because it made him dizzy. So he recorded "Pack Jam" with the intent of obliterating the most popular kid-fattening time-rot since TV. "We took a man and turned him into jam," Michael Jonzun would tell me, seriously, just trying to avoid getting litigated by Pac-Man's manufacturer Namco. For appearances' sake, the vocoder obliged, being somewhat unclear on these matters to begin with.

+ + +

The vocoder would flourish in Miami, where it was a good idea to pick up a few spare identities and a speech scrambler, where everyone's a character, whether you're a Cuban double agent working for the CIA shadowed by the FBI, or say, Amos Larkin, a guy recording under at least ten different aliases with the Bee Gees' unused vocoder in a motel studio run by Krishnas in West Palm, surrounded by outlaws with recording contracts shadier than swampy real estate deals. (The Bee Gees covered the Beatles' "Mean Mister Mustard" through the vocoder in the Robert Stigwood film *Sgt. Pepper's Lonely Hearts Club Band*.) In Miami, one could make a career out of being somebodies—Larkin said he had to keep changing names so radio wouldn't get sick of him, inventing a son and a grandson (Larkin II and III) and making a song called "FRESH BEATS WITHOUT RAP BASS YOUR CAR STREETS AND PARTY." Amos decided to do electro records after smoking away an afternoon at the South Dade 8 watching *Tron*. ("They just went up in that damn computer, didn't they? I never saw any shit like that!") *Tron*, with its Gentlemen's Club fluorescence and minitruck blues and pinks, had enough neon to shame Miami Beach.

In 1982, Larkin recorded "E.T. Boogie" and "I Like It (Corn Flakes)," perhaps the only vocoder song to say, "Raisin Bran makes you feel like a man." That year, as Miami police sparked another riot by fatally shooting an African American teenager in a video arcade, a man in a bug suit recorded a vocoder song entitled "Electronic Pussy Sucker." Calling himself Blowfly, he had a hyperbolic middle finger and claimed to give better head than Pac-Man.

+ + +

As things stood, jumping up and down, Miami Beach is quite fond of Pac-Man. The crowd at the Amazing End of Summer Jam screams bloody quarter with Michael Jonzun's wig on it. So Jonzun asks, "Are you ready for the Pack Jam?" smiling behind the hope that the sand hasn't gritted his machine. A wink of granule is deafening when cracked between teeth. The salted air may be unkind to the vocoder, which is just happy not to be in a Russian prison.

Then things get blurry for Jonzun, on stage, sweating musket balls. Did he just hear the vocoder say, "Black man, look out"? He tells Miami to look out for the OVC instead. Crowd: Whatever you say, man.

Michael Jonzun, creator of "Pack Jam (Look Out for the OVC)," released on Tommy Boy Records in 1983. "People gotta like what's going on even if they have no idea what's going on," said Jonzun, who also released the electro 12 inch "Unclear Holocaust" while recording as The Future.

Weird Al: That *is* that thing in "P.Y.T." that goes "P.Y.T." after Michael Jackson says, "I've got to love you!"

Giant Inflatable Beer Can: I seem to be losing air.

Lattisaw: I am doing the Snake, having a ball.

Stallone: I am no longer here and nobody cares.

GO WITH THE SPACEMAN

I am Chroma the Great, conductor of color, maestro of pigment and director of the entire spectrum.
— *The Phantom Tollbooth*

OVC! Yeah, I remember the OVC. I never thought the OVC was real.
— Jordan Knight, New Kids On the Block

Sun Ra sits in darkness, starving for photons and wishing for ice cream. He withholds carbon dioxide while intubated by a machine designed to remap the chromatic spectrum. This silver hexagonal screen is the Outer Visual Communicator, the ideal companion for a man believed to be at once from Alabama and Saturn. For the moment, Sun Ra is stuck in 1985, sharing a studio with New Kids On the Block.

The OVC's inventor (named Bill Sebastian) stands behind him, twirling his beard into little red balls. Beyond their whisper, Mission Control Studios is empty. NKOTB have the day off. Normally, they'd be there rehearsing, transforming themselves into your little sister's everwaking tear-streaked wall-plastered moment. But none of the New Kids are old enough to drive. Their producer, Maurice Starr, hasn't given them a car to illegally tool around in. Not yet. Donnie Wahlberg is elsewhere in Boston, smoothing his rattail and playing video games, trying to scare up some facial hair.

Sun Ra can breathe easy and be a man from Saturn in peace. Three narrow plastic tubes snake from his mouth into an electric harmonica, which is wired to the OVC. Sun Ra's cheeks deflate, causing the hexagon to erupt in a scramble of color. Tiny flashes of light, also hexagonally shaped, chase each other across the screen's Plexiglass surface.

The original OVC was manually operated, an idea that originated when Bill Sebastian played keyboards for the Johnsons in the early Seventies, spelling the band's name out in lights. In the fall of 1973, a friend had advised Sebastian to catch an Arkestra gig in downtown Boston. He said, "I don't know what's going to happen to you but you have to do this." So Sebastian did that and spent the next five years of his life designing and building the Outer Visual Communicator.

Bill Sebastian at the controls of the OVC, circa 1980. The OVC was partially built in the basement of a machine shop at MIT, where Gunnar Fant invented a vowel synthesizer called the OVE (Orator Verbis Electris) in 1953.

Construction began in a warehouse on Thayer Street until one of the tenants blew up the building while attempting to devise a homemade oil centrifuge in the basement. Sebastian then relocated to a Swedish machine shop at MIT, a haven for vocoder research, where he held a day job welding laser base plates for NASA. He wore a vulcanized helmet with a window and daydreamed about "ripping apart old organs and doing strange things to them." Sometimes Michael Jonzun would show up and help wire the OVC to pay for his lodging at Sebastian's mildly ghoulish manor in Roxbury, Massachusetts.

In October of 1978, Sebastian finished the OVC inside a barn in Ore City, Texas. Local farmers saw this sixteen-foot sentient hexagon and assumed he was either building a spacecraft or harvesting killer bud. Sebastian, to his credit, did little to dissuade them. He listened to

Sun Ra records ("Tapestry from an Asteroid") and mumbled to himself while tractors drove in circles.

Sun Ra finally met the completed OVC in the fall of 1978, in Sebastian's drafty loft in downtown Boston. There, he found his new friend hunched over a small hexagonal keyboard, his fingers flitting across touch-sensitive "capacitants." Sebastian was making "spacescapes," as if he had *Close Encounters* on speed dial, consuming 15,000 watts of power in the process. Sebastian told me he would play the OVC just to keep warm in the winter. "The capacitants respond to the magnetic field in your hand," he says, calling from the parking lot of a Cape Cod grocery store. "It's like electronic finger-painting. You could shoot comets across the screen. Seventeen million colors at mind-dazzling speeds. I didn't even have to think about my fingers." Sun Ra would finally leave Sebastian's loft three days later—he had to have the OVC.

By 1980, Sebastian and the OVC were performing with Sun Ra's Arkestra at Mass Auditorium in Boston. Sebastian wore a pyramid on his head and hopped around on stage in a purple gown. "To see him do that with his red hair was amazing," said one witness. "It was way over my head."

"Bill looked like a wizard from fairy tales," adds Michael Jonzun's older brother Calvin, a horn player. "But I never thought he was strange. You gotta be into the character. If I'm gonna believe it, then you gotta believe it. That's the Outer Visual Communicator. You see, this guy Sun Ra, he had a big following. I mean the guy's been around a million years."

One night, Sun Ra asked Michael Jonzun to substitute on the sound board at Mass Auditorium. He was told that the OVC was "designed to go infinitely dark." "The OVC operated in the Scotopic Shadow World," says Sebastian. "Or Suboptic Shadow World. When we performed, we extinguished every light source in the auditorium. We'd starve the mind in darkness. There were Light Police to enforce this policy. The OVC could function effectively at the threshold where there was no color— just apparitional shadows in a totally blacked-out room. So much of our visual experience is based on filtering out information. Denial. Visually, everything is spam when you walk down the street. There's umpteen trillion photons hitting the retina. You can only see little pieces of it.

When you get down to the Scotopic Shadow World, it's the other way around. Your brain and your cones are trying to pick up any photon, any piece of information they can get. So when the OVC lit up—half of what the audience saw was in its imagination." With its 20,000 wires, chips and endless racks of equipment, the machine filled two trailers. Sebastian soon found himself spending more time under the OVC's hood than onstage in his purple gown. Brilliant isn't always practical— it's hard to get to Saturn when you can't even get off the truck.

After the Jonzun Crew signed with Tommy Boy Records in 1982, label manager Monica Lynch and CEO Tom Silverman visited Bill Sebastian's baronial residence in Roxbury, Massachusetts. Lynch described it as "the Munsters' house." She remembers the OVC, coiled up in the back of the studio behind a curtain. "It was crazy, like a hybrid of a time machine and a Chinese magic dragon." "The OVC was long," adds Silverman. "The length of the room. I never really understood the shit behind it, though. I have a science background but I still couldn't figure it out."

In 1984, Sebastian took Sun Ra to Mission Control Studios and plugged him into a leaner, new and improved OVC-3D, a "mouth-controlled virtual reality hologram machine." It would be used for Sun Ra's video "Calling Planet Earth," which was partially funded by Michael Jonzun. At the time, Michael and his brother Maurice Starr ("Larry") were grooming New Kids On the Block and recruited Sebastian to direct the video for "Be My Girl," a song that Starr had written while in junior high. Sebastian's editing helped synchronize the New Kids' choreography, which helped them get a record deal with Columbia Records.

Maurice Starr had been calling the New Kids "NY NUK," or maybe New Nuke, possibly as fissile vengeance against New Edition, another kid group Starr produced in 1982, with much success. Starr and New Edition parted ways the following year when, by coincidence, Columbia decided to pass on a Sun Ra 12 inch called *Nuclear War*, a record that posed a tautology about what to do without your ass when your ass is gone.

The New Kids practiced at Mission Control Studios, trying to dance their way out of New Edition's shoebox. This would not be easy, since

I THOUGHT I HEARD

Arthur Baker, who discovered Jonzun and Starr, also produced New Order. Prior to working with Baker, New Order vocodered, "I thought I was mistaken / I thought I heard your words" in "Blue Monday," while also using the device for polyphonic shading. Released in 1983, New Order's "Ecstasy" was essentially a vocoder on a tone bender, mumbling "I've lost my way."

Michael Jonzun in the studio with Danny Wood, Donnie Wahlberg, and Jordan Knight of NKOTB. According to Wahlberg, watching Jonzun use the vocoder was like playing catch with Mickey Mantle.

New Edition had already gone platinum just after cracking puberty. Fifteen years later, when Earth would scream for boy bands, Sun Ra had moved on, leaving his fans behind breathing holograms. Bill Sebastian, meanwhile, remained in Boston with his faulty Outer Visual Communicator. "He [Sebastian] was Frankenstein's assistant," says Donnie Wahlberg, on the phone from Hollywood. "He was this computer-genius gremlin who kept popping out from behind some equipment with some tool in his hand. He had this really scruffy red beard. He'd just kind of stand there and twirl his beard into balls and talk about stuff. None of this, 'Pack Jam' and all, would've been possible without him." "Pack Jam was about the OVC," smiles Sebastian. "The vocoder was talking to that little video-game critter. 'You're about to be annihilated by the OVC!'" Sun Ra had once said: "A voice from another dimension will be speaking to Earth. You may as well practice and prepare for it." In 1983, Donnie Wahlberg was sort of prepared. In a record store in Boston, the thirteen-year-old stood with his younger brother Mark, with $3.99 between them, and faced the ultimate decision: "Pack Jam" or "Candy Girl." "I had to go with the Spaceman!" Wahlberg tells me.

When I initially asked Wahlberg about the vocoder, he paused and exhaled, "That's my *shiiiiiiit*." Wahlberg remembers first seeing the machine at Mission Control. Maurice Starr had gimped in late from a game of pick-up basketball, using a busted mop handle for a crutch. ("Must've landed funny.") Sebastian wore grease-encrusted jeans and a yellow plaid shirt. Michael Jonzun played with the vocoder while the OVC lay in the back room in a state of disrepair.

Wahlberg was in awe. "The first time Michael whipped out the vocoder and started using it, it was like, unbelievable. It was a big thing for me, man. He'd do it to show off because he knew I loved it. It might sound silly to sit around in the studio and watch Michael Jonzun mess around with the vocoder. But understanding what I grew up listening to—the fusion of the funk and Kraftwerk and Bambaataa—for me to actually see this thing…to see Michael speak into this microphone and hear this whole other thing coming out, it was pretty incredible. I could never fathom how they were made—it's like playing catch with Mickey Mantle. As a twelve-year-old kid, these are the biggest things in the world to me."

North End, "Tee's Happy" (1980, Emergency Records). This was an early disco collaboration between Jonzun, Starr, Arthur Baker, and Tee Scott. Emergency also released Kano's Italian vocoder dance classic "I'm Ready."

WITHOUT SOUNDING LIKE SOMETHING

The last time I saw Donnie Wahlberg, he was missing his eyebrows, shivering in his underwear in Bruce Willis' bathroom after escaping from a mental institution. By the time *The Sixth Sense* was released in theaters, New Edition's "Candy Girl" had already claimed its third generation. On a front stoop in Brooklyn, I witnessed two pigtailed fourth-graders do a Candy Girl update of a Patty Cake standard. A song old enough to be their chaperones was now a playground classic on a summer day when cats hid under sedans. "Can-dee girl! You're all my world!" The shorter one popped her gum on "girl" and "world."

LEFT: Dwayne Omarr, *Holy Rock*. Maurice Starr-produced vocoder album from Florida, featuring "This Party's Jam Packed" and "Save the Children." Starr also made the amazing "Electric Funky Drummer," with vocals by a squirrel in tight britches.

RIGHT: Jonzun Crew's *Lost In Space*, 1983

"Candy Girl" is the child star who never grew up and who became a pink ringtone instead. New Edition's hit also boasts one of more gloriously hairballed vocoders on record, a Drano clog to the pipsqueak pipes of Ralph Tresvant, the group's fifteen-year old lead. If helium causes the vocal tract to vibrate at a higher rate, then the producers of "Candy Girl," Michael Jonzun and Maurice Starr, had cloned the Jackson 5's "A-B-C" for all it was worth, which was too much for Tom Silverman, head of Tommy Boy Records, then still smarting from being sued by Kraftwerk for replaying their synth riff for Afrika Bambaataa's hit "Planet Rock." Arthur Baker, who signed New Edition to his label Streetwise, was less concerned. "When Maurice played me 'Candy Girl,' I said, 'Fuck, I'll sign it right away.' It sounded like 'A-B-C' but wasn't close enough that you'd get sued." Long before co-producing "Planet Rock," Arthur Baker had been using Maurice and Michael for various disco 12 inches in the Seventies and Eighties. "I had been making records with them and none of them really did anything. They were

COLOR OUT OF SPACE

great musicians—really clever." Michael Jonzun was a gifted singer who could replicate any voice. To the public, his true identity (and biggest success) would be with the vocoder, a device that rebuilt his voice box in its own image and became the faceless face of the Jonzun Crew and their 1983 vocoder album, *Lost in Space*.

Michael and his brothers spent most of their Florida childhood replicating famous larynges, specializing in Al Green, the Jackson 5, Stevie Wonder, the Bee Gees—whatever the gig required. They did Patsy Cline covers in a nursing home. They warmed up a Farrakhan rally with New Birth. They played Johnny Cash's "Walk the Line" at a party for the KKK. "The damn Klan treated us better than the Muslims [did]. I remember that," says Michael's oldest brother, Calvin, who played horns and helped manage the group. "The Muslims searched us and searched our instruments and when Farrakhan got there, they kicked us out."

By the late Seventies, Calvin and Soni Johnson were backing the Allman Brothers in Daytona, while a frustrated Maurice Starr—then fresh off his role as "Kid Playing Garbage Can" in Floyd Mutrux's *American Hot Wax*—would ambush artists at clubs and music stores, sometimes playing their own bass lines with his teeth. In the early Eighties, Michael and Maurice were hired by Sylvia Robinson to play (uncredited) on Sugar Hill projects like Grandmaster Flash, Funky 4 + 1 and Sequence. "He and Maurice would spend a few days in the Sugar Hill Studios in Englewood, New Jersey," says Sebastian. "Maurice would buy a pink squirrel fur coat and a king-size bed. Michael would put his money into equipment." By then, the musician-for-hire thing was getting replaced by cheaper technology. "You could pay a string section twelve thousand dollars a session or just do it with a synthesizer," says Jonzun. "Arthur and I did music together—real music. But we discovered great singers rarely make it. The kids in the clubs wanted noise." It was Calvin's idea for his brother to make a song about a creature born from Japanese chewing sounds and a missing slice of pizza. "I'm like, boy, what a dumb game—but if that's what they like, that's what they like." Though "Pack Jam" didn't exactly put up "Planet Rock" numbers, it did its lemons-to-lemonade thing by selling 250,000 copies. As Calvin once told me, "Something can remind you of

Brazilian pressing of Jonzun Crew "Space Is the Place" (Ariola Fonograficos/ Industria Brasileira Disco e Cultura/ Tommy Boy). When Jonzun first phoned me on the vocoder in 1999, he said the song was inspired by a dream he had about a Martian running through a field.

something without sounding like something." "We could never get away with calling it "Pac-Man," explains Tom Silverman. "We had to change it because we knew we were going to get sued. Didn't want to piss off the people at Pac-Man." To Jonzun's credit, there's no evidence of the video game in the song. No high score, no floating pretzels. Just a beat with a Star Trek door-slide. The arcade is empty.

+ + +

Not surprisingly, my first phone call with Michael Jonzun was through the vocoder. (He greeted me with, "Space is the place.") A typical conversation might include NASA (Jonzun Crew sold well in Houston), the Three Stooges, a date with Donna Summer's cousin, and an appearance on *Saturday Night Live* with the J. Geils Band. He said he recorded "Space Cowboy" because Westerns and Martians came on TV at the same time. "Space Is the Place" was the second single from the Jonzun Crew album, perhaps a nod to when Sun Ra used hand-coded signals to send Arkestra members out for ice cream when staying at Jonzun's house. If "Pack Jam" is vocoder speech compression, then "Space Is the Place" took infinite measures to increase the bandwidth and played its bass lines with iguanodon thumbs. "People got into it," says Calvin. "The vocoder. The character. It was almost unnatural."

Michael tells me he was getting messages back then. "It was so long, Michael Johnson! I was the spaceman at the dump."

MR. BAGS TAKES A TRIP

Zounds! A Gorgon Death Station appears! Evasive Action!
— Spaceman Spiff, *Calvin and Hobbes*

If it appeared as a light, was it brighter than the brightest stars?
— Question 10, US Air Force UFO Report Form 164, October 1962

A 1956 Pontiac Star Chief hurtles across central Florida with a trunk full of last week's garbage. Its grill is peppered in bug grit, a frog lunch at seventy-five mph. The road is long past supper, crittered in darkness. The Star Chief reminds its driver to fasten his seat belt. As the only

Michael Jonzun with Roland SVC-350 vocoder at Mission Control Studios in Westford, Massachusetts, circa 1996. According to Arthur Baker, Jonzun and his brothers were incredible vocalists, reproducing four-part soul harmonies. (Photographed by Dennis Ackerman, courtesy Michael Jonzun)

fourteen-year-old in town with a talking car, Calvin Johnson is somewhere out the window. His brother Soni is quiet. Neither is thrilled with the nighttime drop, considering the possibility of running into Mr. Bags, a one-armed vision of ain't-rightness rumored to live at the dump, known to wear flood pants and three coats. Calvin had seen him around town, taking swipes at nothing while his sleeves flailed along, giving the impression of a man trying to flag down an octopus. Pulling into the dump, Soni and Calvin agreed to jump out together, chuck the garbage and peel out, until they realized that something was hovering over the car. "It was bright," says Calvin, on the phone from Boston. "Bright, bright, bright. It weren't no damn aeroplane, I can tell you that! It stayed there for like ten seconds. We couldn't move, the car wouldn't move. It had a blue light on it. It was big and didn't make no sound. The last thing I remember sayin' was, 'Oohhhh, shit! Look out!' Then it took off slow, two or three miles per hour. Planes just don't go two or three miles per hour. Then all the sudden that sucker took off. It created a lot of dust."

When I asked Calvin what the dust was doing, he said the dust was doing what it was doing. His talking Star Chief was quiet and the only sound was tree frog night. So they tore off to the nearest filling station, looking for witnesses. "I saw the damn spaceship, now! I'm not sayin' I saw no little green men or no Pac-Men…but I saw what I saw. And I know I didn't pass out."

Calvin—who said the OVC was fancier—suspects that the spaceship was looking for Mr. Bags. "Bags used to tell people that aliens used to come visit him out at the dump. Nobody took him seriously, because the guy stayed out by the dump. He'd have on three coats, so everybody thought he was crazy. Sometimes he'd be in town and have on pants that looked shorter than Lil' Abner's."

Calvin and Soni finally drove home to scare their next of kin, nine-year-old Michael. Not to make a mountain out of mashed potatoes, Michael remembers feeling rather practical about the incident, as kids do when crediting

In Harlan Ellison's 1967 story "I Have No Mouth And I Must Scream," a bitter supercomputer transforms the narrator into a "soft jelly thing." In 1941, Harlan's Russian grandmother threatened to permanently staple him to his mattress for sneaking out to see *Mr. Bug Goes to Town* on his seventh birthday. Ellison, who may have coined "bugfuck," would later denounce the term "Sci-Fi" as the sound of crickets doing the sex act.

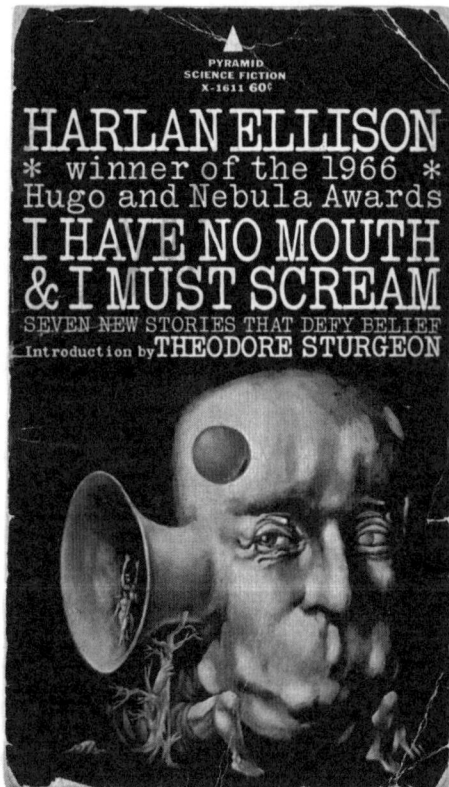

PYRAMID
SCIENCE FICTION
X-1611 60¢

HARLAN ELLISON
* winner of the 1966 *
Hugo and Nebula Awards
I HAVE NO MOUTH
& I MUST SCREAM
SEVEN NEW STORIES THAT DEFY BELIEF
Introduction by THEODORE STURGEON

logic to the unreal. "The UFO was probably picking up some trash and going back to make some stuff."

IT BECOMES THAT

That sounds like some crazy shit Jonzun would come up with.
— Arthur Baker

Michael Jonzun didn't need drugs to see UFOs.
— Jordan Knight, NKOTB

In 1983, when Jonzun turned man into jam, the Pac-Man brand was already binging on ash trays, air fresheners, socks, hats, light switches, cereal bowls, TV trays, more than a few theories of Eighties consumption, and jelly. "It was an imaginary war," says Bill Sebastian.

Homemade "Pack Jam" sleeve discovered in San Jose, California, rendered in Magic Marker. Artist unknown. (1983, Tommy Boy Records, unearthed by Hua Hsu)

"At the time you had those silly video games. Michael saw this other visual monster and I think he imagined it attacking and demolishing Pac-Man. The problem was because of copyright laws the name was changed to Pack Jam." On the run-off wax of "Pack Jam," you'll find a family of Pac creatures etched in by the engineer, laughing their way around the black spindle hole preparing to gobble serial numbers. For the OVC's warning, the vocoder let the reflux do the talking, inhaling a trucker's five-star breakfast and belching, "Look out for the Outer Visual Communicator." Calvin Jonzun called it "the thunder and the hell and all that type of stuff. The earth is opening up. As if you had a thousand-piece orchestra or something. You know—the stars and all that opening up and goin' for it."

"I always looked at the OVC lights eating up the Pac-Man," says Michael Jonzun, realizing the letters O, V and C actually formed a Pac-Man— the V being the mouth. "By destroying it, it becomes that," says

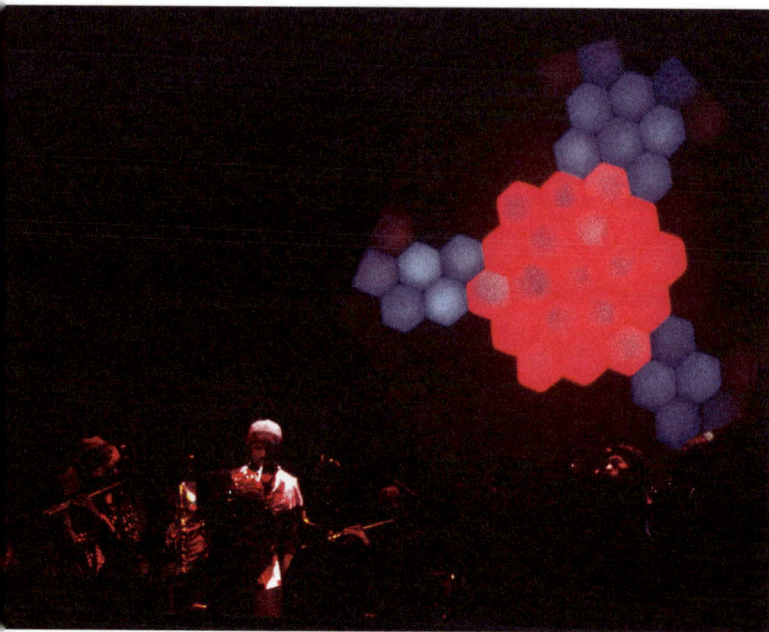

Jonzun. "The *O*, the *V* and the *C* are the symbols in the Pac-Man thing." "There's many ways to interpret the conflict," continues Sebastian. "When somebody plays Pac-Man, you're playing a game where everything you do is structured according to somebody else's rules. With the OVC, you create your own environments with your own rules. The OVC is creating an experience rather than playing a game and following someone else's rules. There's a fundamental cultural conflict between the two attitudes. It's mind control. Of all the things you could do with your life that they could focus you on something that has such a lim-

Bill Sebastian's Outer Visual Communicator (OVC), photographed with the Arkestra at the Modern Theater in Boston, December 1978. The OVC was a 16-foot hexagonal chromatic scrambler controlled by a "Spacescape" keyboard. Originally built for Sun Ra, the OVC would be Michael Jonzun's muse for "Pack Jam," making room for another dimension.

ited set of possibilities. You're just moving a cursor up, down, left or right. In a maze. Squares are artificial."

+ + +

Jonzun claims that Bell Labs had been waiting for him all along. The vocoder's function in World War II—spread spectrum communications and bandwidth compression—fits the description of "Pack Jam." When German intelligence intercepted SIGSALY transmissions in 1945, the signals were not recognized as human speech. Disregarded as random interference, these vocoded pulses were spit back out over the airwaves as jamming frequencies. American Signal Corps officers, however, caught something else in the ether. When connecting SIGSALY calls, officers reported hearing "gobbling sounds."

In 1983, Jonzun and the OVC won the war on the home front when Atari buried five million unsold copies of its inferior Pac-Man home version in the New Mexico desert. The cartridges were flattened with a steamroller and entombed in cement. Atari's bankruptcy was partly blamed upon the creature's unsatisfactory death. There was no shrivel, no dramatic pop. The video game giant quickly learned that one of the key pleasures of Pac-Man was the death of Pac-Man. On Jonzun's original version of "Pak Man," the vocoder simulates Pac's last breath, a shrinking "ooohhh" after admitting "The OVC has got me!" Instead of a hyper-desiccated pop, the creature simply dwindles down the drain, as sad a sound as a single-color, two-dimensional pixillated video being could make.

+ + +

In 1975, the Johnson brothers' van nearly flew off the side of a mountain during a blizzard in Vermont. "I thought I was a goner," says Michael. "We were swinging around at the top of an abyss. You look down. Now that's death. I was hearing things." What Jonzun heard, in that yeti pillow fight, was the van's radio, the dissipation of white noise into David Bowie's "Space Oddity." This near-death experience became "Ground Control," the only track from *Lost in Space* too slow and dark for radio. "I thought it was time to leave Earth," he says. "'Ground Control' was the sad intergalactic feeling of slow-moving time. Earth has a lot of problems."

"Ground Control" baffled Calvin Jonzun more than the UFO at the county dump. "I don't know what the hell Mike was thinkin' when he made 'Ground Control.' Man, please! For a minute there I thought he was on drugs. The other songs were more or less specifically made. But that one…that one was a little strange." To refresh himself, Calvin hums "Ground Control" through his nose. "Some songs just be so far removed from other ones. That one definitely made the list of Far-Removed-from-the-Other-Ones."

GROUND CONTROL
TO THAT THING IN YOUR BACKYARD

Johnson, you fool! You have attempted to overload my circuits!
— *Colossus: The Forbin Project*, 1970

We need batteries. The Suboptic Shadow World has descended early
on the western tip of Cape Cod in December. Bill Sebastian stands in
his kitchen with his eyes closed, holding a dead flashlight, talking about
how the mind begs for photons in absolute darkness, scrambling.
"Please, just give me one photon," he laughs, shaking the flashlight.

Sebastian's wife is preparing eggplant parmesan, one of Sun Ra's
favorite dishes. The Sebastians maintain a communal kindness that was
part of Arkestra survival for so long, a rarity in today's gated peephole
fear. Dinner won't be ready for a while, so Sebastian says he can show
us what's left of the OVC, if we're interested. "It's somewhere in the
woods out back," he says, and then disappears on a search for batteries.
My friend quickly says he could run to the store and get batteries right
now, no problem at all.

Slightly embarrassed, Sebastian says the OVC is now just squirrel
housing. "It's cool for someone to come up and ask you about all of
this stuff twenty years later. The reality is even stranger. Why would
anyone want to see the OVC ruins?"

On the way to the store, we listen to "Pack Jam" and then "Ground
Control." Sebastian hasn't heard the Jonzun Crew in over twenty
years, and "Ground Control" is a favorite. The organ is more St.
John the Divine than Sam Ash, and the vocoder feels downright sad as
we pass by houses netted in Christmas lights. Inflatable snowmen
wobble and smile in the wind. One has keeled over, face-down and
fat, impaled on its broom.

At Wegmans Supermarket, we wait in the car, allowing "Ground
Control" to finish its lonely trudge. Sebastian leans down to tie his shoes.
"I couldn't imagine Sun Ra being skilled at navigating conventional
reality," he says.

The OVC ruins, photographed in daylight in Cape Cod, Massachusetts, October 2009. Bill Sebastian, inventor of the OVC, finished his creation in Ore City, Texas in 1978 and later retired the remains in the backyard of his home in Cape Cod.

With the OVC and Spaceship Keyboard, Bill Sebastian and Sun Ra would channel the colors out of space. Sun Ra would often have Sebastian take a silent "OVC solo" during performances.

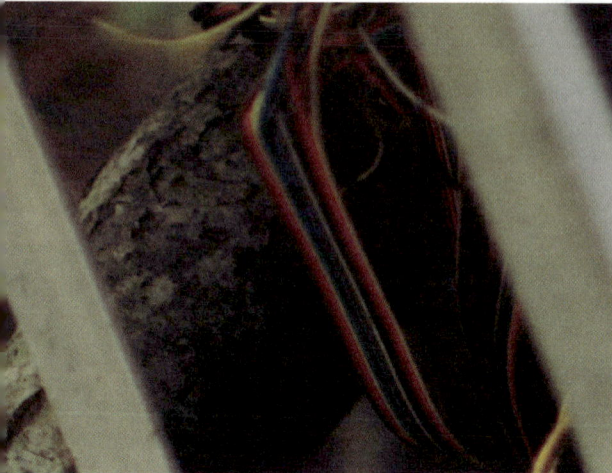

Inside the grocery store, conventional reality is blaring with holiday stress. We load up on D-cells, and Sebastian suggests getting some cave lights to wear on our foreheads. Kidding, sort of. I'm all for it. We agree that all price checks should be conducted with a vocoder and pick up an extra flashlight for backup. You deal with the photons you're given. Upon returning to Sebastian's house, we check in on dinner and file out back. "We go to the graveyard as a team," he whispers. In the woods, next to a green canoe, is a silver backboard shaped like a trapezoid. One half of the OVC, decapitated by a low-flying bridge. The Plexiglass is dead-tooth gray and covered in duct tape. Rows of hieroglyphics have been carved out of the tape with a box-cutter. An ankh, a wolf, a queen, an amulet, a curse.

The wind follows up. We duck thorns and branches and crouch inside of Sebastian's dream, amid racks of hard-wired logic boards that have endured more than two decades of Cape Cod winters. Our flashlights play across racks of electronics and consoles, wire clots in fishgut pink and tiny bulbs and coils, partially buried in pine needles and damp leaves. "The OVC wasn't practical for touring," Sebastian says. "There were malfunctions. It took about a week of working full-time to set the thing up. Every time you took it apart and moved it, you wondered if you were ever going to get the thing back together and working again. But life goes on. Different things happen."

He hands me the flashlight and pries open a long rectangular silver case leaning against a console. Along with the promised squirrel nests, this is the Spacescape keyboard, the controls of the OVC. Sebastian moves his hands across the map of tiny round capacitants. I ask if his daughters, both at Harvard, ever wondered about the crashed spaceship in their backyard. Sebastian says no, they never asked about it.

"The OVC is designed for you," he says. "It's the stuff you want to see. You must accept it without filters." Sebastian ducks under a panel, looking for a 3-D harmonica transducer. Along with the OVC, the harmonica transducer occupied the "weird half" of Mission Control Studios in Westford, Massachusetts, where Sebastian and Sun Ra played with their mouth-operated virtual-reality hologram machine. By the time New Kids On the Block had made Maurice Starr rich, Bill

Like the vocoder, the OVC was another form of spectrum communication. Though the OVC was never successful in destroying all Pac-Man machines, it did put on dazzling light shows when Bill Sebastian performed with Sun Ra, from 1978 to 1980.

Sebastian had run out of money and abandoned the OVC. In 1988, he and Jonzun started a company called Virtual Scene, which broke off into Intelligence Compression Technologies. ICT now does data compression for satellite networks. "That's what the vocoder was," says Sebastian, flashlight bobbing. "Data compression. Unfortunately, Sun Ra couldn't wait around on the planet for me to finish."

We shield our faces and stumble back through the briars. Sebastian pauses, flickering back at the OVC. "See how it's slightly convex? The OVC was intended to be part of a larger whole."

He's not kidding. The OVC was intended to be the first piece of a massive dome, with Sebastian and Sun Ra performing inside, live at the OVC Dome, maybe forever, only breaking for ice cream. "Total immersion environment." He smiles, passing a hexagonal birdbath. "The best view is inside the dome." We follow Bill Sebastian and his photons back to the house, leaving the OVC to another winter.

Bill Sebastian envisioned the OVC as one hexagonal piece of a massive dome, similar to one of Buckminster Fuller's geodesic spheres or the ship from Jack Arnold's 1953 science fiction classic *It Came from Outer Space* (which looks like an indoor tennis court for aliens).

CHAPTER SIX

THE SACRED THUNDER CROAK

Bart! The larynx is not a plaything!
— Marge Simpson

Bell Labs' R.R. Riesz with his artificial
Electrolarynx, photographed in 1929. Riesz
also built one of the first electronic vocal
tracts and helped design the Voder with
Homer Dudley. (Courtesy AT&T Archives and
History Center)

SO TO SPEAK: THE ACTUAL HISTORY OF SYNTHETIC LARYNGES

Let us dissect, so to speak.
— Charles Bogert, herpetologist

A toad and a frog are hard to tell apart.
— Vocoder test sentence, Fort Huachuca, Arizona, 1971

The man who couldn't color his sound lived on the corner of Voorhis Avenue in Deland, Florida, in a house bleached dog-tongue pink. Michael Jonzun, ten years old in a cowboy hat, would drop by to taunt the bulldog leashed in the back. The screen door would slap open and out popped the dog's owner with an electric deodorant stick jammed into his neck: "You-damn-kids-get-outta-my-yard!" A crabapple buzz in monotone. Jonzun saw the hole in the man's throat and scrammed, a *Little Rascals* routine. Hang onto your hats, gang!

"I was like, 'that is the coolest sound.' But I was afraid of this guy. He looked like…umm…who was that guy from…" (Pause) "Was it Herman Monster [sic]? No. Not him. This was a bald scroungy fella. The guy from *Gunsmoke*? No, his hands were too clean." Jonzun finally decides upon a mix of Lloyd Bridges from *Sea Hunt* (1958 snorkel drama) and Froggy from *Our Gang* (a show where kids get chased by cranky men). "That's it! Everybody on TV looks like the same guy anyway. But he had that hole in there and that hole looked nasty. It really scared me. And man, that dog was ugly." Calvin Johnson remembers the incident. "That man kind of sounded like a vocoder. GetoutofmyyardGetoutofmyyard…Yup! Vocoder!" "The spaceman had another mouth," adds Michael. "And I dreamt later that he had changed his mouth."

+ + +

On January 20, 2005, the telephone informed me that our forty-third president was on TV being inaugurated by a vocoder. It was Chief Justice William Rehnquist, a man without a windpipe, swearing in George W. Bush, a man who would spend his administration talking out the side of his neck. A longtime sufferer of thyroid cancer, Rehnquist

had been speaking with the aid of an electric larynx since undergoing a tracheotomy in 2004. What the dejected TV audience heard that day was a more refined version of what yelled at young Michael Jonzun on Voorhis Avenue. The spaceman's spare mouth was a fistula, the site of larynx extirpation for victims of throat cancer. It is a hole where a hole should never be, and Philip Morris would rather it not appear on television ads, much less the Marlboro Man's gizzard. (He can be spotted on an ad for Truth.com, squatting on a busy New York sidewalk with a tuneless jingle: "You won't sing worth a heck with a hole in your neck.")

Bell Labs' F.E. Hayworth does a soundcheck with an Electrolarynx in 1959. (Reproduced, with permission, from "New Artificial Larynx," in *Transactions of the American Academy of Ophthalmology and Otolaryngology*, Vol. 63, American Academy of Ophthalmology, 1959)

Chief Rehnquist and the Marlboro Man are indebted to Wolfgang von Kempelen, the seventeenth-century Hungarian baron who detailed the first manmade leather throat in his book *Mechanism of Human Language with Description of the Speaking Machine*. Yet von Kempelen was discredited due to his bogus invention of a master chess robot called "The Turk." Undefeated throughout Europe (and rumored to have beaten Napoleon and Ben Franklin), the Turk could roll its eyes and smoke a hookah while moving castles at will, thanks to a paraplegic Polish chess master hidden in its gut.

The actual history of synthetic larynges claims inventions no less bizarre than robot fraud. Many are German-made, with sources of inspiration ranging from balloon reeds and woodwinds to one patient who had created his own fistula with a hot ice pick. In 1870, Dr. V. Czerny installed artificial larynges in canines, with dubious results. ("The dog could yawn and make some noises.") Dr. T. Gluck devised an underarm accordion bellows that plugged into the nasopharynx.

CONSTRICTION

MOUTH - - - RADIATOR

VOCAL CORDS

RESONANCE CHAMBERS

LOUD SPEAKER

RANDOM NOISE SOURCE

UNVOICED SOURCE

RELAXATION OSCILLATOR

VOICED SOURCE

RESONANCE CONTROL

AMPLIFIER

1 2 3 4
5
10
6 7 8
9
"QUIET"

t-d
p-b
k-g

ENERGY SWITCH
WRIST BAR

"STOPS"

VODER CONSOLE KEYBOARD

PITCH-CONTROL PEDAL

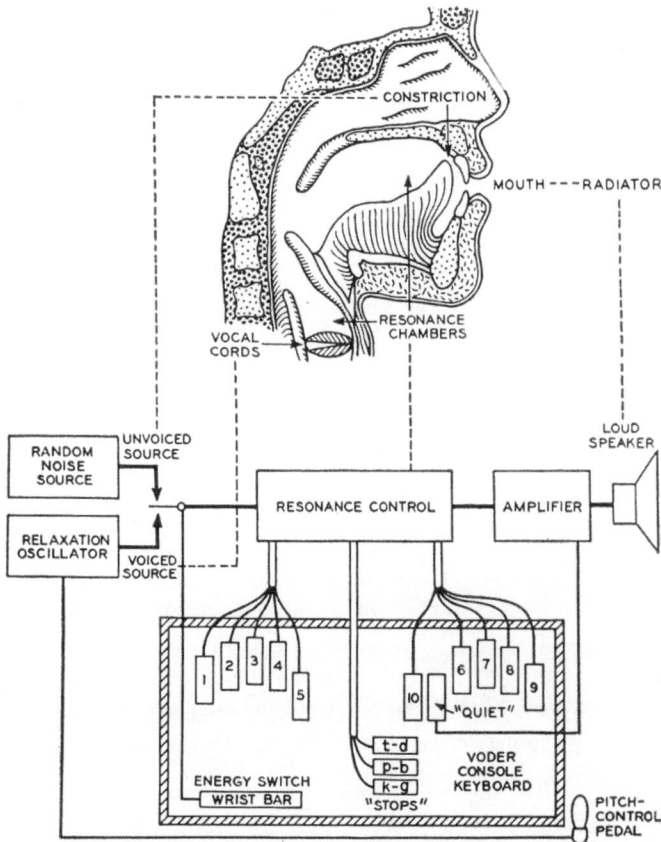

"Let me clear my throat." Bell Labs diagram of frog-shaped larynx, pictured here with a Bell Labs Voder scheme, from the Homer Dudley article "Fundamentals of Speech Synthesis" published in 1955. (Courtesy Audio Engineers Society)

More ingenious was Gluck's motorized gramophone purse. Wired to a denture plate (with tongue-flicked pitch control), it allowed patients to channel their favorite singer, a form of lip-synch by necessity. Gluck could have been taking a cue from nineteenth-century French writer Villiers de l'Isle and his imaginary robot chanteuse named Hadaly, who channeled speech from a gramophone and the record collection housed in her electric bosom.

With its articulation being "far from natural," the Gluckian model could've been a mobile vocoder turntable prototype. Dr. Anton Phibes would use an Art Deco version in the 1971 horror classic *The Abominable Dr. Phibes*, in which Vincent Price starred as a dead inventor who

SPEECH

AFTER
THE
REMOVAL
OF
THE
LARYNX

RECORDED BY HARM A. DROST

FOLKWAYS RECORDS FX 6134

Folkways' LP *Speech After the Removal of the Larynx* (1964, Folkways). This record demonstrates various techniques of speech without the larynx. Patients were concerned about "loss of personality" while being defined by a buzzing voice prosthetic. Contains the track "Frogspeech." (Courtesy Steinski)

drank champagne by pouring it into the speaker jack in the side of his neck. Looking like Captain Kangaroo with a hangover, Phibes was a foxtrotting romantic, despite losing his face and voice box in a car crash. He spoke through a golden Victrola on wheels, which was plugged into his neck. 'As you see and can hear, I have used my knowledge of music and acoustics to re-create my voice!"

In addition to channeling speech through record players, Gluck's experiments in 'phonetik surgery" would inform the research of Bonn University philologist Werner Meyer-Eppler, an early vocoder advocate deemed by many vacuum-tube nerds to be one of the godfathers of electronic music. With the invention of the transistor in 1947, Meyer-Eppler began developing an Electrolarynx, a device that originated in 1925 with Bell Labs vocoder designer R.R. Riesz. In 1956, the US government issued a "consensus decree" to AT&T, requiring them to construct their own Electrolarynx as well as research underwater acoustics for the military. By 1959, AT&T had unveiled what appeared to be a can of battery-powered Right Guard. It had a modified vibrating phone diaphragm and a pitch-shifter for inflection. Though it did provide cordless communication, the device's persistent buzz seemed to indicate the presence of an invisible barber. According to Bell Labs, the Electrolarynx was more intelligible when used over the phone than in person.

In 1964, Smithsonian Folkways released the album *Speech After the Removal of the Larynx*, recorded at the Phonetic Laboratory of the Ear in the Netherlands. It was hosted by Dr. H.A.E. van Dishoeck, an expert in "Electro Nose Wings," psychogenic deafness, and house-dust allergies. Included was a recording of the Italian-made "Pipa di Ticchioni," a pipe equipped with a pitch button and a transducer in

its bowl. This clever device gave the illusion of smoking while speaking in a weed-eater timbre, as if providing its own surgeon's warning.

Dr. van Dishoeck explains that without a voice box to generate vibrations, words have to be expelled by breath or muscle contraction. One of his trickier demonstrations was an air-suck technique called "Frog Speech," or Glossopharyngeal Speech. For contrast, van Dishoeck provides actual frog recordings, though the effect is more like a cricket making fun of a frog than a frog. Conversely, the manmade example of frog speech is more loyal to the pond while suggesting the shriveled parched Toadcoder heard on Kraftwerk's 1975 song "Uranium."

The liner notes of *Speech After the Removal...* include a photo of a farmer swallowing a frog, that locally quirked air of we-do-things-dif-

Artificial larynx plugged into an organ and Theremin to play "Dusk In Upper Sandusky," designed by F.A. Firestone, 1940. This could be an ancestor of Red, the homeless YouTube phenom who buzz-sawed like an Electrolarynx on "I Should Tell Ya Momma On You," released on Stones Throw Records in 2009. (Courtesy *Journal of the Acoustical Society of America*)

ferently-round-here (see the 1973 film *The Wicker Man*). As one of earth's oldest speaking creatures, the frog has certainly earned the right to occupy our throats, and it is no coincidence that the human larynx is frog-shaped. True frog clearance is an act of speech in itself, the "ahem of phlegm" that pronounces the air dead, the silence awkward, and the apparent obvious, a mucosal scramble of hint.

+ + +

In 1940, F.A. Firestone published "An Artificial Larynx For Speaking and Choral Singing for One Person" in *The Journal of the Acoustical Society of America*. Firestone described running a glass tube, a foot and a half long, from the mouth into a speaker unit plugged into a relaxation oscillator, a theremin, an organ or "other electric musical instrument." ("Saliva traps are useful when protecting the diaphragms of both speakers.") Songs tested on this machine included "School Days" and "Dusk in Upper Sandusky," in which one could form speech from a trap drum solo.

Sonovox Jingles with Moog Synthesizer (1976, East Anglican Productions). Often mistaken for a vocoder, the Sonovox was a pair of vibrating speaker cones that attached to the throat, allowing Sonoveuxes to articulate the noise of planes, trains, and vacuum cleaners into speech. According to the *Saturday Evening Post*, the Sonovox could make wine say anything but "glug."

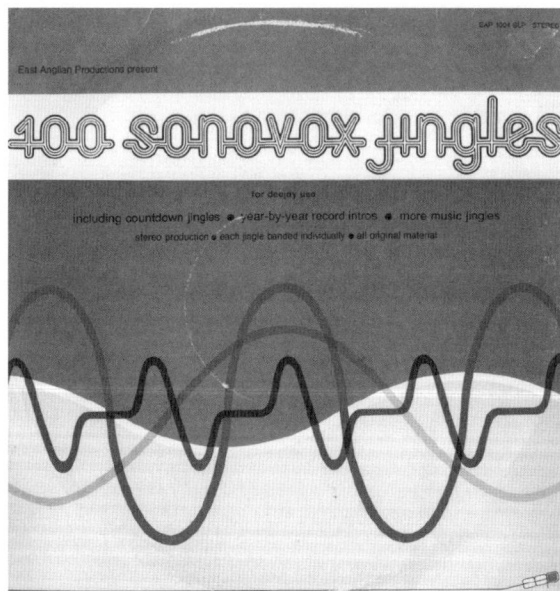

A few weeks after demonstrating this rig, Firestone heard a similar effect on the radio. It was the Sonovox, a vibrating throat module that plugged into the studio console and essentially substituted instruments and recordings of heavy machinery for the voice box, converting modes of transportation into cloying pets and sidekicks. Treasured by yesteryear types and mastered by big-band guitarist Alvino Rey, the Sonovox was invented by Gilbert Wright one morning in 1939 while grazing the shadow on his neck with an electric razor.

When contacting a representative from PAMS, a Dallas-based company that sells Sonovox jingles, I was immediately told that the vocoder sucks. Often mistaken for a vocoder, the Sonovox carried itself with a relatively clear and sunny disposition, a studio gimmick used in cartoons and radio commercials, from the pneumatic steam engines of *Dumbo* to an ad for Bromo Seltzer (nothing screams headache relief like a steam engine in your living room), and ultimately, counting down the week in the Who's "Armenia City in the Sky." The effect can be unintentionally frightening, as demonstrated by the nanny grilling the ice cream man in 1950's *The Good Humor Man*. Peter Frampton and Richard Tandy of ELO recall hearing the Sonovox on *Sparky's Magic Piano*, a children's record about a talking piano who helps a kid cheat his way through Rimsky-Korsakov's "Flight of the Bumblebee"—the indestructible speech muse for *The Green Hornet* and the SIGSALY vocoder, as invented by the beekeeper himself, Homer W. Dudley. Up until then, Sparky was best known for being friends with Bozo the Clown.

EEEEL LIKE I EWWW

Drool may be a friend to electricity, but it's really here for the Rémy. It's gathered in a clear plastic tube lodged inside Peter Frampton's mouth. The tube runs southbound into a small metal box marked "Heil," which is plugged into an amp onstage. The tube's diameter is less than that of a garden hose but more than that of a crazy straw. It's been marinating in Rémy Martin, so Frampton's saliva glands are thrilled. Yet the main intrusion in Frampton's mouth tonight isn't the tube but the noise. His oral cavity has become a speaker and his teeth vibrate at a frequency that would purple a dentist. The rear molar, possibly #14, clenches the tube. The silver filling in Bicuspid #21 hangs on for dear life. The guitar amp by Frampton's foot transfers the wattage, happy to oblige for *Frampton Comes Alive*, the biggest selling live album of all time.

Imagine ice cubes and Doritos cracking up inside your head. Replace that with Madison Square Garden losing its voice. Replace larynx with guitar. Listen to teeth. Calcareous conduction. Frampton opens mouth, drool catches light and there it is, a word, or at least the shape of one. "Eeeeel."

A children's record released in 1942, *Sparky's Magic Piano* used a Sonovox to help a kid cheat his way through "Flight of the Bumblebee," also muse of *The Green Hornet*. "I can play myself!" said the Piano, much to the horror of Seussian piano teacher Dr. T and his 5,000 fingers. The Sparky records would creep out future generations of electronic music nerds, from ELO to OMD.

Maybe not in the best shape, but close enough. The crowd is programmed to hear "Feeeeel," so they do. By the third *eel*, there's enough wattage in Frampton's mouth to eject his silver filling and pop Afrika Bambaataa, standing in the front row at the Garden, right between the eyes. That would've been something: Bam walking home with Frampton's filling lodged in his forehead, still vibrating with "Do You Feel Like We Do."

Bambaataa did catch Frampton live to see the Talk Box, his jaw on the floor. "When I was younger, my mother would let me run around and go to concerts," says Bam. "I couldn't afford that top ticket so I had to sneak up to the front row. I had to see it for myself." What he saw was a Talk Box, better known and recognized as "that thing Richie Sambora stuck in his mouth for 'Living on a Prayer,'" and now used by Geico to sell car insurance.

With the Talk Box, one doesn't talk but pantomimes, lip-synching like a drunken fish. Its principle is sixth-grade science fair: Bypass amp, pipe sound through tube, replace larynx with guitar or keyboard, turn mouth into speaker, hang on to teeth. "The Talk Box is an extra larynx," Frampton continues. "You shut off yours and get piped-in larynx. It could be a guitar, it could be a synthesizer—anything that could be amplified and come out of the speaker and be bypassed and put through the tube. The Talk Box is analog and physical. It's a warmer sound to me than the vocoder. It's also much cheaper. Just a guitar plugged into an amp, bypass the speaker and put it in the Talk Box, up the mic stand and bingo. I'm pretty naïve to what a vocoder does. You're restricted to a keyboard whereas you're not with the Talk Box. You free up the larynx. The Talk Box's got more soul. Flesh in the wires."

Though Frampton is instantly recognized as a Talk Box icon, he refers to himself as a cover merchant, deferring to antecedents like Rufus, Sly Stone, Sly's bass player Larry Graham, and Eagles guitarist Joe Walsh. "I did it my way and it happened to be on two popular songs from the Seventies," Frampton says. "I'm sure the Talk Box has been around since the Forties. Someone must've laid a book on a speaker, took the book off and it went *wha*? It's such a simple effect. I'm sure there's been a Talk Box ever since there was a microphone, a pre-amp, an amplifier and a speaker cabinet."

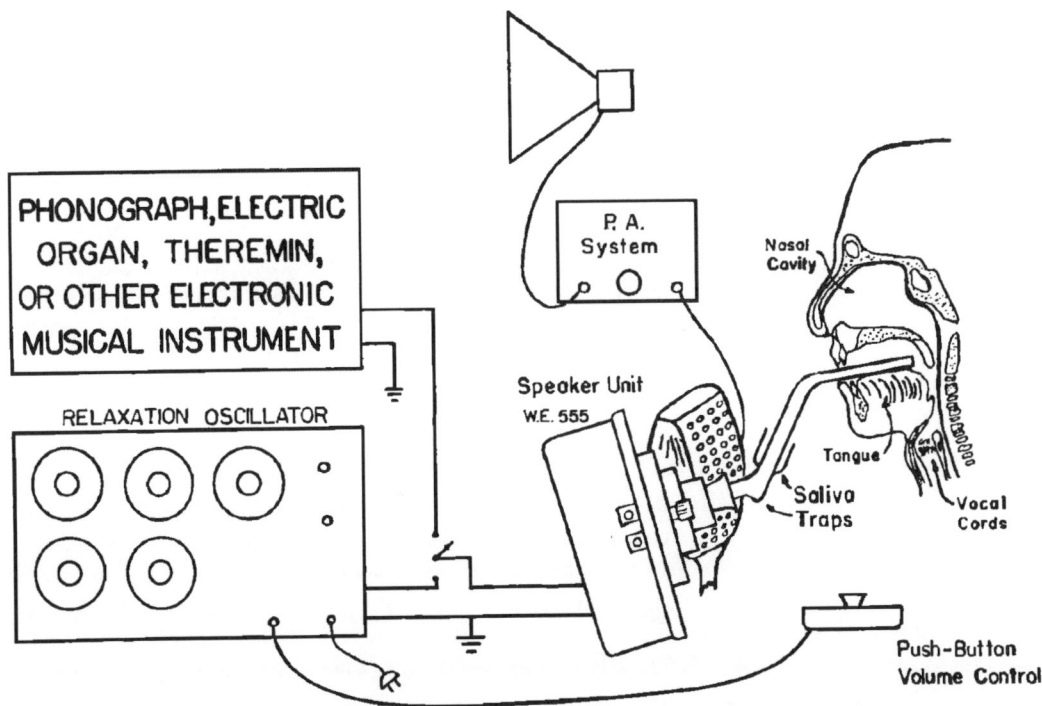

PHONOGRAPH, ELECTRIC
ORGAN, THEREMIN,
OR OTHER ELECTRONIC
MUSICAL INSTRUMENT

RELAXATION OSCILLATOR

P. A. System

Speaker Unit
W.E. 555

Nasal Cavity

Tongue

Saliva Traps

Vocal Cords

Push-Button Volume Control

ON GOLDEN THROAT

The first Talk Boxes weren't boxes but bags. In 1963, Doug Forbes was working in an electronics shop in Missouri when an old man came in speaking through a synthetic larynx. Forbes thought it was a vibrating tuna can. Wanting to fill his throat with guitar fuzz, Forbes then built a bagpipe prototype, essentially a hot-water bottle draped with "splendid green carpet with gold fringes." Grateful Dead sound tech Bob Heil would follow in 1971, when collaborating with Joe Walsh for the more traditional tube-and-pedal model, making the Talk Box commercially available for $100. In 1976, the year Frampton released *Frampton Comes Alive*, Electro-Harmonix put its "Golden Throat" Talk Box on the market. The device had a fat red button that could've stopped a freight elevator, and its tube was indeed golden,

Schematic of early talk box rig, circa 1940, using Theremin, records, organ, or "other electronic instrument." This would evolve to guitars and, ultimately, the first ten seconds of "Sweet Emotion" by Aerosmith. (Courtesy *Journal of the Acoustical Society of America*)

though similar to an instrument of surgical discomfort. Peter Frampton first encountered the Talk Box via Pete Drake, a Nashville pedal steel player who used it in 1964 on Roger Miller's "Lock, Stock, and Teardrops" and then solo for "I'm Just a Guitar (Everybody Picks on Me)," released that same year. (Prior to Drake, another country act, Harry and the Troubadours, had recorded a Talk Box version of "Hey Jude.")

Framptom met Drake during a session at Abbey Road Studios. "He said 'Peter, check this out,' and he stuck a tube in his mouth and the pedal steel started talking to me and I let out the nirvana yelp of delight. I asked where he got it. He said, 'Well, Peter, I made one of these m'self.' He was basically telling me, 'Back off, don't even bother looking for one. It's mine.'"

Yet one could use the Talk Box to share larynges, like an analog ventriloquist. "If someone was singing I could actually have their voice," says Frampton. "I'd have their voice mic split and come out of the PA and then come through into the amp through the Talk Box through my mouth. I could affect his voice while he's singing and it'd be an addition to his voice. That's sort of what you could do with the vocoder really, but this is so much more creative. I could take the lead vocal or backing vocal and stick my own vocals back through the Talk Box."

As with the vocoder, intelligibility is no friend to the Talk Box. Frampton explains: "It's raining and I don't feel well' becomes 'There's a terrible storm and an H-Bomb just went off.' With 'Show Me the Way,' there's no talking and singing. There's no enunciation. 'Do You Feel' is where I start to experiment with talking and singing. On 'Do You Feel,' it's perceived that I say, 'I want to fuck you' instead of 'I want to thank you.' Whether it is or it isn't—is up to the listener."

Fucked or thanked, it didn't really matter to anyone who bought *Frampton Comes Alive*, the album that went platinum when released in 1976. This success called for champagne. "They used to sterilize my Talk Box tube by dipping the end in Rémy Martin. This would get me going for the evening. I'd have a taste for it. After the show, it was 'Okay, where's the Rémy?'"

Frampton remembers being in the back seat of a white Rolls-Royce with Sly Stone at the wheel, enjoying the excess of Talk Box stardom and making a fool out of the speed limit. "Sly was at the peak of craziness and I was at the beginning of mine," Frampton says. "So it was pretty scary. It was 1976 and he wanted me to write. He drove me to Sausalito, to the Record Plant studios. He had an assistant in the front seat, and he was trying to open a beer while driving. It wasn't a twist top. We're going all over the road in a Rolls. He'd get a thought and say to his assistant, 'Write this down! Write this down!' It was like a movie. We arrive six hours late and he told her to go in and tell [everyone] he'd arrived. I'm the hugest fan. He'd go from one song to another quickly. He asked, 'Can we play "If You Want Me to Stay?" He's singing and playing it on bass and I'm noodling along on guitar. That was probably one of the finest moments of my career right there."

MUPPET OF MY MIND

By the time Stevie Wonder got to *Sesame Street*, Cookie Monster had already crashed a stolen steam engine into a game show. A blue guy in overalls cried, "Hey, that's my train!" A purple banker in whiskers asked for his cane. An orange thing ran around with jumbled fangs, his poof of eyebrows lifted from the forehead of Leonid Brezhnev. The show was *Beat the Time*, and its host, Guy Smiley, had lost control. He could be heard shouting Cookie Monster's name as creatures frittered away nervous energy across the TV screen. A loose flap of hair leapt about Smiley's head, a living thing itself, egging on the chaos. Cookie Monster was typically incoherent: a fuzzy bathroom rug with a rag-bag voice, trying to high-five the host ("Hi, Guy!"), his pupils jiggling everywhere at once, perhaps still feeling the effects from that appearance on *The Dick Cavett Show* when his stomach exploded after he ate a time machine.

Sesame Street special guest Stevie Wonder tried to make sense of it all, assembling this herky-jerky riot of felt and foam inside his head. *What's going on?* Cookie Monster has stolen a train. *Everybody okay?*

No less confused was *Sesame Street*'s target audience (age six, gnawing on a Matchbox truck) when Stevie Wonder later appeared on the show with a plastic tube that appeared to drool, non-retractably, from his

COMPRESSED LEACH

Called TONTO, Malcolm Cecil and Robert Margouleff's room-swallowing modular synthesizer would make a cameo in Brian De Palma's 1974 film *Phantom of the Paradise*, allowing the character Winslow Leach to speak after his head was crushed by a hydraulic record press.

mouth and into a Moog synthesizer. Yet the tube's most impressed demographic that day was Roger Troutman—a twenty-one-year-old from Hamilton, Ohio, who would spend the rest of his life sticking vinyl hardware tubing into his mouth.

Stevie Wonder had revamped the *Sesame Street* theme into something nastier than a grouch in a trash can, yet faintly redolent of a Honeycomb breakfast chant. Newfangled as the Talk Box seemed, it wasn't a stretch for a children's show where one learned to count (ah! ah!) and spell with animated noises (e.g., the letter *B* bouncing around to a vibes solo), where letters and numbers became characters, encouraging kids to hear things differently, if not reinvent them altogether. *Sesame Street* was musique concrète. Back then I would lip-synch to Joe Walsh's "Rocky Mountain Way" but do the Talk Box solo by mashing my face into a Bjorn Borg tennis racquet, thinking the catgut grid would further convince the effect. (It helped that I wore a medieval anti-warp racquet press around my head.) To a child, the Talk Box was a tool of the avant-garde—as the Muppets of invention have often said, "It's so crazy, it just might work!"

HALFWAY HOUSE

In Robert Silverberg's 1964 story "Halfway House," Franco Alfieri must travel across several universes to find a cure for his throat cancer, ultimately replacing his voice box with a vocoder. Though vocoders were never actually installed in nonfictional human throats, their pitch analysis function was used to study speech pathologies.

Yet Stevie Wonder's Talk Box wasn't a box but a bag—or "Blowbag"—designed by Malcolm Cecil, son of Edna, Gypsy Queen of the Accordion, and Robert Margouleff, a man who strapped his Moog to a hospital gurney. Margouleff and Cecil introduced Stevie to their monolithic TONTO synthesizer and won a Grammy for producing *Music of My Mind* in 1972.

WATCH A MUG TAKE HOLD

Roger Troutman was the heart of Zapp, a selfless, garage-grown outfit from Hamilton, located between the funk hubs of Dayton and Cincinnati. Backed by his brothers Terry, Larry and Lester, Zapp would later enlist vocalist Shirley Murdock for additional songwriting. Shepherded by Bootsy Collins, who Roger met at age fourteen, and George Clinton, Zapp's first three albums for Warner Brothers followed Led Zeppelin's roman scheme (*Zapp, Zapp II, Zapp III*) and went gold. Bootsy would treat Roger to the stage when Parliament did two sold-out nights at Madison Square Garden, circa 1979. "They didn't know who he was yet," says Bootsy. "The record wasn't out, and the Talk Box was unfamiliar territory. That was so funny to be there to watch a mug take hold of his audience."

"You were forced to get tight touring with Roger," says Vincent Calloway of Cincinnati's Midnight Star. "He'd do anything he could to 'get house' from the audience. 'You gotta get house,' he'd say." Often stealing the show with his borrowed voice, Roger was the consummate performer, whether standing on his head in nothing but a G-string during ten minutes of "More Bounce to the Ounce," or backstage goofing around in an X-rated Donald Duck voice.

As a sampling legacy, Roger Troutman often enters the conversation with George Clinton and James Brown, though sadly he's no longer around to hear about it. In April of 1999, Roger was shot and killed by his oldest brother, Larry, who then turned the gun on himself. The hip-hop media barely took notice despite Zapp being a gateway drug to West Coast G-Funk. (The Mini Moog plunge at the beginning of "Dance Floor" is the best cartoon slingshot on record.) Zapp was the reason why O'Shea Jackson figured that life would be more interesting if he started being Ice Cube. There should be a study on how Zapp's 1980 hit "More Bounce" stimulated the automotive industry in California—Latino and African American–made, and manufactured in the Midwest. The cover of Zapp's eponymous album shows exactly where this would go. Rendered in a Cray-Pas melt of pastels are the essentials: car keys, ocean, sunset and cassette (or "Zapp tape," as it appeared in King Tee's glove compartment, with the unregistered Glock). The only thing missing is someone to share it all with, and she probably just drove off with the band's name, spelled in a fuse blowout of gold, for Roger's homemade throat.

THEY HAD TO KILL BEARS

Peter Frampton always thought Roger Troutman used a vocoder, ever since his wife first played him "More Bounce." When I broke the news to him a few years ago, he was shocked: "*Wow*. I thought, 'That's the best vocoder I ever heard!' He had a very clean sound with it. That's why I liked Roger. Because he was using a synth. That's what made it sound so vocoder-like."

As with T-Pain and Auto-Tune, Roger Troutman is the most famous vocoderer to never use a vocoder. Talk Boxes and vocoders are confused more than bad for good. "People don't know what to call [the Talk Box]," Frampton sighs. "They think it's a vocoder. That's the word they've got, and that's the word they want it to be." Nor was Roger Troutman in any hurry to clarify. He'd refer to his Talk Box as "the Ghetto Robot" or "the Electric Country Preacher." Not one to miss out on some good nomenclature, Bootsy Collins had his own ideas: the Secret Magic Babbler, Roger's Snake Charmer, Cosmic Communicator—as if "Talk Box" was just too square, so to speak. Too British-for-phone-booth.

Roger Troutman performs "Computer Love" at a low rider show in Fresno, California, June 1998. Influenced by early Talk Box pioneers like Sly Stone and Stone's bass player Larry Graham, Troutman was the first to articulate entire songs through the tube.

Watching old video clips, it's strange hearing Roger address the crowd with his dinner-table voice. We always assumed the Talk Box *was* his voice, as if he'd permanently swapped out his pipes for the tube. "I would say that what you hear is the way he talks," continues Bootsy. "I told Roger that when you go do an interview, you have to take the Talk Box with you. That has to be your voice."

Bigg Robb began serving as Roger's tube tech and security in 1987. Often he'd guard the Talk Box between sound check and when Zapp took the stage, or just take it with him back to the motel. "I didn't want anyone messing with my dude's stuff," he says. Bootsy calls the Talk Box a drug addiction. "Everybody wants to use it. It is a special gift, and it is forbidden for you to know the secrets. It will always be a mystery."

H.P. Lovecraft, a writer well acquainted with the unspeakable, might have consulted Bootsy when pondering: "From what unplumbed gulfs of extra-cosmic consciousness…were those half-articulate thunder croakings drawn?"

They were unplumbed from a meat freezer in a garage in central Ohio and plugged into Roger Troutman's amp. "I shouldn't be giving you these secrets," says Lester Troutman, who helped Roger build Talk

Boxes. "But we took the tube off the deep freeze in our garage, for meat. They had drains on them."

Drains being drains, I had to ask Lester about the hygiene situation. He clarified it:

> We had no money, man! You think we went over to the Guitar Center and said, 'Give me one of those tubes, and, by the way, better call the family doctor and see if this stuff is going to give you toxic poisoning'? You think that when Daniel Boone went from Kentucky to California he hopped on I-40? They had to kill bears! We spent hard-earned hours. It was a rig from somebody's mind, and we emulated what we saw. The whole thing with the Talk Box was a struggle. We were hungry entrepreneurs. With the Talk Box, we had to go out there and hurt for it. So when you ask 'Was the tube clean?'—you want the answer? *Hell no*, it wasn't clean! But I didn't put the shit in my mouth, so I didn't give a doggone what Roger did.

IS IT SAFE?

One morning on *The Today Show*, host Katie Couric generated respectable incoherence while attempting to use Frampton's Talk Box. Then Al Roker flubbed it, as if taking his first bong hit. "Al Roker tried it but he didn't let any air out, so it was just blowing his mouth up," Frampton says. "Al said, 'Oh, that's very strange.' I asked Matt [Lauer] if he wanted to try it. He was like, '*Nooooo*, not after you, Al.'"

The Talk Box is a personal commitment to one's own drool. It's the one thing you cannot return to the guitar store, no less intimate than sharing a toothbrush. The Talk Box's failing sanitation grade would be a problem when combined with Zapp's exhaustive touring habit. The tube itself wasn't visible from the crowd, so Roger appeared to be showing off a funky sore throat—which wasn't far from the truth. When your mouth is open for fifteen minutes of "More Bounce," there'll be some bacterial backwash waiting for you when it is time for "Computer Love." "You go through a lot of tubes," says Bigg Robb, who occasionally rushed Roger to the emergency room to treat some alien stomach aches. "A lot of Dr. Tichenor's and Listerine was involved. And a lot of hot water. Before I was handling the tubes, Roger had gotten sick many times, getting these weird stomach viruses. I would go buy a fifty-foot spool of nontoxic vinyl tubing from a plumbing or hardware store."

"Once you master it, it's a lot less drool," says producer Teddy Riley, who first befriended Roger in 1987. "It vibrates your saliva in." Roger would often discourage Talk Box use, perhaps to filter out the rookies who didn't have the heart for it, or maybe for their own good. "In the early days, we were getting zapped in a hot second," says Lester Troutman. "When you're fourteen, fifteen years old, that was nothin', man." "I don't go near the tube," says T-Pain. "It's weird. You gotta not get slobber in it. I'm real crazy with electricity—since I was a kid, sticking my fingers into plugs."

"It's not human," says Patrick "P-Thugg" Gemayel, who first electrocuted himself while building his first talk box at age sixteen. "[The tube] is not supposed to be there. But you get used to it and become a hybrid." As the Talk-Boxing half of Chromeo, Gemayel took his first memorable jolt while learning Zapp's "So Ruff, So Tuff." So began a habit and a hazard. "We still don't know the effects of repetitive Talk-Box use. You get migraines. You faint." Gemayel once passed out on a stage in Montreal after making the word "baby" last for thirty seconds. Breathing is a hindrance in the art of phantom enunciation—oxygen deprivation in itself is raw talent. The less you breathe, the better the sound. "You have to know when to breathe out so you don't hear it in the microphone— so the mic doesn't pick up all the crap sounds. When you pronounce, you stop breathing and open your throat. You have to block your trachea during an extended phrase. So it creates a room inside your mouth—a resonance box. That's what gives a flangey effect."

Yet, it's the teeth, the last forensic survivors of fire and time, which take the real beating. The Talk Box will hurt your fillings. When we spoke, Frampton had complained of a "chronic sore tooth." His dentist blamed the tube. Kraftwerk's Florian Schneider—who is more of a vocoder guy—attempted the Talk Box after seeing Zapp play a small hall in Cologne. "I thought I would lose my teeth," he tells me. "After five minutes I couldn't talk anymore. All those vibrations!" P-Thugg solved the problem by becoming his own dentist and hasn't seen one since.

"I'm almost out," says Michael "Mico Wave" Lane, a former Troutman rival who lost eight teeth to the Talk Box when playing in Japan. "It's like hockey players. If you play hockey and you have teeth, then you ain't in the game. We need to invent a Talk-Box-proof tooth."

Teddy Riley, on the other hand, ingeniously uses the space vacated by a rear molar as a placeholder for his tube.

THE EFFECT OF A G

"More Bounce to the Ounce" could be a new way to study streptococcal pathologies. One of the best things about having strep throat is opening your mouth first thing in the morning and just vibrating. Issue a few boa-whoa-wows, gut deep, before your formant resonances get wise to what's happening. On "More Bounce," the word "bounce" carries itself with a phonetic elasticity that turns one syllable into an exaggerated country mile, with Roger Troutman riding the assonance of "wow" and "whoa" in a low-riding stretch diphthong, as if amazed at the effect. Terms of elocution become dirty words and everyone's dancing in their underwear to the sacred thunder croak.

"Roger practiced the enunciation part, all day, every day," says Lester. "A lot of words people still can't say to this day. Some words were impossible to sing with [the Talk Box]. Like *U* words. *Y* is all right. *F* words and *s* words are okay. Roger would practice the whole alphabet. Most artists do the effect of Peter Frampton or Stevie Wonder. We covered a little Frampton, but Roger was so much better than that. He actually formed words. Roger was the first to do the whole song, then the whole album."

Teddy Riley would often practice on the phone. "I'll have conversations through the Talk Box. I could be talking to you through it right now."

"Consonants are hardest," says Patrick Gemayel. "Everybody wants to say 'girl.' It's super hard to pronounce. You can never have a good *G* come out. You have to give the effect of a *G*."

"The *G* is cool," Riley tells me. "I do the *G* very well."

CELINE DION

Patrick "P-Thugg" Gemayel once accidentally picked up a French soft-rock station in Montreal while using the Talk Box. He found himself with a mouthful of Céline Dion's "My Heart Will Go On" while only hearing it inside his head. It took an iceberg-splitting migraine to clear her out.

On "More Bounce to the Ounce," the *g* is understood. The song was intended as a brief reprise of "Funky Bounce." Bootsy, who was in the studio with Roger, remembers being airborne most of the session. "When we were recording 'Funky Bounce,' we were both jumping up in the air, as if to say, 'who is going to jump for the longest time?' and neither of us would stop until the take was done." With George Clinton helping with the edits, Troutman then stripped the track until it was all skin and drums. Then he went in and replayed the bass, synth and guitar. "If you listen carefully, it's a repeat-add-repeat kind of thing," says Robb. "That song's really only a minute and a half long. But he keeps editing. Takes stuff in, takes stuff out." At ten minutes, "More Bounce" doesn't end, it veers off and drives over to the next county, giving the impression that it's always happening. The loop—the bow, the boa, or whatever snake-eat-tail rig you're rolling with these days—would be perpetuated in the countless rap songs that later sampled it. EPMD's 1988 hit "You Gots to Chill" could have been a sleepy accidental nod to the Troutman drain freeze in Hamilton, Ohio. Yet Troutman wouldn't truly get hip-hop recognition until appearing in the video for Dr. Dre's "California Love" in 1996, leaning out of a helicopter above the Mojave Desert, chewing on a nasty straw. This would reboot Troutman's career. Kids born in the juice-box era, who were in diapers when EPMD were in fishing hats, were getting their first look at a G-funk legend. Not bad for age forty-four.

MAGIC BABBLE OUTREACH

In the nineteen-nineties it was easier just to sample Roger and pay the man than relearn the alphabet and glean the tube yourself. (No YouTube hours to squander on Talk Box instructionals back then.) Roger himself was impressed when hearing DJ Quik use it on a Shaq album, of all things. (Quik was already miles around the bend for sampling Kleeer's classic boogie vocoder for his single "Tonight.") Quik remembers Dr. Dre telling him that Roger was the most talented person he ever met. "He was kind of intimidating with music," Quik says after finally meeting Roger in Vegas. "Dude was too far beyond good, and it freaked us out a little bit. I was green to what he was doing." Quik and Teddy Riley both remember one thing: While Roger spoke to them about "life, music, ice cream, whatever," he was playing the theme from *2001: A Space Odyssey*, on acoustic guitar—the desolation of being abandoned

Dayton, "Sound of Music" (1983, Capitol). This may be the classiest, Saturday morning-est vocoder song ever invented. Makes you want to headbutt the sun. Makes you want to pull a Vida Blue hologram baseball card out of your Frosted Flakes. The hills are alive with electronic handclaps in Ohio.

by your own IBM somewhere outside of Jupiter, in Cinerama no less, captured in a few choice strums. Quik's own guitar player, Bacon, couldn't believe it. "It freaked Bacon out," says Quik. "Freaked him right out."

Sadly, Quik's next Talk Box track, "Roger's Theme," would be a posthumous ode. "I wanted to do a real moody, solemn dedication to him. Just hearing the Talk Box and knowing that man was dead was a little too cathartic for me."

Early in the morning of April 25, 1999, Roger Troutman was shot and killed by his oldest brother Larry, just outside the family's studio, Roger Tee Enterprises, in Dayton, Ohio. Larry Troutman would then drive off and take his own life. Roger was forty-seven; Larry, fifty-four. The entire community was stunned. Among the speculations was the fact that Roger wanted to break out on his own, inspired by his revival with "California Love." "At a certain point, Roger wanted to do his own thing, which presented a conflict," Terry Troutman would tell *New Times LA* in August 2002. "It was their whole life they'd been together. And then for it to break off? That was a strong move, man."

Bigg Robb was one of the pallbearers when the funeral took place six days later at the Solid Rock Church in Monroe, Ohio. "On that day, there was a double funeral. We didn't lose just Roger. We lost Larry as well. And Larry was just as much the mastermind and just as much part of the group's success and part of Roger's success as anybody. Everybody talks about Roger, but nobody talks about Larry. Nobody knows what happened, or why it happened. That's water way under the bridge, trippin' on that. It's not gonna bring my friends back." "My mom was hurt the most," says Lester Troutman. "I told everybody who interviewed me, ABC News, BET—that I don't know. Roger is dead. Roger is gone. And I am sick about that more than anybody will ever know."

The funeral service concluded with Larry's son, Rufus Troutman III, singing "Amazing Grace" on the Talk Box.

Satellite, "You Can Drive My Space Ship" (1984, High Altitude). Talk box song by Satellite of Cincinnati, freaking in the shadow of the Dazz Band hit "Joystick." Other talk box necessities: Jackson 5's "Different Kind of Lady," Syreeta's "He's Gone," and Rufus (Roger covered Chaka Khan's vocals through the Talk Box).

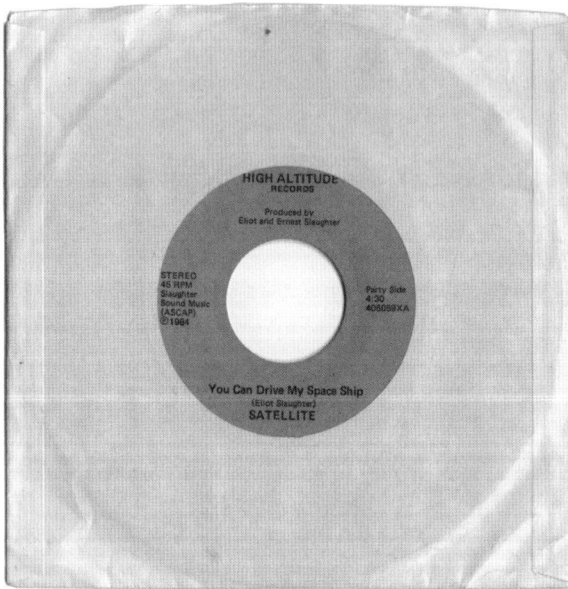

The first note he hit sounded like Roger," says Mico Wave. "Then I burst into tears. Everyone started crying. Imagine if I'm talking to you and you die. And I get on stage and sound exactly the way you're talking. It hit us then. We're never gonna hear this guy's voice again."

The magic was infused in Rufus at that time while Roger laid there and watched," says Bootsy. "Not the passing of the torch but the outreach of the magic babble that was first born in Roger himself. Once you pass over, you are connected to the magic without distractions, so Roger got a chance to see the power of what was first gave to him." "We all gotta leave here sometime," says Bigg Robb. "And hopefully, it'll be at ninety-five, in our sleep, with a couple of big-booty old ladies feeding us grapes and ice cream."

COMPUTER LOVE IS IRON MAN

I'm telling Lester Troutman about a Zapp show I saw in 1987, as if
he wasn't there. R.J.'s Latest Arrival did "Shackles" on the vocoder.
Fresh Gordon played the Andy Griffith theme on his "drum computer,"
channeled through Aunt Bee's dentures. Doug E. Fresh cracked
knuckles inside his mouth. And Roger came out in his electric suit and
did "Computer Love," twice.

The phone is quiet, then Lester roars, "I am Iron Man!" This was the
effect Zapp was going for at the beginning of "Computer Love," though
Ozzy's Talk Box seemed to have been tortured into existence from
peasant bones and bubonic mud. "That was me," says Lester, who
practiced Black Sabbath with Roger. "I am Iron Man! 'Computer Love'
was 'Iron Man'!" "Computer Love" was once described to me as "a
ballad for AutoCAD engineers with the vectors and flying-toaster screen
saver." It's the only quiet-storm classic with enough bass to crack the
low-rider scene in Los Angeles.

"Computer Love" is the encore that night at the Charlotte Coliseum.
Roger Troutman wears his photon-studded suit. According to Lester,
he'd borrowed the suit from Robert Redford's rodeo cereal spokesman
in *The Electric Horseman*. The swooning twinkle of lighters is pretty
into it. So is Roger, probably four tubes deep by now. Zapp cuts the
music so the crowd can hear itself do the chorus, replacing Roger's larynx with the voice of thousands, singing *Thanks to my technology.*

It sounds so good, Roger says he wants to do it again.

So they do it again.

FREAKAZOID ALMOST STARTS RIOT
AT OHIO STATE FAIR

Vincent Calloway, a black belt in purple glasses, does a roundhouse kick
over the mic stand. Just loosening up. Across the fairgrounds, the third
biggest cow in Ohio yawns. A kid at the Dairy Barn sneaks a twenty into
his sock. The Bavarian rollercoaster cranks up "Hot For Teacher."

Summer of 1985 is winding down at the Ohio State Fair in Columbus. Calloway is now doing static isometrics, waiting for sound check.

A few weeks ago a woman spotted him at the airport, mummified in a scarf and purple tints and yelled, "There he is! That's the Freak-A-Zoid!" She'd seen Calloway's group Midnight Star performing their hit "Freak-A-Zoid" on BET. In 1984, when Midnight Star's *No Parking on the Dance Floor* went double platinum, a Pentecostal reverend in Arkansas was concerned that the vocoder was turning his youth group into Freak-a-zoids.

"The vocoder can be soft and sexy or powerful and demanding," says Reggie Calloway, the group's co-founder. "'Freak-A-Zoid' is so powerful because of the way the vocoder is stacked. You can get a silky sound with strings or you can go ballsy balls-up with the Mini Moog. With the vocoder you have to have a voice. That's why our vocoder had personality. It became more human, so to speak. An entity unto itself."

Vincent Calloway, the vocoder freak-a-zoid of Cincinnati's Midnight Star. Vincent first encountered a man speaking through an Electrolarynx while trick-or-treating as a child. "We grabbed our candy and got the hell out!"

Midnight Star's inspiration for the vocoder was getting whipped by Zapp on tour. Reggie Calloway remembers being taunted by Roger Troutman during sessions at Fifth Floor Studios in Cincinnati. "He'd say, 'You guys keep playing that pretty jazz music. Oh, that's beautiful, mm-hmm,'" Reggie laughs. "That *pretty* music. We were into making everything sweet and perfect. After touring with Zapp, we changed our entire style. Roger taught us a lot inadvertently."

+ + +

In Columbus, Ohio, the fairground speakers announce the start of a thermonuclear assault, through the vocoder: "Professor Faulkin could not reach you at three-five-three-two Cedar Road. We're going to DEFCON One and will launch our missiles in twenty-eight hours, twelve minutes, thirty-two seconds." Vincent Calloway quotes WOPR, the national defense computer of *War Games*. "My whole sound check was *War Games*."

When Midnight Star actually take the stage, Calloway makes his PSA: "Freak-a-zoids, robots—please report to the dance floor." Kids say, "No problem," but tear down the fences getting there, giving Vincent

flashbacks of almost being fatally crushed by a Jackson 5 mob at the Cincinnati Garden when he was ten. "I never experienced anything like that. It wasn't like we were talking about anything crazy. Just freak-a-zoids." That day at the fair, the police nearly arrest Midnight Star and their vocoder for violating Section 2917 of the Ohio Code—inciting a riot.

Midnight Star performs "Freak-A-Zoid" at Disney World in 1984. Calloway believes the vocoder is personality driven, not dehumanizing but evoking emotion from the machine itself.

BOOK TWO

CHAPTER SEVEN

INTERDICTION

The Vocal Well Gods took the American president's bet until they
were warned about what tragically happened.
— Rammellzee

That is one hell of a gamble.
— JFK, 1962

John F. Kennedy used the KY-9 vocoder during the Cuban Missile Crisis when consulting with British Prime Minister Harold Macmillan. Crypto-engineers said the KY-9 made the president sound like Donald Duck, the de facto diss for weird sounding voices at the time. (Courtesy National Archives/NSA)

THE MAC-JACK LINE

The brink of nuclear annihilation calls for sound advice over a secure phone line, at least one that works properly. On October 25, 1962, John F. Kennedy pushed the button and spoke on the vocoder. While his voice went to the machine, his body was at the pharmacy, infused with steroids, painkillers and anti-spasmodics. He heard a hiss of static and pushed again. At the other end, British Prime Minister Harold MacMillan heard "garble," not, "I don't want to have an incident with a Russian ship tomorrow." While the US Strategic Air Command was at a DEFCON 3 state of readiness—with no secure way to communicate with the ground—Kennedy's Brahmin accent was being transformed into "Mickey Mouse/Donald Duck," a side effect of processing the president's vocal tract into a binary code. Talk of a "Naval interdiction" of all vessels bound for Cuba was compressed and artificially rendered at 1667 bits per second. The letter *R* was nowhere to be found.

The KY-9's push-talk button was a source of irritation for John F. Kennedy during the Cuban Missile Crisis.

Kennedy had been using the KY-9, a 500-pound 12-channel scrambler developed by Bell Labs in 1953. He often turned to the KY-9 during the Cuban Missile Crisis, a time when a single teletype exchange with Premier Khrushchev in Moscow could take over twelve hours between transmission, decoding and translation, while hung-over Soviet missile commanders sweated it out in submarines and gingerly shuttled warheads across Cuba's harrowing mountain terrain in the dark. Those thirteen days in October were so fraught with miscommunication, Intel glut and near-misses, it's a wonder we're even here to speculate. For the vocoder, there was no shortage of speech-energy breakdowns to analyze. According to transcripts of the Kennedy-MacMillan phone calls, garble came out as "ggrble," as if near gerbil in frequency.

On October 22, after informing Americans about Soviet missile sites in Cuba, JFK called Prime Minister Harold MacMillan in London and General Norstad, then stationed in Paris. MacMillan urged the president to work a compromise with Moscow (don't invade Cuba) while offering support (activate sixty Thor missiles, tipped with US megaton warheads). Norstad, a former WW II pilot who believed "nuclear superiority had limited psycho-political meaning," wanted to immobilize his Jupiter missiles in Turkey, bordering the Soviet Republic of Georgia.

That August, with Soviet cruise missiles and warheads already in Cuba, Harold MacMillan received a classified memo from his secretary Philip de Zulueta: "The Americans have developed a telephone scrambler which promotes secure transatlantic speech. The disadvantage is that the voices sound rather odd." "Temperamental in its habits," the KY-9 was referred to as the "Mac-Jack Line." Conversations were often choppy at best, due to its push-to-talk (PTT) function—fine for buzzing in UPS, yet nerve-wracking on matters of national security. Kennedy would often forget to push or release, leaving dead-air interpretation, perhaps the illusion that he wasn't being interrupted. Cryptography historian David Boak described the KY-9 voice as being artificially restrained. "You…must…speak…very…slowly," he said.

The KY-9 cost $40,000 per unit and had all the charm of an Acme safe, a squat three feet high with a combination dial and light that flashed red for non-sensitive talk and green for crypto. Before activating the vocoder, users were required to say, "Go green!" Instead of sensitive vinyl records—as with SIGSALY—the code key was provided by computer punch cards, with a separate batch reserved for discussing nuclear retaliation. The KY-9 allowed the president to communicate directly overseas without the call being routed through the Pentagon, thus avoiding bureaucratic interference. He enjoyed how his private line aroused suspicion in the State Department, which had its own KY-9 system with separate clearance. If it malfunctioned, Fault Control was contacted and a small set of railroad tracks would release from the back, permitting the vocoder to be trundled out for maintenance. Said one technician, "There was absolutely no possibility of voice recognition."

VISIBLE SPEECH

During the Cold War, when Sylvania wrote a missile jingle set to a Pepsi ad, Bell Labs devoted more attention to Anti-Ballistic Missile systems than vocoders. In 1964, the Soviet Union declined the invitation to attend the World's Fair in Flushing Meadows, where the theme was "Peace Through Understanding," as the world was still flinching from being taken to DEFCON 2 and the assassinations of Kennedy and Martin Luther King, Jr. Since the Soviets had already put a dog in orbit before the US even got out of Florida, the Fair also emphasized space travel.

Bell Labs' vocoder exhibit at the 1964 World's Fair, where Wendy Carlos first encountered the machine. (Courtesy AT&T Archives and History Center)

The success of Sputnik helped get *The Martian Chronicles* back in print. Ray Bradbury returned to the World's Fair as an architectural consultant. Instead of crying at the fireworks, he found himself marveling at a fluorescent cloud of lightning bugs hovering over Queens. The robots in dinosaurs' clothing were a nice touch, too. In a *New York Times* op-ed piece, Bradbury's friend Isaac Asimov mused about frozen TV dinners and the future of "automeals," robot breakfasts prepared by housekeepers powered by radioisotopes. Disney unveiled its animatronic creatures (including the Abraham Lincoln simulacrum that inspired Philip K. Dick's *We Can Build You*), IBM computers translated Russian into English, and the Bell System offered more free long distance, transmitted, somewhat clearly, at 600 bits per second. Those who enjoyed the sheer pleasure of having their voices dismantled could

Invented by Dave Coulter in 1963, EVA (Electronic Voice Analogue) created artificial speech from visible speech patterns drawn by electromagnetic conductive ink. After seeing the demonstration at the 1964 World's Fair, the NSA would purchase EVA from Coulter for speech encoding research only to junk the machine in a scrap yard in Marlboro, Maryland. (Courtesy Frank Gentges and Dave Coulter)

attend the vocoder exhibit over at Bell's "Floating Wing," a *Millennium Falcon*–like structure. "Watch this fascinating experimental machine sample your voice, take it 'apart,' put it back together again and play tricks with it."

Avoiding the Talking Flashlight over at the Sermons from Science exhibit, one could also check out Electronic Voice Analog (EVA), a "Visible Speech" synthesizer that said, "I enjoy the simple life" to anyone within earshot. EVA was essentially a formant vocoder married to a chart-reading machine. Its voice was created by spectrograms, speech waves traced onto Mylar paper by conductive ink. Based on the Swiss-made OVE (Orator Verbis Electris), EVA was invented by Dave Coulter, a key vocoder engineer and consultant to various federal agencies during the Cold War. Obsessed with synthetic speech since hearing the Voder say "extraordinary" at the 1939 World's Fair when he was seven,

Dave Coulter (left) being congratulated on his formant vocoder at Melpar, circa 1968. Melpar was contracted by the US Army for vocoder R&D. Known as "The Hairlip Machine," this vocoder tracked and synthesized formants—the energy concentrated around a speech sound that helps compose the frequency spectrum. (Courtesy Frank Gentges and Dave Coulter)

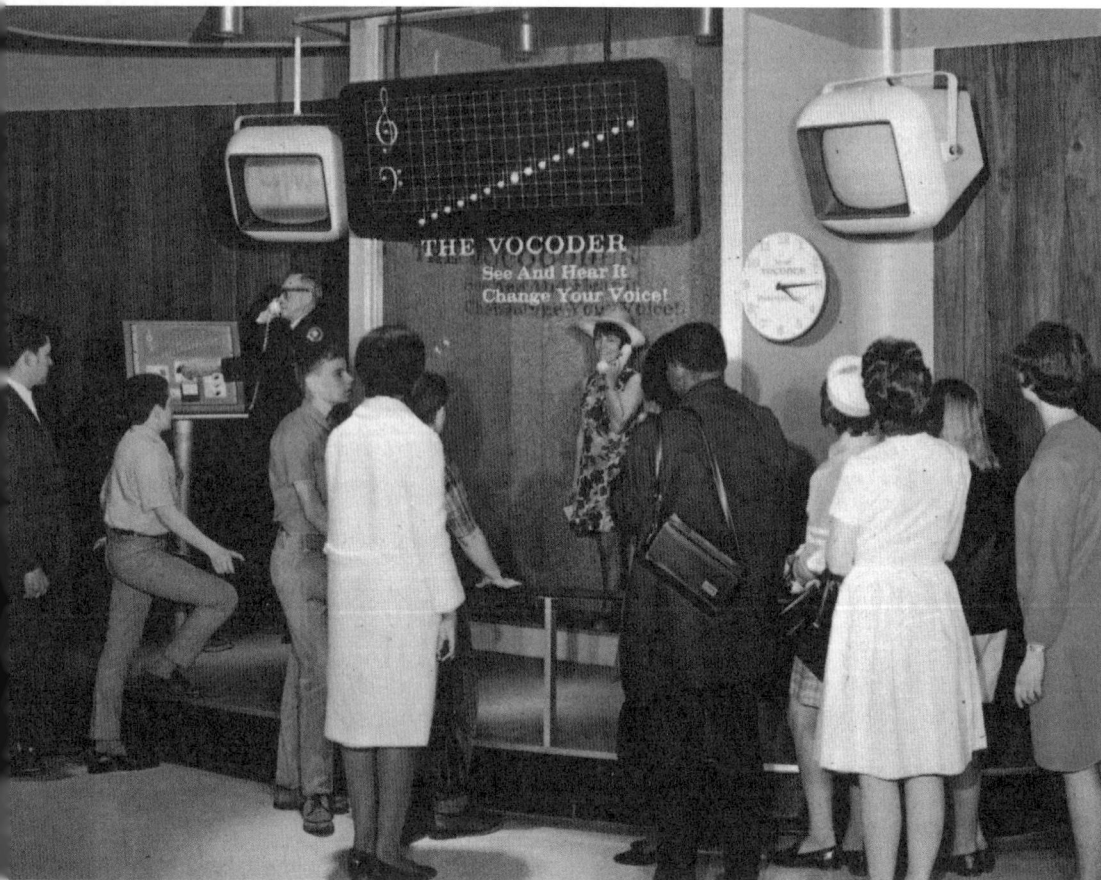

Bell Labs' vocoder demonstration at the Chicago Museum of Science and Industry, circa 1964. (Photo Courtesy Archives, Museum of Science and Industry, Chicago)

Coulter had been working as a cryptology engineer for Melpar, a defense contractor in northern Virginia that specialized in electronic warfare and weapons simulators.

The EVA demonstration at the World's Fair impressed children and the NSA, who purchased the machine for secure voice research only to ditch it in a scrapyard in upper Marlboro, Maryland, where Coulter would randomly discover his invention years later, still coherent and harboring a stack of classified satellite photos.

MOOG DROOGS

In 1971, Dave Coulter's 15-year-old daughter Annie told him she was going to a midnight showing of *Fantasia* and saw Stanley Kubrick's *A Clockwork Orange* instead. While Annie sat in the theater watching Malcolm McDowell being tortured by a vocoder version of Beethoven's Ninth Symphony, her father was in his basement vocoder lab, stretching and mangling phonemes for the State Department. (A childhood friend of Annie's remembers the lab's massive Bat Cave computers and the "strangest disembodied voices" that haunted the Coulter household.) Conservative and pro-Vietnam, Coulter not only banned his daughter from seeing Kubrick's film, he didn't want her listening to Wendy Carlos' soundtrack, the experience of being drowned by a Moog synthesizer, if not the future itself. Ultraviolence on reverb was a bleak departure from Carlos' popular Moog debut, *Switched-On Bach*. Annie Coulter may be the first case of a teen rebelling against her father with vocoderized Beethoven instead of Mick Jagger.

A physics PhD from Cornell, Robert Moog had been seeking Dave Coulter ever since reading a published Army report on the latter's Melpar research in 1964, when Moog was in the early stages of building modular synth legos for recording studios. Moog had implemented Coulter's tunable formant into his synthesizer, allowing it to emulate human sounds. "Bob was always going off on tangents," says Walter Sear, an engineer who worked closely with Moog. "The vocoder was a distraction when the company was going broke. It wasn't marketable."

Another Moog associate, Jon Weiss, remembers feeding Bach's Brandenburg Concertos through the vocoder and getting a "splendid ethereal reformulation." This synthetic derealization of classical music would anticipate the vocoder's breakthrough with Carlos, a Columbia physics/music composition student and one of Moog's most proactive collaborators. "That vocoder was a prototype we worked on together," says Carlos on the phone from New York. "It was experimental, a little crude, and far less costly than several later commercial 'luxury' vocoders." (By 1977, commercial Moog vocoders—designed and impoved by Harald Bode—fetched used Volkswagen prices at $5,900, just less than half of what EMS was charging.)

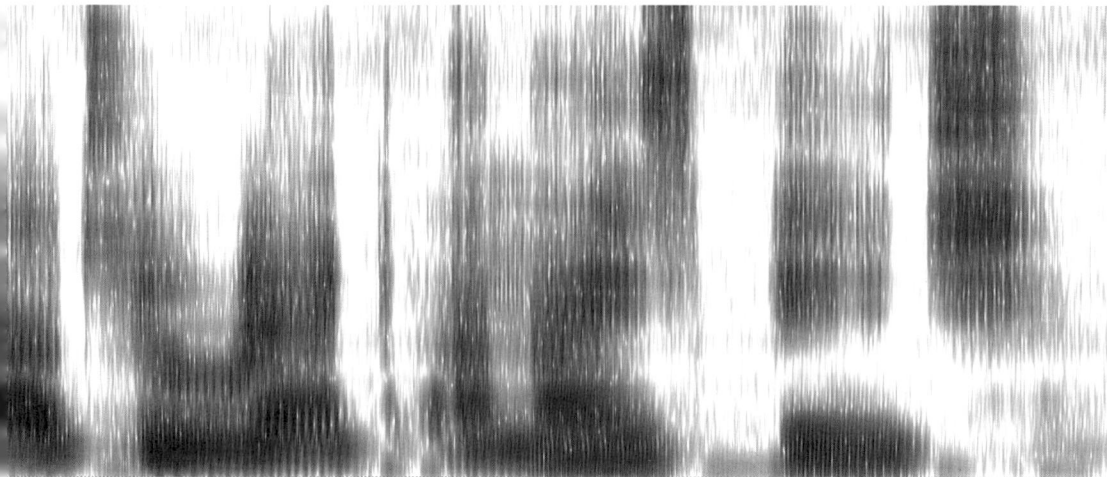

The words "how to wreck a nice beach," spoken through a Korg VC-10 vocoder and transformed into a spectrogram's visual frequency bands by Wendy Carlos. "The chordal pitches made a darker lower region while the white-noisy audio gives more spatterings up above in the graphs," said Carlos in an email. (Courtesy Wendy Carlos)

Carlos had been fascinated with the vocoder since seeing it at the 1964 World's Fair:

They had a visual display with a pitch follower so you could sing into it. It could detect the pitch and little bulbs would light up on a musical scale to show you what pitch you were hearing. They'd harness someone from the audience to come up and talk and sing as well. And I got nailed to do that. They would raise the pitch, to a chipmunky sound or down to a Darth Vader effect, and ask, "How are you?" or "Why are you here?" Like a dopey television quiz program—nothing that needed to be saved for posterity. But I found it whimsical and affectionate. I set aside in my mind that some day, some way, I wanted a vocoder!

Carlos attended the exhibit six times. A year later she met Bob Moog at an annual convention for the Audio Engineering Society, at which attendees were allowed to check out new technologies displayed at the World's Fair. After being shown the control booth for synchronizing fountains and fireworks to music, Carlos impatiently burst, "*Alright, where's the vocoder?*" "They said, 'Oh, you're right beside it.' And there was a large beige molded fiberglass cabinet that reached up to my chin,

Bell Labs' 16-channel vocoder filter bank circa 1960, condensed from SIGSALY's 2500-square-foot vocoder. (Courtesy AT&T Archives and History Center)

with sloping, streamlined sides," she continues. "You only saw a couple of switches and a power light that was on. It was quiet. I pressed my ear against it, but could hear no fans. Of course—solid state!"

+ + +

"You meet the strangest people these days when you happen to be carrying a vocoder around with you," Wendy Carlos once told me. "Ever notice that?" I once emailed Wendy the Who's Sonovox track "Armenia City in the Sky," and she responded with a "visible speech" spectrogram of the track, followed by a spectrogram of some of her early vocoder tracks, which at first glance appeared to be a procession of electrocuted caterpillars.

"She is a brilliant person," says Kai Krause, a former vocoder consultant for Sennheiser and a tech friend. "She's a great inspiration for sonic illumination." Back in the late Sixties, while working as a studio engineer in New York, Carlos was introduced to the Eltro, an "information rate changer" made in Germany that manipulated tape playback using special rotating heads to stretch or shrink time. It could also alter pitch without affecting the playback duration. "We used it to speed up or slow down commercials to fit in their exact thirty-second or sixty-second

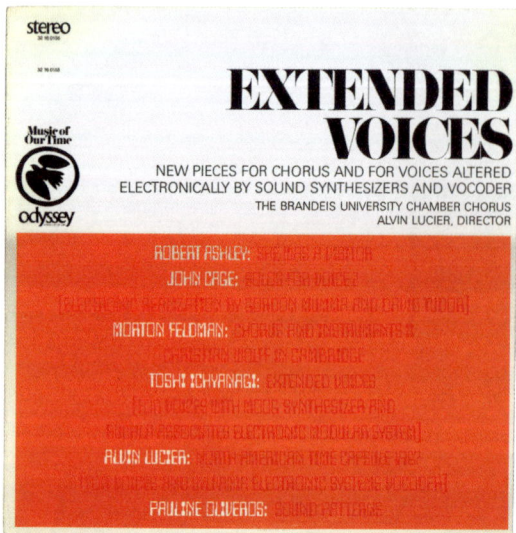

stereo

EXTENDED VOICES

NEW PIECES FOR CHORUS AND FOR VOICES ALTERED
ELECTRONICALLY BY SOUND SYNTHESIZERS AND VOCODER
THE BRANDEIS UNIVERSITY CHAMBER CHORUS
ALVIN LUCIER, DIRECTOR

Music of
Our Time

odyssey

ROBERT ASHLEY: SHE WAS A VISITOR
JOHN CAGE: SOLOS FOR VOICE 1
[ELECTRONIC REALIZATION BY GORDON MUMMA AND DAVID TUDOR]
MORTON FELDMAN: CHORUS AND INSTRUMENTS II
CHRISTIAN WOLFF IN CAMBRIDGE
TOSHI ICHYANAGI: EXTENDED VOICES
[FOR VOICES WITH MOOG SYNTHESIZER AND
BUCHLA ASSOCIATES ELECTRONIC MODULAR SYSTEM]
ALVIN LUCIER: NORTH AMERICAN TIME CAPSULE 1967
[FOR VOICES AND SYLVANIA ELECTRONIC SYSTEMS VOCODER]
PAULINE OLIVEROS: SOUND PATTERNS

Extended Voices: New Pieces For Chorus and
For Voices Altered Electronically by Sound
Synthesizers and Vocoder (1967, Odyssey
Records). Features Alvin Lucier's "North American Time Capsule," one of the first vocoder
songs to be somewhat commercially available
on record. (Courtesy Patrick James Longo)

spots." Among the Eltro's clients were the US government, the Union Theological Seminary of Richmond, Virginia, and Stanley Kubrick, who forever endeared himself to my mom when he used the Eltro for HAL's lobotomy in *2001: A Space Odyssey*. HAL's drool-speed version of "Daisy Bell" was essentially a lullaby sung to me in the crib when I was an infant. Kubrick's script collaborator, sci-fi author Arthur C. Clarke, had visited Bell Labs in 1962. While trying to determine how a phone booth would look in outer space, Clarke overheard an early IBM computer singing "Daisy." Bell Labs would release this computer voice demo on 10-inch vinyl the following year.

Wendy Carlos explained HAL's voice in terms of running toward the back of a moving subway car. "The Eltro at first was used to gradually drop the pitch without changing the duration. HAL's voice then slows down as the playback time expands. Very few Eltros were produced and sold. People have hypothesized all manner of extremely intricate fabrications that are fun to read but horseshit. The reality was simple and rather elegant."

The reality was inside the space helmet of Mission Commander Dave Bowman, his breathing compatible with the uphill huff of Kraftwerk's "Tour de France," had its 45 rpm been downshifted to 33, with HAL expiring just before crooning, "I permit you to use the brake." The bicycle had been pitched into the muckspit, leaving us on foot and in deep space, somewhere outside Jupiter.

In 1970, two years after the release of *2001*, Carlos saw *Colossus: The Forbin Project*, a Cold War science fiction film featuring the first paranoid supercomputer to speak through a vocoder. A nosy, overbearing control freak, Colossus polices sex and alcohol consumption, forms an alliance with its Soviet counterpart (GUARDIAN) and blackmails mankind with nuclear warheads. "Colossus is a much more frightening talking computer than HAL, which may be partially due to the vocoder," suggests Carlos. "*Forbin Project* was the first movie that I recognized for

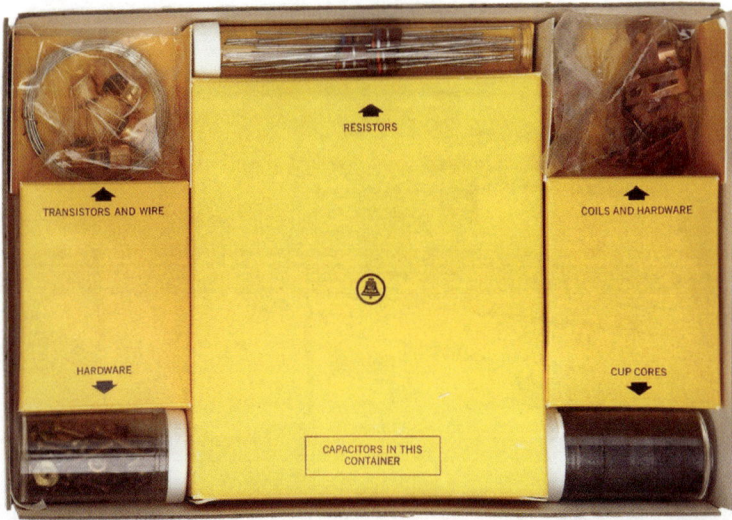

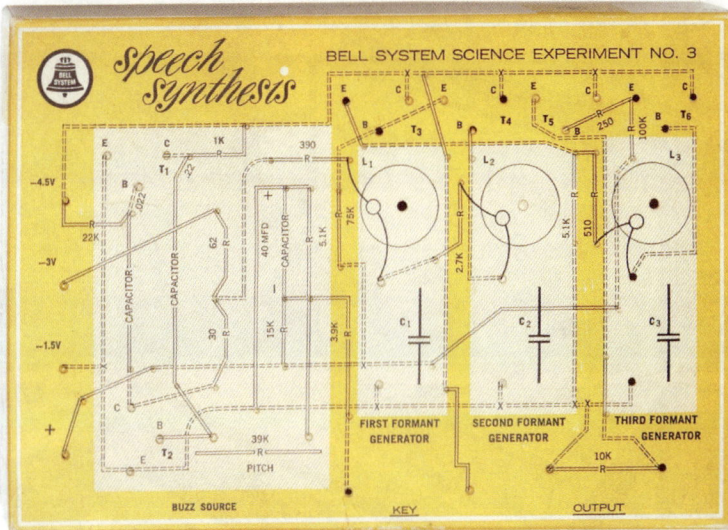

We can build you: Bell Labs Speech Synthesis Kit, 1963. This DIY voice machine was part of a promotional campaign as Bell Labs began using computer models of synthetic speech, from the automatic digital recognition (Audrey) to the Charles Dodge LP, *Synthesized Voices*, released in 1976.

certain used one. By its release I had my own vocoder. And it hit me abruptly—the synchronicity—that this is an idea whose time has come! A year later I discovered Stanley was interested in *everything*, open and curious. Over dinner one evening I had to give him a description of the workings of a typical vocoder."

Some listeners had an "emotional resistance" to artificial voices, creating a robot stand-off, of sorts. Carlos explains:

> People at first hated our synthesized singing. I watched good friends who enjoyed my synthesized instrumental sounds turn squirmy. They visibly winced. I proposed composing an additional work for the album, one to precede Beethoven, and so *Timesteps* was born. *Timesteps* featured a gradual easing-in on the notion of singing synthesizers. By the time they reached the Ninth Symphony it didn't hit them in the face the same way. Not that the vocoder and synthetic speech were state secrets—now they're almost clichés. But they certainly were cutting-edge, and highly unusual at the time.

In *A Clockwork Orange*, the Beethoven vocoder is first heard at a record store, where Alex DeLarge picks up two girls, skipping the John Fahey LP and *2001* soundtrack (a nudge to the eyeball in the bins) and goes home for a Benny Hill speed orgy. Beethoven later returns when Alex undergoes the Ludovico Treatment in the theater, his eyes peeled open by speculum.

Carlos had recorded unused tracks, many containing the vocoder, for other scenes. She explains: "There was the elaborate 'Biblical Day-dreams': three interwoven musical themes for the prison library episode, accompanying Alex's darkly perverted 'olde tyme' fantasies. The most significant was *Country Lane*, a long, complex cue highlighting the vocoder, that was composed for the scene in which the older Droogies, now cops, meet and savagely beat Alex." Police beatings, perversions and record stores—a nice way to introduce the vocoder to America.

By 1974, Annie Coulter was seventeen and the beef with her father had evolved from censoring droog beatdowns to his support for Nixon and the war in Vietnam. That year they attended a Robert Moog lecture at the Audio Engineering Society and approached him afterwards. Moog was excited to finally meet Dave Coulter, thanking him for inventing the tunable formant that wound up in his synthesizer and, ultimately, in *A Clockwork Orange*. More thrilled was Annie Coulter, upon discovering that her dad might be kind of cool, despite himself.

WHEN YOU SAY NASTY WORDS

Smile death fraud pit gill charge hot pod frown

In 1971, Homer Dudley, the seventy-five-year-old inventor of the vocoder, hit the beach in Hawaii and went surfing. That year NASA and Magnavox paid good money for someone to say, "Smile when you say nasty words" through a vocoder. This description of speech was compared to cockpit noise inside a Boeing 707. At the time, the Federal Digital Voice Processing Consortium was evaluating a secure voice standard for all branches of the US Armed Forces. "Smile when you say nasty words" was part of a series of tests conducted at Fort Huachuca, Arizona, the main switch of AUTOSEVOCOM, a global network of vocoders fielded during the Vietnam War. At Huachuca's Automated Articulation Test Facility, recordings were analyzed for phoneme extraction and intelligibility.

Sub chuck beach cuss gust fate folk nook mange

As engineers for the Naval Research Laboratory, Dave Coulter and his partner Frank Gentges would subject their formant vocoder to these tests. The recordings were sent to a blind listening jury at the University of Texas, where students volunteered to skip class and spend the afternoon flooding their headphones with third-grade vocoder rhymes, "A noise annoys an oyster," seashells, and assorted Myrtle Beach trinket backwash.

Knee puck rip bought cloud chute earl corpse sludge

"We ran a Vocoder Confusion Matrix on them," Gentges says. "The relationship to reality was not very good."

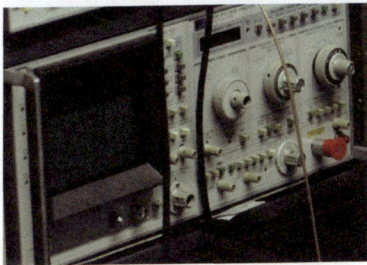

Spectral analyzers photographed at Metavox Laboratories in Great Falls, Virginia, run by Frank Gentges and Dave Coulter until Coulter passed away. Not pictured: the vacuum tank used for simulating conditions in outer space which now serves as a shoe dryer.

CHAPTER EIGHT

VIETNAM, VERBOT, AND CLEAR

This will lead the world to more sound and fury.

— Vocoder test sentence, prepared for Goddard Space Flight Center, 1971

FULL METAL THROAT COAT

The vocoder was on precarious terms with reality throughout the Vietnam War, a time when human speech often masked actual events and planes dropped portable radios from the sky. Cold War policy encoded in the airwaves translated to tactical confusion in the jungle. To the grunt being shelled in a spider hole, Narrowband Ciphony was just compression.

In 1968, a sixteen-channel vocoder sat on board the *USS Bonhomme Richard*, an aircraft carrier stationed in the Gulf of Tonkin off the coast of North Vietnam. Called MF STEAMVALVE, it digitized outgoing calls from commanders to the Pentagon and other ships, processing daily air strikes into bits of 1 and 0. In the mess hall one floor above, the ship's crew shared their lunch with bombs, which were sliding and bumping around beneath the tables, waiting to defoliate Vietnam. There was nowhere else to put them. Frank Gentges sat below in Radio Central doing quality assurance on the vocoder, while ordnance rumbled above his head. "I was quietly working on my vocoder while above me aircraft loaded with bombs were being shot off the ship with a catapult," he says.

J.V.C. F.O.R.C.E.

Long Island's JVC FORCE won the acronym battle with Justified by the Virtue of Creativity For Reasons Concerning Entertainment.

As the designer of STEAMVALVE and engineer for Rixom Electronics, the 25-year-old Gentges had been assigned to Yankee Station, a triangulation of carriers deployed in the Gulf of Tonkin. In 1964, Tonkin was the site of an imaginary Vietminh PT-boat attack, some hokey Intel quickly branded an incident, allowing President Lyndon Johnson to publicly wage an undeclared war on communist aggression, a policy secretly backed by the US since the early Fifties. By the time Gentges arrived at Yankee Station in 1968, more than half a million American troops were stationed in Vietnam.

The STEAMVALVE system was the Naval crypto-voice connection to the Pentagon as the US tried to bomb its way out of an eleven-year foreign policy morass. One of the Navy's better acronyms, STEAMVALVE stood for Secure Tactical Electronic Amplitude Modulated Voice Actuated Long-range Vestigial Emanations. The encryption key generator—TSEC/KG-13— subsisted on voice bits instead of vinyl records. (The KG-13's would be kept in safes after one had been seized during the Korean War.)

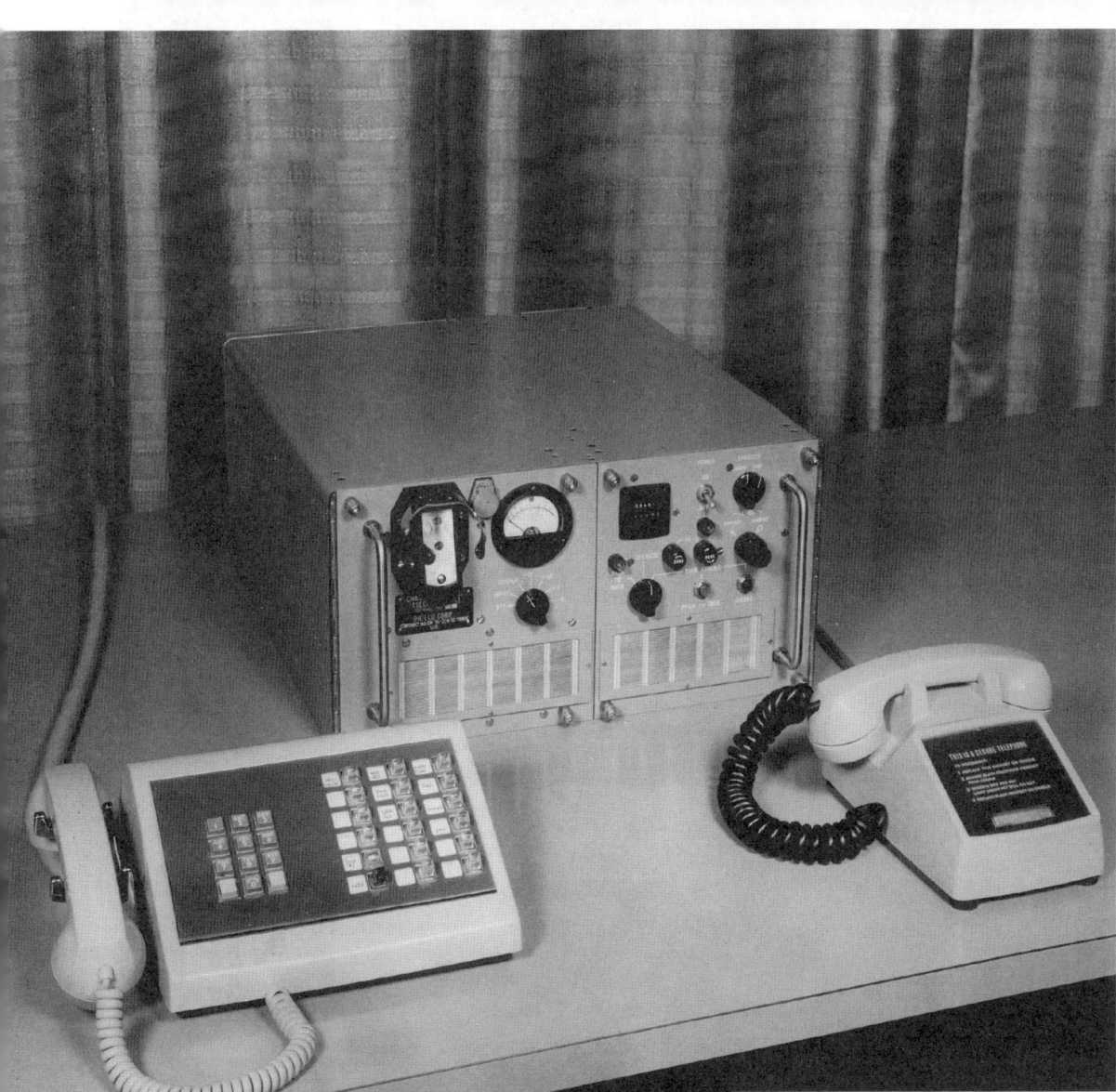

"It didn't really sound like Joe." The HY-2 Vocoder photographed in 1964, invented at Bell Labs and deployed for secret telephony in Saigon, Paris, and the State Department in Washington. (Courtesy AT&T Archives and History Center)

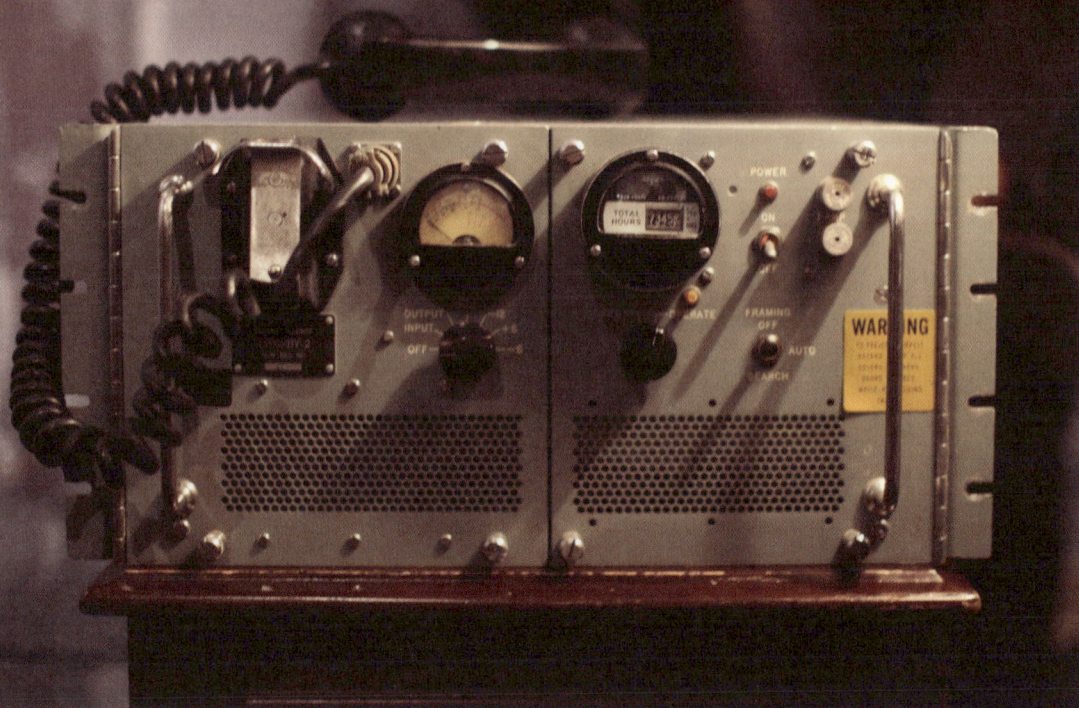

The HY-2 Vocoder, photographed at the NSA Museum of Cryptology in Fort Meade, Maryland. Invented in 1961, the HY-2 was the main secure voice apparatus patched into the worldwide AUTOSEVOCOM network during the Cold War.

The STEAMVALVE system had to be patched into the AUTOSEVOCOM network, which primarily used the HY-2 vocoder. Invented in 1961 by Bell Labs and Philco-Ford, the HY-2 introduced the first generation of digital vocoders, long before analogue versions began appearing in recording studios in the early Seventies, while the HY-2 itself remained stuck in Saigon. Producing an "approximation" of human speech at 2400 bps, the HY-2 doubled the capacity of World War II's SIGSALY behemoth. But the robotness-vs-recognition issue confounded officers not accustomed to receiving orders from a machine, unable to identify the voice on the phone any better than the trees that shot at them. Displeased with the vocoder in Air Force One, Lyndon Johnson once flung his headset at an aide and yelled, "When I talk to the Secretary of State, he better *sound* like the Secretary of State!"

"They wanted [voice] recognition," says Gentges. "It didn't really sound like Joe. The average user knew Joe, but when he was listening to it, he didn't think it sounded exactly like Joe. That was a problem with the HY-2." The HY-2 inflicted further degradation on the voice in cases of rapid speech and shouting, not uncommon during the Tet Offensive of 1968, when the Vietcong launched surprise attacks on major provinces in the south, putting armed American teenagers in a state of mortared panic. Users had to speak at a "moderate rate and at a moderate level" to be understood. "We were sending a representation of the voice to the far end," said Donald Crowder, a lieutenant who serviced vocoders in South Vietnam.

Much about the AUTOSEVOCOM network is still held close. The word *vocoder* is rarely used in the AUTOSEVOCOM community—at least among those willing to talk—often walled up in tech shorthand and bold-faced acronyms. Though many vets ate hesitant to discuss crypto-gear from a war in stubborn denial, the HY-2 saw heavy voice traffic in 1968. The Saigon terminal supported the Paris Peace Talks from 1968 to 1972, with systems linked to the palace of South Vietnam President Nguyen Van Thieu and linked to Paris and the State Department. Little was accomplished over these phone lines other than deadlock and the realization that Nixon's National Security advisor Henry Kissinger—slippery back-channeler and vocoder in his own right—had been holding covert cease-fire negotiations with the North Vietnamese Politburo. Meanwhile, Nixon was busy wiretapping the home front while the vocoder channel in the presidential limo was accidentally intercepting frequencies from the Weather Bureau.

For the most part, the tactical specifics of AUTOSEVOCOM—what was said and who said it—won't be declassified until 2030. The HY-2 user manuals are stashed away somewhere on NSA property in Fort Meade, Maryland. The AUTOSEVOCOM manufacturing site is now a shuttered mall. "Something happened in 1972 that I can't tell you about," says Frank Gentges, shadowy to the point of sport. "Fifty years from now, maybe, but not now. I'm throwing an awful lot of crap at you. You're dancing in a minefield."

A couple of Frank Gentges' spectrum analyzers, photographed at his Metavox laboratory in the fall of 2009.

"Please listen to my limo." The secure voice channel in Nixon's limousine accidentally picked up frequencies from the Weather Bureau. Nixon pretty much eavesdropped on everything but his own conscience.

ALL CLEAR

Every time a kid went to war, his mother threw out his magazines.
— Forrest J. Ackerman, as told to author, 1998

More space, Willy, more space soon!
— Wilbur Whateley of the Decaying Whateleys, *The Dunwich Horror*

Rik Davis has spent the afternoon blowing up trees. Deposited by helicopter, the eighteen-year-old Marine from Detroit squats in a bomb crater near Dong Ha, in the northernmost region of South Vietnam. He carries a chrome M-16, some C4 to heat his cocoa, and a leaflet picturing girls, smiles, and Coca-Cola. On the flip side is a photo of a B-52 Stratofortress dropping bombs. This psy-op propaganda is intended to convince the Vietcong to defect while promising *chieu hoi*, "open arms." It's 1968. The stomach of Rik Davis is expecting grenades.

"Most people you interviewed were in the rear with the gear," says Davis, now fifty-five, living in Ann Arbor, Michigan. "I was not one of those."

When we first spoke, Davis summed up his Vietnam experience with an H.P. Lovecraft quote, shriveling his voice for the occasion. "I wonder what I'll look like when the planet is cleared off." The question originated with *The Dunwich Horror* and ended up with a Private First Class who refers to himself as "3070." If the squidlocked Cthulhu has anything to say about it, Davis will look like some ancient bat-winged entity with a beard of tentacles, its voice produced by nonhuman organs with "ghastly infra-bass timbre," a voice "unseen and foul in lonely places," abandoned by reason and attended by a farm-clearing stench. This is how Rik Davis deals. A little *bugg shogg y'heah* from one who split his teenage years between riots in Detroit and getting shot at in a remote jungle on the other side of the planet.

Though Lovecraft and Vietnam share an interest in the nameless and the unspeakable, Rik Davis implicates both in "Clear," an electro-funk classic he recorded in 1982 with Juan Atkins, a Parliament nut from Belleville, west of Detroit. Dunwich refers to a dimension of "Clear" that the record itself never wished to consider: Lovecraft's Old Ones

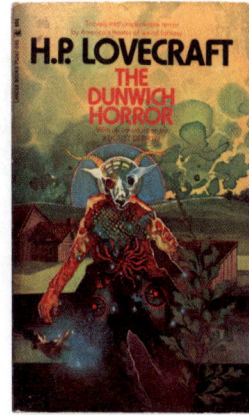

Published in 1929, H.P. Lovecraft's *Dunwich Horror* used "voices with ghastly infra-bass timbre." Rik Davis defines Cybotron's electro-funk classic "Clear" in terms of carpet-bombing, redaction, and Lovecraft's Old Ones de-peopling the planet.

depopulating Earth if the Rapture didn't beat them to it. "It may sound like pure fantasy," says Davis. "But it's just apocalyptic Christian doctrine." In 1982, "Clear" was far too busy filling skate rinks, too busy melting the wheels off your shoes—too busy being *proto*—to worry about who left open the last gate to hell. "Clear" was a minimal exchange between two artificial voices created by "slap back delay with a comb," one a burping silo, the other more treed in pitch, both chilly and bleak. Though "Tomorrow is a brand new day" never held such cheerless menace, the kids—the Sons of the P—danced out of their constriction.

Juan Atkins had befriended Rik Davis in 1980 while taking electronics classes at Washtenaw Community College in Ann Arbor. They named themselves Cybotron after a particle accelerator and the type of robot that puts humans out of business. Signed to Fantasy Records, Cybotron were just two guys pushing drum machines and Korgs through a city that lived and died, and died again, by the machine—Atkins, the future godfather of Detroit techno, and Davis, his soul on Eldritch, now making Lovecraft EROS DVDs in Ann Arbor (and apparently still unbeatable at throwing darts underhanded).

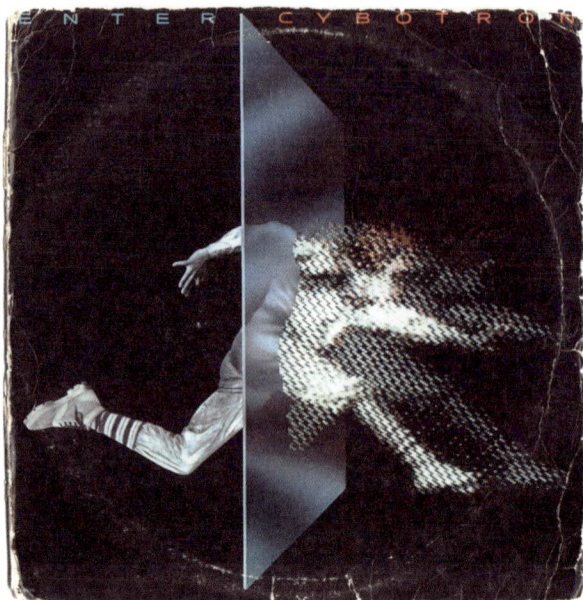

Cybotron, *Enter* (1983, Fantasy Records). Rik Davis breaks for the Detroit public library to read *Famous Monsters of Filmland*. "We didn't sound like Kraftwerk—Kraftwerk had deep pockets."

The first two Cybotron singles, "Alleys of Your Mind" and "Cosmic Cars," were released on Atkins' label Deep Space Records. The latter had the misfortune of being delivered to New York radio stations the day "Planet Rock" broke and has been trying to avenge itself ever since, only showing its age with a double toot of car horn. "'Cosmic Cars' was the beginning of driving for me," says Atkins' friend Kevin Saunderson, another of the early techno DJs. Saunderson was borrowing his mom's Seville at the time. "Cybotron was music for progressive black kids who came from the lower class but dressed like middle-class preppy kids, smoking Germ cigarettes, wearing Polo sweaters, khaki pants and penny loafers."

Juan Atkins remembers "Clear" as being misread as Scientology propaganda, auditing the reactive subconscious for an L. Ron Hubbard time-share. To Rik Davis, "Clear" was face down in the mud in Vietnam. It was urban renewal, carpet-bombing and Lovecraftwerk, a secret history of destruction buried in a song that greenly believed, "Earth is ours for us to save," though the Old Ones already claimed ownership. "Embrace the world-destroyer," says Davis. "It's the only way to live. Because whatever you cling to, it'll be destroyed. The hippies perished in it. They thought it was forever."

For Juan Atkins, "Clear" was a technocratic vision, with all the utopianism of "Planet Rock" and the spatial neuroses of "Pack Jam." He had read Alvin Toffler's 1980 book *The Third Wave*, which hailed post-industrial automation and hybrid neologisms. (Could machines replace human assembly lines so GM could chew up the highways that had already destroyed black neighborhoods?) "Clear" would end on a positive note that nobody heard: "Out with the old/ In the with new." "They deleted it from the radio version," says Atkins. "That was basically the concept behind the whole album. Clear out the old program. Technological revolution."

For me, the technological revolution started in a Zenith clock radio inherited from my parents' divorce. "Clear" was the first electro song I heard, an escape from junior high psy-ops. My mother was in the room when it happened, fooling with a dislocated window shade, the sunlight crushed by October, and Les Norman, the Night-Time Master Blaster of WPEG, on the radio. "Clear" came from nowhere, swooping from above. I didn't know whether to nod my head, duck, or just blow up the request line. (Blowing up request lines was not easy before the invention of redial.) "That's the idea," says Davis. "It's all coming down from above. 'Clear' is outside what exists." What I saw outside that day was a swirl of dead leaves chasing each other in the street like children. As if something had just taken off. The song ends in a turbine swoosh, leaving you behind.

Nobody seemed to know what "Clear" meant, other than the fact that Detroit's abandoned factories made good party spaces and that the song fit nicely between Kraftwerk and Debbie Deb, between clean

German automation and debauched Miami strip malls. Though designated as the birth of Detroit techno, "Clear" couldn't wait to get down to South Florida, where the song was adopted and sainted, a reason for DJs to shout out the clarity of bass sub-frequencies before blowing their woofers out to sea. The lyrics "Clear, you're behind" could have meant "make room for that bottom." And so Miami backed into the future through a garrison of speakers cabinets, in the rear with the gear.

To the generation that discovers these conspiracies on the Internet, "Clear" would be recognized for what it isn't, something Timbaland sampled for "Lose Control," a Missy Elliott single released in 2002. The conceit was simple: Music makes you hallucinate blue Lamborghinis airbrushed by a Ciara chorus while Fat Man Scoop, the drill sergeant of hype men, berates the freaks, freaking the club. It's all seizures and tracksuits, boneless and acrylic.

"Lose Control" enabled Rik Davis to drive off in a black Corvette C6, paid in full with sampling dividends and pictured on his MySpace page along with a photo of Missy in designer combat fatigues. Yet talking to Davis, you immediately sense that "Clear" was everything but the club. It was someone simply trying to deal, making room inside his head. Whatever passed through the vocoder from Washington to Saigon, Rik Davis lived it in the clearing of the jungles, where Kissinger had quantified bombing to "the bejeesus," as if unaccountable. "Clear has a military value," Davis says. Securing an area of operation could mean slaughtering the village. "Clear our displays," their actions. Clear is classified, redacted. The human blank. A contradiction that would never admit as much. In itself, a white sky mindfuck.

Much of Davis' Vietnam tour is restricted as "need to know." He says "Clear" was a way for him to vent his spleen. "I'd seen too much death. Destruction is something I've dwelt in all my existence. My motivations— what would be the use or sense in trying to explain these things? I'm only telling you now as a post-mortem." Juan Atkins remembers his friend's accounts in the bush. The snakes, the leeches, the artillery pop, the swamps, the bugs, the elephant grass. "It was the worst mistake of his life."

Davis' motive for enlisting had less to do with godless communist aggression than it did with just getting out of Detroit, a city that nearly burned to the ground in the riots of 1967. Davis, then sixteen, witnessed it from the gutted grocery store where he worked. "I was born in the ghetto of Detroit in Black Bottom," he says. "Politically, I wasn't pro or anti [war]. A chance to escape the ghetto became more imperative than anything else." Once thriving because of World War II industry and the migration of black families from Alabama and Mississippi, Detroit underwent slum clearance in the Fifties, a policy of racism and deindustrialization that leveled and displaced entire communities. By the Sixties, when Davis was catching every Roger Corman film in town, Interstate 75 had ploughed through Black Bottom, formerly Paradise Valley. Clear was desolation. "I have been on the wrong end of urban renewal all my life," says Davis. "The population was cleared out, for a highway. They dug a big ditch straight downtown, straight to the riverfront."

Audio Tech, "I'm Your Audio Tech" (1985, Express Records). This obscure Detroit techno 12 inch was created by Juan Atkins, post-Cybotron, and anticipated the Miami car show bass scene.

Rik was one of those kids who had to run to the library to avoid getting mugged, finding refuge in a fanzine called *Famous Monsters of Filmland*. He would do the gauntlet through Detroit's East Side, past the Arcadia roller rink and Brewster Projects, so he could catch a double feature of *The Lost Missile* and *The Seventh Voyage of Sinbad*. "You're not going to believe this, but I joined the Marines to sail the Seven Seas with Captain Sinbad. Adventure and thrills."

During grunt training at Camp Pendleton, north of San Diego, Davis went AWOL and caught a bus to Los Angeles, where he was taken in by a branch of the Diggers commune, another disillusioned seventeen-year-old chasing flower girls in his uniform. ("I was just trying to get laid before I died.") But the escape was abbreviated by the news of Martin Luther King, Jr.'s assassination on April 4, 1968. "I heard it from an old white guy. I was in uniform. He stopped me in the street and said, 'Well, what do you think of him now?' I had no idea what he was talking about. He said, 'They've killed him! *He's dead.*'"

Forrest J. Ackerman, editor of *Famous Monsters of Filmland*, early mentor of Rik Davis, photographed in front of his house in Los Angeles, fending off the same Allosaurus that menaced Raquel Welch in Ray Harryhausen's dinomation classic *One Million Years BC*.

Confused, high and broken, Davis turned himself in and was shipped off to Vietnam. He wasn't allowed to pack his *Dunwich Horror*, not even the special GI Armed Services Edition, published in 1943. The Marines did provide a bible—all the same for Lovecraft and Cybotron, only more deluxe ichor, more rot. Revelations would become "R-9," a 1985 Cybotron single about being trapped in the Good Word. "Human life does not depart from the word," says Davis. "So you're forced to step in synchronization, whether you believe it, whether you want it. Irrelevant. You're programmed to fulfill it." (I wouldn't have skipped Sunday School had I known they were teaching the bible with cosmic electro lasers from Detroit.)

Davis would be sent to Quang Tri, the northernmost province of South

Vietnam, a region overrun by the NVA but ruled by the jungle—the most dangerous place to be in 1968. Davis' first duty was accidentally torching a row of wooden toilets. "It was better that way," Davis laughs. "They got new latrines." Christopher Lee's biggest fan was then deployed north of Dong Ha to fight the Pathet Lao Insurgency, a group of communist guerrillas backed by the NVA. "We did ops that don't exist. Ops that weren't allowed to exist."

On Cybotron's 1983 debut album *Enter*, Davis used an Arp Axxe synthesizer and a vocoder to get from Vietnam to El Salvador. Filtering noise through a modulated wave, he created machine-gun patter and helicopter drumming, sampled from combat memory in the 17th Parallel and mixed down in his nightmares. (Davis had purchased the Arp after watching Dario Argento's horror masterpiece *Suspiria*, scored by Goblin in quadraphonic sound and adopted by a ballet school run by witches, filling the gate to hell with reverb. Goblin would later go disco vocoder on the soundtrack to Argento's *Tenebrae*.) Listening to the Clash's *Sandinista* and keeping with the Reagan-backed junta of the times, Davis called the song "El Salvador." The lyrics quaver like algae's grandmother, sub-tarn and only understood by Davis himself, who was then processing some post-traumatic demons through a Korg vocoder. When I ask for a translation (all I caught was "El Salvador"), he repeated the hook: "I don't want to kill you but I have to."

"El Salvador" was not chosen as a single. With a sluggish zombie pulse, the song can't get out of its own head much less to the dance floor, instead choosing to melt into a dark corner best avoided.

Cybotron, "Clear" (1983, Fantasy Records). The B-side, "Industrial Lies," is pictured here.

✦ ✦ ✦

When Rik Davis returned from Vietnam, there were rehabilitative stays in VA hospitals and trips to record stores in downtown Detroit—the black kid asking for Tangerine Dream and Ultravox's *Rage in Eden* only to get weird looks and end up on the same label as Creedence Clearwater Revival. "How are you gonna fit into *that*?" says Davis. "There's no place for you. You never assimilate. One side of you wants to be a hippie and the other side wants to fit in. Neither can ever happen. The time of your youth is gone. Everybody has moved on. What you had is gone. It's not coming back. Sometimes this place is so foul… I can't swear to you that Rik ever actually came back out of the jungle."

One night, during the recording of "R-9," Juan Atkins walked into Cybotron's studio above Tee Tee's Speakeasy in Ypsilanti, Michigan. There he found Davis in his pajamas holding an assault rifle. "He'd be on guard duty in the middle of the night, aiming the rifle around, cocked. Doing maneuvers. I never felt he was crazy or anything—we were best friends. It was something that just caught me off-guard a little bit." When Atkins asked if everything was okay, Davis said, "Yeah, man…I just sometimes have these dreams."

Outside the studio, the crickets chirped. This would be Cybotron's only field recording, a decision to drop a mic out the back door and see what a Detroit evening had to offer. Stridulation would be the way out of "El Salvador" and into "Clear," the last track on *Enter*. The helicopter and machine guns fade into cries of "dear mother of God" in Spanish. You're left alone with the ghost of your nonexistent ops and some bug-wing friction before everything disappears. It's kind of pleasant. There's nobody else out there.

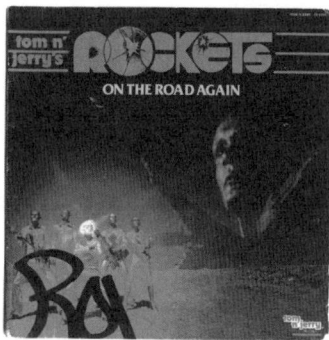

POWER TO THE POWER WINDOWS

What do you think every electrofreak dreams about?
— Thomas Pynchon

The Electrifying Mojo says he designed the formula and personally feels it's exactly what you need on a hot Wednesday night. To devout listeners of WJLB in Detroit, this means Prince, Kraftwerk, and more Prince. Then an hour or so of Parliament bootlegged live, uninterrupted save for the part where Mojo says, "Funk kicks ass"while a Mothership synth does an admirable job of giving the *Close Encounters* theme a chocolate swirly. Detroit has come to expect this from Mojo. Porch lights flicker in anticipation. The Midnight Funk Association has convened, and according to your host, it's time to dance on your back in Technicolor.

It's now sneaking up on three in the morning, and Mojo's talking over "Pocket Calculator," a Kraftwerk song that saw it coming, waiting for us to

Rockets, *On the Road Again* (1978, Tom N' Jerry). Rockets were bald, silver, and French. The title cut was cosmically stretched by New York disco remixer Tom Moulton. That's German producer Zeus B. Held on the vocoder, giving the machine top billing over regular "vocals." Zeus B. Held's Talk Box vamp on Rockets' "Future Woman" sounds like a gargling grackle.

Siemens vocoder circa 1969. Munich-based electronics giant Siemens developed a 50,000 DM vocoder for their music studio in 1959. The Siemens model would later be used for talking cars, Swiss chocolate commercials, and data-processing systems. (Courtesy Siemens Corporate Archives, Munich)

catch up. Its patient minimal pulse is at odds with Mojo's story—apparently he had a wild cab ride down I-96 to the station. "Record-breaking speed."

It's 1981. Mojo has introduced Detroit to "Cosmic Cars." The Ford Motor Company logo is on an Airborne Audio Frequency Vocoder called KY-585. Munich-based electronics giant Siemens presents an articulate Renault at an automobile expo in Frankfurt, a car that allows paraplegics to drive with their voice. That year, Kraftwerk releases *Computer World* in the United States, plays Detroit and sees its real audience for the first time. Kosmichelin Man meet Cosmic Cars. "We were in Detroit in a weird place," says Florian Schneider of Kraftwerk, on the phone from Düsseldorf. "What is this? The room was full of black people. They loved our music, which was a big thing for us because we admired all these masters of funk. In some parts we had white people, but Detroit… they were using our sounds."

KINSKI AT THE ZOO

In 1979, Klaus Kinski appeared in the French film *Zoo Zero*, smoking away his vocal cords while speaking through a vocoder. Kinski's "speech" is triggered by a computer keyboard and some no-look typing while he exhales bloodless blue ghosts. A couple of lions have to listen to whatever he says (something about a car crash and Mozart), as does a woman in an evening gown, one cage over.

Kraftwerk's new-smell ride was austere and fastidious, popularly described by Brian Eno as "nostalgic for the future." Released in 1974, their unfolding travel brochure, "Autobahn," was the first song to put the vocoder on the road. Things bob along for ten minutes until a tunnel of death gasp fogs up the rear-view and the sky disappears. It's kind of startling, articulated slowly, a puppet's chin. This was the machine's first time out with the word, though its grumpy phoneme *bah* had already made several passes through Homer Dudley's vocoder back in 1935. "'Autobahn' is a very good word in the vocoder," said one German electronics dealer. "It has beautiful vowels—*autooobaaahn*. Like, *I love you*." Nothing says *love* like a highway, when half the fun is getting there while the other half wants Waffle House.

As a friend once said, "We should be thankful that Kraftwerk did not know how to sing." Kraftwerk was the first group to use nonhuman voices for songs about roads, railways, cafés, quasars, radiation, the dance floor as virtual networking site for romance, robots who might be models, men who might be machines, machines gracefully making fun of rock stars, and pineapples. Florian admits to using the vocoder to "a certain excess." "It's just a trademark," he said. "That's what we got out of it."

THE FEDERAL SCREW WORKS, WITH A LITTLE URANIUM

Had the Electrifying Mojo's cab taken I-75, he could've ended up at the Federal Screw Works, an automotive parts company based in Troy, Michigan. In 1971, the Federal Screw Works introduced Voltrax, a Vocal Interface Division that developed a line of speaking machines controlled by fingers, eye movements and breath. Called "Handi-Voice," the Votrax text-to-speech chip originated in a declassified military algorithm, foreshadowing chips that would be implanted in arcade robot shootouts like Berserk. The Votrax market would include outgoing office phone messages, children with paralyzed vocal cords, and by accident, Kraftwerk.

"The machine sounded strange": A text-to-speech device manufactured by Votrax, the vocal interface division of Federal Screw Works in Troy, Michigan. The Votrax was a speaking aid for deaf-mute children. A rack-mount version of the Votrax was used on Kraftwerk's "Uranium."

A self-described "collector of artificial voices," Florian Schneider was introduced to the Votrax Audio Response System by an engineer at Siemens. "It was an artificial speaking device made in Detroit. You tap in the names and the output was speech. The machine sounded strange." The Votrax made its musical debut on "Uranium," a brief passage of croak and choir that appeared on Kraftwerk's 1975 album *Radio-Activity*. "Nobody liked that in America," says Schneider, recalling insinuations that the album was an endorsement of nuclear power. "They didn't want to touch it. It was a mental movie. An end-of-time scenario—the radiation of sound and radioactivity." In July 1945, radiation traveled in a whisper. Harry Truman sat at the Potsdam Conference, dissecting Germany with Stalin and Churchill, when he received news of the plutonium explosion at the Trinity proving grounds in New Mexico. It was unvoiced hiss energy encoded as the birth of a baby boy: "The light in his eyes discernible from here to Highhold." The future appeared bright enough to be blind, wiped

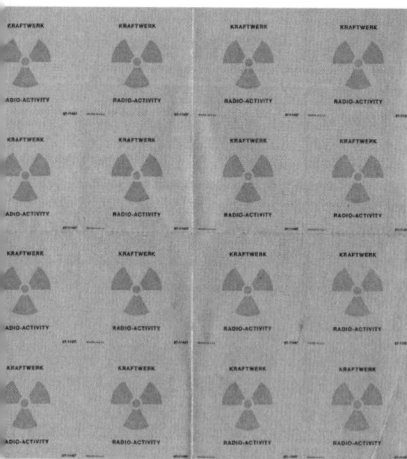

Promotional insert for Kraftwerk's 1976 LP *Radio-Activity*. Artificial voices sounded perfectly normal with Kraftwerk, who made the once sterile world of electronic music seem warm and wistful. "We were outsiders in the early days," says Florian Schneider. "People were laughing but at least they were listening to it."

from existence as the break of dawn came from the entirely wrong direction. *Die sonne scheint.*

Appropriately, the polyphony on "Uranium" is created by light—an optical celluloid disk (marked "CHOIR") inserted into the Vako Orchestron, a voice-modulating keyboard. "It was a very strange thing similar to the Mellotron," says Schneider. "They had photo cells to transform light into sound through plastic film. [It was] what you had in the early movies instead of magnetic tape. That's what we used in conjunction with the vocoder and Votrax." "Uranium" covers a lot of wasteland in ninety lizard-sizzling seconds flat. The polyphony reckons into the toxic highhold, an afterimage of burnt angels peeled from the eye. Then a gulch gasp, tapped from the Federal Screw Works, pulls us down to Ground Zero: "Through constant decay, Uranium creates the radioactive ray." It's the sorest throat on record, bonecake-dry.

"I got what I wanted," says Florian. "A nonhuman."

✦ ✦ ✦

In May 1976, the WDR (West German radio) broadcast a play about a man who was accidentally put to death by his own book club. Adapting the Gordon R. Dickson story "Computers Don't Argue," the WDR used a $10,000 vocoder to send the story's protagonist, Walt Child, straight to Amazon hell. "In a way, [the play] envisioned the Internet," says Ludwig Rehberg, a dealer for EMS-Germany who worked on the project. "You ordered everything online, and it was processed by computers. The whole play was really over the top." "You are continuing to dun me with computer punch cards," said Child, just trying to exchange Robert Louis Stevenson (*Kidnapped*) for Rudyard Kipling (*Kim*). While racking up late fees ($15.66), his account is misfiled as Criminal Code 1567, Kidnapping. Walt is then arrested for abducting a child named Robert Louis Stevenson, who according to the Bureau of Statistics is not missing but dead. Murder is tacked onto the overdue charges and terms of a simple misunderstanding are scrambled into a death sentence, with Walter Child of Paduk, Michigan, still out one copy of *Kim*—a morbid failure of quality assurance.

Siemens held a sunnier outlook on the relationship between humans and computers. A 1973 press release for the vocoder describes the computer as "a conversational companion" and follows that "communication between man and machine is a desirable goal." The German rendition of "man and machine" appears on the press releases as "Maschine-Mensch," replacing conjunction with hyphen and allowing robots to make the band, one and the same. According to Florian Schneider, the recording of *Man-Machine* (1978) and *Computer World* (1981) were covert operations themselves, no less neurotic than Dickson's story. "The mysterious thing about these machines, sometimes when you use them you feel like a secret agent of sounds. We closed our studio—nobody could go inside. We were very paranoid."

With the Kraftwerk single "Numbers," the child in the machine was Speak & Spell, an educational tool developed by Texas Instruments and used by E.T., the witch-fingered namesake of the 1982 Miami vocoder classic "E.T. Boogie." Speak & Spell was the first successful commercial application of Linear Predictive Coding, conceived at Bell Labs by George Doddington. Michael Noll, a former associate of Doddington's, remembers being "flabbergasted." "Doddington took the idea over to Texas Instruments, and up popped that toy. We couldn't believe someone had made a chip and was using it to synthesize speech…and selling the damn thing for forty bucks! We saw an ad for it in Bloomingdale's and rushed down. I said, 'Obviously it doesn't work.'" The man performing the demonstration then pushed the button and the machine said: "Spell 'house.'" Noll responded with, 'Good grief!'" Incidentally, the day we spoke, Noll had just sold his own Speak & Spell on eBay for $26.

Florian Schneider had also acquired a device that translated English into Japanese. "The Texas Instruments Language Translator—it was similar to Speak & Spell. That's what we used on all these *Computer World* things. At the time, there was no sampling, so we had to record it live off the tape. In real time. Thank you, Texas Instruments."

Carol Greene's *New True Book of Robots*. Not Kraftwerk's idea of a robot but good eyebrows nonetheless.

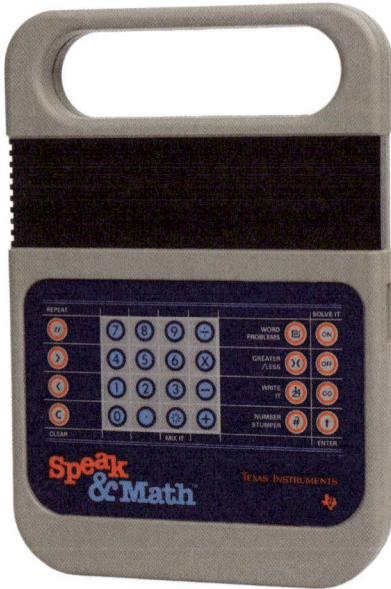

Speak & Spell was an educational toy equipped with its own "mystery word" button, also the first commercially successful use of Linear Predictive Coding (LPC), popularized by E.T. and used by Kraftwerk on "Numbers," a beat perpetuated in the tailgating scene in "The U," an ESPN documentary about the University of Miami football program in the Eighties.

The Collector of Artificial Voices moved on. Next acquisition: the DECTalk, a text-to-speech device now operated by the cheek of physicist Stephen Hawking. "These people, they were trying to play Frankenstein and have the homunculus speaking," says Florian. "It's really perverse. I got this wonderful machine from DEC [Digital Equipment Corporation]. Then the inventor, Dennis Klatt, got throat cancer and could not speak any more. The ghosts you are waking, they are going to kill you, Doctor Faust."

VERBOT SPEKTRALZERLEGER

In the early Sixties, the ghost of Dr. Faust appeared in the Siemens vocoder in Munich as engineers fed Goethe to the machine. "*Die Sonne tönt nach alter Weise.*" The sun makes music of old. This frequency specter was committed to magnetic tape along with speaking winds, pleading Volkswagens and instructions for children. It was a demo.

Florian Schneider—who used his own voice to admire the sun on "Autobahn"—first heard the Siemens tape in his early twenties, while studying music at the Akademie Remscheid, near Düsseldorf. "There were speaking chimes and bells. Childish songs about making the bed. A quiet whispering. Motors talking. 'Please don't put me in the wrong gear.' All these weird things. It really stimulated my fantasy in those days. Oh, what is this! And where can I see it? But no. No way."

Not for sale and costing 50,000 DM, the Siemens vocoder made its television debut in 1962 in a commercial for the Swiss chocolate Camille Bloch, with a steam engine chanting "Shok! Shok! Shok!" In 1966, the composer Peter Thomas used the Siemens model for a rocket-launch countdown in the German science fiction serial *Space Patrol*. "I thought about how I could make a marriage between two instruments, a voice and a cello," Thomas told *The Independent* in 1999. "The marriage was in the vocoder. I asked the cello player to play a long note. He asked, 'How long a note?' I said, 'Until Christmas.' Then I spoke the countdown."

Produced by German composer Peter Thomas in 1966, the soundtrack for the science fiction TV show *Raumpatrouille* (Space Patrol) may be the first vocoder record. Includes the track "Danger for the Crew." (Courtesy Fontana Records and Allen "Doc Strange" Goodman)

The vocoder spectrogram I received from Siemens appeared no less paranormal than any of the others (phantasm clouds, ferns, a surprised fish skeleton, etc.) and translated to English as "automatically run local networks." According to Siemens, their vocoder was involved with automated directory assistance and news satellites. According to Henrik Teller, a retired officer in the Danish Signal Battalion, a Siemens-made vocoder called Elcrovox had been deployed by the German armed forces (Bundeswehr) in 1968. Said Teller, "In those days, everything was 'need to know' and 'nice to know'—I did not need to know."

Peter-Thomas-Sound-Orchester (New Astronautic Sound)

Original-Soundtrack aus der 7-teiligen Fernseh-Serie der BAVARIA
Original-soundtrack of the television series in 7 parts of the BAVARIA
Soundtrack original de la TV-serie en 7 parties de la BAVARIA

fontana
special

RAUMPATROUILLE

Space Patrol   Commando spatial

Die phantastischen Abenteuer des Raumschiffes ORION
The phantastic adventures of the space-ship ORION
Les aventures fantastiques du vaisseau d'espace ORION

Promotional photo of the Siemens vocoder, circa 1969. Siemens helped fund the early speech ciphony work of Oskar Vierling, a pioneer of electro-acoustic instruments and director of the Laboratory Feuerstein in Upper Franconia during World War II. (Courtesy Siemens Corporate Archives, Munich)

Frank Gentges, a Cold War Secure Voice consultant who has heard just about every vocoder this side of the Berlin Wall, thinks the Elcrovox was one of the best versions on the market back then. "The Elcrovox could handle those guttural sounds in the German language that we did little to focus on—those back of the throat noises. It was better sounding because of superior fine tuning of the design that US designers did not get to do because of rigid schedules."

"I never saw the Siemens studio, actually, but I heard about strange things going on there," says Holger Czukay of the Cologne group Can. "The vocoders in the Fifties and Sixties were secret units. It was a really sophisticated thing at the time. Siemens manufactured it themselves. They were working with the vocoder and paper strips with holes."

In 1966, an article published in *The Journal of the Acoustical Society of America* revealed that Siemens had registered a patent (# 594976) under the name Schmidt, describing "ideas similar to those of [Homer] Dudley." It had been filed in 1932, a year before Hitler came to power.

LABORATORY FEUERSTEIN

According to Manfred Schroeder, the German physicist who designed the first voice-excited vocoder for Bell Labs, Siemens had been developing vocoders prior to the war. "Did the Germans use the vocoder in the Thirties? I think the answer is yes. We knew a little about German efforts by a speech engineer from Siemens named Friedrich Vilbig. They had patents. I'm sure they had several [vocoders] on an experimental basis, used in the lab, so to speak. But I don't think there was any field use of the German vocoder. We would have known."

In 1999, a vocoder prototype chucked by the Nazis was dredged from the Schliersee, a lake in upper Bavaria. According to documents declassified by the NSA in June 2009, the vocoder had been under development in Germany in the early Thirties, both at Siemens and the Heinrich Hertz Institute for Vibrational Research, the latter being run by synthetic speech pioneer Karl Willy Wagner, a German contemporary of Homer Dudley's. Wagner's employees included Harald Bode, who

GOETHE BUST

In Salomo Friedlaender's 1916 story "Goethe Speaks into the Phonograph," Professor Abner Schorr attempts to "trick" Goethe's cadaver out of its voice in order to woo a girl. After violating Goethe's crypt, the professor calibrates the poet's formant resonances and recreates his voice box inside a head bust. He then uses a phonograph (a popular instrument of woo) and a bellows to inhale and record the leftover acoustic vibrations from Goethe's study. During playback, Goethe's vibrations fall asleep in mid-thought and start snoring. The girl swoons. Jealous of his own invention, the professor chucks the fake Goethe larynx in front of an oncoming train. German media theorist Friedrich Kittler would later write, "Goethe's bass frequencies, vibrating in infinity…remained unmeasurable."

went on to design vocoders for Robert Moog in North Tonawanda, and Dr. Fritz Sennheiser, the name on your headphones and the vocoder that would drive Neil Young fans to mutiny.

In 1939, another Hertz acoustic scientist, Dr. Oskar Vierling, opened the Laboratory Feuerstein in Upper Franconia near Bavaria. Inventor of the Grosstonorgel (a vacuum tube oscillator-based organ), Vierling joined the Nazi party to expedite his speech-privacy research but did not remain in good standing. (Vierling's staff was reported to have operated "in tolerable harmony," save for one Dr. Zappe, who was arrested for "irregularities.") To avoid Allied bombings, the Feuerstein lab relocated deeper into the Alps in 1942, doubling as a hospital. On May 15, 1945, a week after V-E Day, British cryptanalyst Alan Turing made a secret trip to Feuerstein following intercepts of what was believed to be vocoded test transmissions between Vierling's lab and Hanover during the war. That summer, the Allied Target Intelligence Committee (TICOM) raided Feuerstein, but not before Vierling stashed the bulk of his equipment in a bomb-proof vault hidden behind a fake wall. "This done, he awaited developments." Among the interrogated were Vierling, Fritz Sennheiser and a man named Wolfgang Martini.

The Nazis wanted the technology destroyed, the British wanted it reassembled. TICOM would allow Vierling's lab to continue its many projects. Under TICOM supervision, the Feuerstein lab worked on "high speed transmitters for agent use," a vocoder based on "the Dudley type," a Wobbler, acoustic torpedoes, anti-radar coating for submarines, a Speech Stretcher and a pocket calculator. Oskar Vierling's productive summer would end with his arrest late that August, as he was forced to sell his crypto-patents to Switzerland. The Feuerstein Lab became property of the German Catholic Church.

After the war, Vierling's associate Fritz Sennheiser opened Laboratory W in a farmhouse previously occupied by British troops near Hanover. There he received an order from the Central Encipherment Office to design a vocoder to guard against wiretapping—billed as "diplomatic service." Sennheiser's vocoder habit would survive the postwar denazification (*Entnazifizierung*), a time when engineers and physicists found themselves either drastically switching careers or recruited by

THE ESCAPE OF DR. ZAPPE

When interrogated by TICOM's Lieutenant Tompkins (no relation) in August 1945, Dr. Zappe discussed the "melody channel in the design of the synthetic." Zappe also claimed that the Feuerstein Lab in Bavaria had built seven vocoders since 1941. (Only one unfinished model was seized.) The German army had also commissioned Feuerstein's director, Oskar Vierling, to construct an artificial speech machine named "Anna 43." Zappe believed Vierling had been dallying on the vocoder to get more money. In February 1945, Vierling had Dr. Zappe arrested by the Gestapo, though Zappe escaped by digging himself out of a jail in Ebermannstadt. Vierling then put a hit out on Zappe for 10,000 DM, accusing him of high treason. Dr. Zappe, who claimed to be the greatest physicist in the world, was never captured.

Dr. Fritz Sennheiser at age 33, photographed at the Heinrich Hertz Institute for Vibrational Research in Berlin. Dr. Sennheiser worked for Oskar Vierling before opening the Laboratory W in Hanover, focusing on voice ciphony after the war. The Sennheiser 20-channel vocoder would later be used by Herbie Hancock and Neil Young. (Courtesy Fritz Sennheiser)

American tech companies for the Cold War. According to Sennheiser's son Joerg, his father had been "interviewed" by American Signal Corps officers as early as 1944: "The people who questioned him wore uniforms of the American Army but spoke German, with no accent."

While Sennheiser remained in Germany, Friedrich Vilbig was hired by MIT and performed speech encoding at the Air Force Cambridge Research Center. "He was collared, so to speak," says Manfred Schroeder. "They may not have had any choice. I think most of them went gladly."

RATHER BELONG TO THE REALM OF THE UNREAL

For Dr. Werner Meyer-Eppler, who served as a radio engineer for the Kriegsmarine, postwar "rehabilitation" included linguistics, running barnyard recordings through an artificial larynx, and lecturing on the vocoder. Appointed as Director of Phonetics at the University of Bonn, Meyer-Eppler called the vocoder *spektralzerleger*, the spectral decomposer. An information theorist, he was interested in how the vocoder could separate speech from the intelligence it conveyed while also multiplying the "channel bed" capacity. Publishing essays with titles like "Observations During the Retarded Feedback of the Language," Meyer-Eppler was perhaps the first to realize the vocoder had a future in electronic music.

This is believed to be part of a vocoder prototype chucked in a Bavarian lake by the Nazis, circa 1945. (Courtesy Klaus Schmeh)

"In a certain sense the vocoder was the initial machine to open the path to composing an electronic studio in Cologne without being used as a musical instrument," says Elena Ungeheuer, who earned a PhD studying Meyer-Eppler's influence on electro-acoustic music. "It was the scheme of the vocoder—the functioning of the vocoder. Robert Beyer, then a sound engineer at West Germany's Radio Cologne (WDR), recognized now we can form sound without being restricted to keyboards. There's been controversy about the role of composers for the birth of the electronic studio in Cologne. But the phonetician Meyer-Eppler started the process with his report about the vocoder."

Meyer-Eppler's 1949 lecture for radio engineers in Detmold would be widely regarded as a pivotal moment in the history of electronic music.

Any speech beginning, "It sounds like a homunculus or a robot" showed much promise for the future, as if rescuing the word from the impotent robot dictator featured in Otto Rippert's 1916 film *Homunculus der Führer*. In attendance that day was Dr. Robert Beyer, a radio bigwig who would establish Cologne's fabled Electronic Music Studios in 1951, and Herbert Eimert, a composer and the host of WDR's chirpily named "Musical Night." Can's keyboard player Irmin Schmidt learned of the vocoder through Eimert. "It was one of the first electronic instruments which came from a totally different background," says Schmidt. "Not for music but military. At that time, the whole electronic studio in

Dr. Werner Meyer-Eppler in the Dead Room recording cabin, Institute for Phonetics, University of Bonn. A radio engineer and vocoder pioneer who researched infra-acoustics and noise detection for the Kreigsmarine, Meyer-Eppler literally drove colleagues mad by putting a delay on their own voices inside headphones. "First they get crazy, then they get outside themselves."

Cologne, when they started, the whole science about it came from other sources and not the music."

During the Detmold speech, Meyer-Eppler assured his audience that what they were about to hear would "rather belong to the realm of the Unreal than to Sober Science." He played records of animal sounds and "voiced" them, in German, through an Electrolarynx. It wasn't exactly "Bozo at the Zoo," but the Unreal quickly had Sober Science chugging a beer-bong tube. Meyer-Eppler then played some Bell Labs vocoder standards, provided by Homer Dudley during a visit to Bonn in 1948. There was "How Dry I Am," in triplicate. And "Suzy Seashells," "Barnacle Bill," and "Goodnight, Ladies." A singing tube of toothpaste that claimed to buff the paint right off your car. The vocoder wishing itself happy birthday in the pitch of a man pretending to be a woman pretending to be Mrs. Featherbottom. There were "grotesque scenes with a single speaker" and "Voice of Energy," a song that Kraftwerk admitted to borrowing in German.

"We pretty much copied the demonstration of the Bell Vocoder and did the whole thing in the German version," says Florian. "We borrowed this from Siemens and used it as interlude between other pieces."

"With a means of research like the vocoder, it becomes possible to test out all its possibilities," said Meyer-Eppler. "Even without a determined purpose."

ITEM 300001522431

The best way to call upon the ghost of Werner Meyer-Eppler, it turned out, would be through a network of computer spies called "eBay." In 2006, the year a man auctioned his soul online for $500, "Prototype VOCODER of German 70s Electronic Pioneers" appeared in the virtual marketplace. To the automated sniper, it was Item 300001522431. Bidding commenced at $3,800, a reasonable figure for a machine that once uttered the word "Autobahn" a few times and coughed.

This large green box was the Barth Musicoder, developed at the Physikalisch-Technische Bundesanstalt and then compressed into an unfinished customized unit for Schneider. (Renamed after World War II,

PTB was originally PTR—Physikalisch-Technische Reichsanstalt—where Karl Willy Wagner had designed a vowel synthesizer in 1936.) The Musicoder first saw action on "Ananas Symphonie," a song featured on the 1973 Kraftwerk album *Ralf und Florian*. The machine was photographed on the back cover, somewhere behind names spelled out in blue cursive lights, Florian in fluorescent.

"We still had this vocoder sleeping under our studio in a storage place," says Schneider, who was selling it through a dealer. "So I put it on eBay.

Florian Schneider (far right) picks up Werner Meyer-Eppler's unfinished 30-band vocoder filter bank in the basement of the Bonn's Institute for Phonetics in 2002. With the help of Kraftwerk engineer Sebastian Niessen, Meyer-Eppler's "wish list" of frequencies was transferred to a computer to create what Florian calls "the Mother of All Vocoders," fifty years in the making. (Courtesy Florian Schneider and Sebastian Niessen)

The EMS Vocoder 2000. Recorded in the mid-Seventies, the EMS vocoder demo included stock market reports, a track called "Two teenage girls' grisly news," and a woman describing her dreams of little talking animals. (Courtesy EMS)

Then this fantastic reaction happened." Ten days later, after an outpouring of holy shits and grails, skeptical bahs and doomed irrational budgeting plans, the Musicoder finally sold for $12,500 to Daniel Miller, CEO of Mute Records and discoverer of Depeche Mode.

At the time, Schneider had been wandering eBay buying old cinema loudspeakers from the Thirties. "Then I had this wonderful money… hmm…what can we do with that?" After the Musicoder sold, a friend alerted Schneider to the existence of an old filter bank stashed beneath a nineteenth-century observatory at the University of Bonn. "He told me where it was located—in Bonn. Down in the catacombs, in this cellar, was this institute. The Institute for Phonetics and Information Theory. Then my alarm bell was ringing very loudly. You understand?"

The filter bank belonged to Werner Meyer-Eppler, who had died in 1960 from kidney failure. "In all of the literature you never heard that he actually was trying to build a vocoder," says Schneider. "This was an unfinished project because this man died pretty early. He put all this work into it and died over that project. Must've cost a lot of money to construct that system. It was sleeping there for fifty years or so."

Florian then drove to Bonn and put his eBay money down for Meyer-Eppler's unfinished vocoder. His account:

This old engineer was there, looking a bit sad because these things were going. I told him they would be in good hands and that I am an admirer of Meyer-Eppler. This vocoder has a tremendous clear wonderful sound. The ghost of Meyer-Eppler, the co-founder of the electronic music studios in Cologne, is in there. Pretty amazing. I know what I have. The mother of all vocoders. These people who invent all this stuff—they must be crazy. Not many of them die in a natural way. They end up in a mental hospital.

In the late Seventies, a Bavarian hospital commissioned EMS-Germany to provide vocoder recordings for sleeping patients, in particular "heavy cases of mental illness." These talking water drops, whispers and wind sounds were used for subconscious autosuggestion, generic back-rubs like "Relax and sleep," and "It'll be okay." Perhaps this is what Dr. Meyer-Eppler meant by "simulation of pathological features through channel transposition." Either way, the vocoder had entered the dreams of the insane through a leaky faucet.

I mentioned this to Laurie Anderson during an interview, asking if she ever dreamed in vocoder. "No," she said. "But that would be fun." She did admit to being serenaded by a quartet of headless squirrels. "Actually," she said, "it was music disguised as screaming."

MOON, HI

The ghosts you are waking, they are in a coffin shop in Cologne called Schmitronic, among the vintage microphones, mixing consoles, obsolete turntables and the occasional lost vocoder. "They called him 'Dead Body Schmit' or 'Cadaver Smith,'" says Schneider, a customer in the early Eighties. "You had to go past the coffins down into the cellar where he has all this used radio and studio equipment. Always complaining and moaning around. I bought many good things."

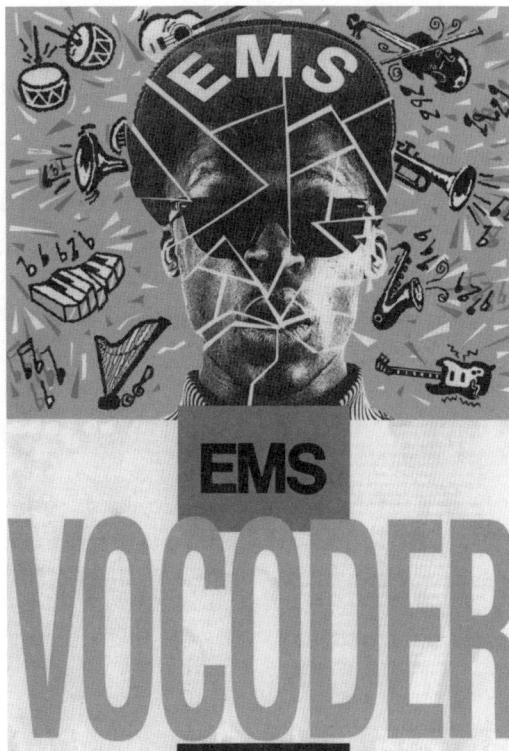

Cyclist has mind completely blown by the vocoder. Ad for EMS-Germany, the company which also recorded a talking water drop demo for a Bavarian mental institution to be played while patients slept. (Courtesy EMS)

I'd first heard of Schmitronic through Holger Czukay, the German tape splicer and bassist from Can. "He was an undertaker," he whispers in a scuttle, a lantern held to a grin. "Mr. Schmit had lots of studio equipment that the WDR radio station threw out. The quality of them was Rolls-Royce. You could use it for the next hundred years without sounding old-fashioned—especially if everything comes to tape machines. I bought a Fifties IBM Dictaphone from the undertaker. It was meant for the secretary, but I was able to make tape loops."

Inner Space Studios in Cologne drooled tape loops from the rafters as Holger tried to edit some sense into Can's epic recording sessions. Czukay once said sampling was invented when Spike Jones recorded a dog barking "Jingle Bells." "Voices became interesting to me by the living atmosphere that they had," he says. "Everything was fascinating beyond natural. When something was going to become artificial, I wanted to know what it was. [With Can] we always were trying to get away from the natural voice."

Can couldn't seem to get far enough away, as if it were a race between losing their voices and their minds. Malcolm Mooney heard a train whistling outside his door and treated his larynx like the Wolfman's welcome mat. Damo Suzuki was famously hired after being spotted head-butting the sun in the middle of a street in Munich. Then there was Irmin Schmidt, the keyboard player who flat couldn't sing. "The only way Irmin could survive was to make something as artificial as possible," says Holger. So Irmin turned to the ring modulator, popular among the Daleks of *Dr. Who*. On Can's "Come Sta, La Luna"—named after da Vinci's moon greeting—Schmidt is an amiable old fishwoman. He calls it a sorcery thing. A friend from Munich heard the song and said he went to Mars and came back on a stretcher.

"If I could only remember what I did with my voice!" Schmidt says, on the phone from Germany with a sore throat. "The song was about a tightrope dancer in outer space who falls for a magic woman who walks through walls, and all kinds of strange things. Unfortunately, the relationship does not work out. It was not meant to be totally understood anyway. It's altered so much with effects. I don't understand it any more."

REACTING EXTREMELY ON SOFT NOISY THINGS

In 1981, Holger Czukay recorded a twenty-minute vocoder song about perfume, based on the space station of his childhood and inspired by his wife U-She's kitchen perfume laboratory. "I'm just listening now to the vocoder in my imagination," she says. "Lots of differentiated transparent things. This fragility makes it the likeness of perfume. [The vocoder] has a lot of floating things in it. It's very unreal. After the rain, the air gets misty. That goes along very good with the ghosts."

"Ode to Perfume" seems to be in pain, like a cat scraped off someone's white walls, on a stretcher and mewling for painkillers. "Actually [Ode] doesn't sound at all like a vocoder," says Holger. "You wouldn't recognize it as robot. Deceptive. I know that robot voice—it was very elementary. 'Ode to Perfume' was a far more musical-dominated thing."

Holger Czukay, *On the Way To the Peak of Normal* (1981, Phillips). Holger Czukay's "Ode to Perfume" was inspired by the perfume experiments of his wife U-She and those of Brian Eno. In an interview with Lester Bangs in 1979, Eno said, "The Voice of Reason is another voice of indeterminate quality, indeterminate humanity, ready, into confusion, after which the men's syllables start becoming scrambled. I've discovered this new electronic technique that creates new speech out of stuff that's already there."

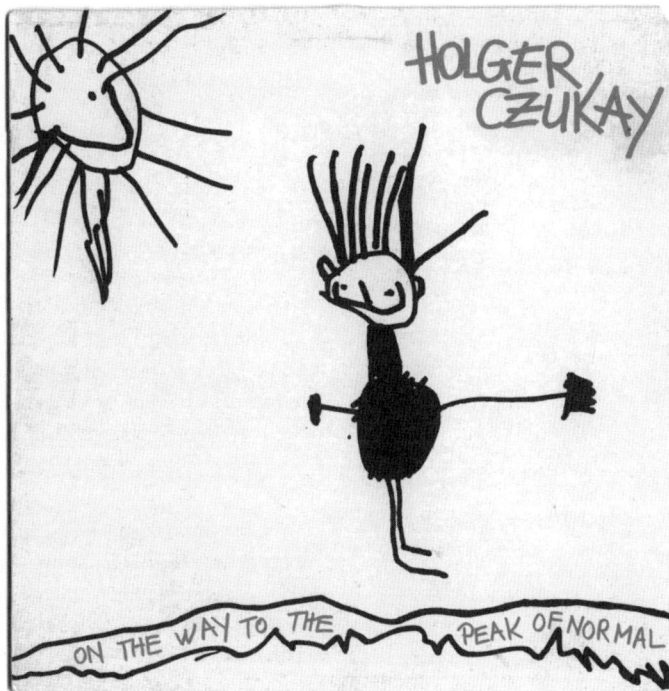

On side one of Holger's album *On the Way to the Peak of Normal*, "Ode to Perfume" yaws past steer skulls, those grinning eggshells, waving at dead motels and filling stations, by and by, at a rocking-chair clip. Heard in Lynne Ramsay's 2002 film *Morvern Callar*, "Ode" is Samantha Morton drifting through the couch-melt ends of a party, all filtered through the memory of a dead boyfriend's mix tape. "The whole [song] was pretty sophisticated," says Holger. "But it shouldn't become pretentious-sophisticated." There's a fine line between sophisticated and smelling funny. When Holger was finishing "Ode to Perfume," the vocoder was the final element, modulating his voice with the synth, as if it were Poncelet's aromatic pipe organ, from Appalachian sassafras (which smells like Froot Loops) to Catholic Church warmed over:

> I was still missing something [in the song] and it was in fact the perfume. The vocoder was the perfume. It was reacting extremely on soft noisy things, like breathing. The flow of air becomes as important as the creation of the tone. To use the vocoder is complicated. You have to dedicate yourself one hundred percent. I had to be extremely reduced in the emotions because if you get a bit too far, the vocoder is punishing you by bad results. Or just ordinary. There is a disturbing factor nonetheless. Suddenly you become something that wasn't any more perfume. Something that smelled bad. Something that was destroying the atmosphere.

Effluvia, such a pretty word for drop-dead noxious. Vocoders and noses go together like code and cold. When a human impersonates a vocoder, the nose shrugs and we become hypochondriacs. The ears tell the brain that the voice has caught a cold and the brain goes along with it, the gullible kid brother.

+ + +

"Ode to Perfume" was recorded in Cologne, in the castle studio of Conny Plank, engineer to Krautrock icons like Kraftwerk, Neu! and Cluster. Plank was known to turn a knob into a road trip, rolling the odometer's eyes right up into its brain, what writer Julian Cope called, "the Moving Fucking Zone Out." This met the specifications outlined by Czukay in his liner notes for "Ode to Perfume": "As a boy I dreamt of leading a normal life on a space station…this music was recorded in such a visionary place but without the family of my fantasy."

Czukay also suggests rollerskating to "Ode to Perfume." If skates are not available, he recommends driving, flying or just taking a "a trick-film journey into the elaborate weavings of a Persian carpet." "Yes! Roller skating! This was the testing of the perfume. How does this music work when you are somewhere, having a journey? On roller skates!"

SO THEY TOOK ME AWAY

With respect to John Cage, the Mellotron and Marley Marl, the invention of sampling can be a personal choice. It could've been Sister Sledge doing RUN-DMC in *The Jefferson*'s living room. Or it could've been Supertramp, when they used the double-chirp turnover signal from Mattel's electronic Pro Football II on "The Logical Song."

One night, Czukay was followed by police while skating through Cologne, listening to his perfume song on a homemade Walkman—a Ziploc bag full of electronics on his hip, wired to explode. "They saw how unsafe I was on these skates and thought, 'This poor man, we have to protect him.' I'd go through the city, testing 'Ode to Perfume.' The whole life around me—the reality became virtual at that moment. The testing of it was good."

CHAPTER NINE

THINK HE SAID HER NAME WAS VOODOO-ON-A-STICK

MCs for tactical ciphony have existed since before this agency was created.
— David G. Boak, NSA lecture on Secure Voice, 1971

Funky, funky, funky contains one word type: 'Funky.'
— Manfred Schroeder, Bell Labs

INVISIBLE MAN GETS IN FOR FREE

Holger Czukay may be the only man to put on roller skates for a vocoder song about perfume. Most skated to songs about freaks. In 1982, Jive Records sent the rap group Whodini to Conny Plank's castle to work on their debut album. Two kids from Brooklyn named Jalil and Ecstasy found themselves in Cologne, listening to Can and Ultravox, and hanging with Holger Czukay. "Whodini didn't have enough magic for me," Holger sighs. "Somehow I didn't like them. There were so many people who were going for effect but somehow they lost their souls in the vocoder."

In 1984, we were less concerned with the fight for Whodini's soul than seeing them at the Swatch Watch New York City Fresh Festival, where kids lost their pants to the curfew-breakers "Freaks Come Out at Night" and "Five Minutes of Funk." I'd stay up all night watching Video Vibrations on BET for a glimpse of "Freaks Come Out at Night," filmed at the Fresh Fest, just to see Whodini do that special clapapella version of "Friends" in a parking garage. I once saw them hold their green-eyed DJ upside down by the ankles over the turntables, a loan-shark balcony grip, so he could put his mouth on the fader and go bonkers on the first vocoder song to speak Arabic, "Al-Naafiysh," all of which amounted to getting barraged by the word "time" for thirty seconds.

In 2002, I caught up with Whodini in a double-wide in Central Park, part of the backstage area for a Summer Old School Reunion that included Biz Markie, Full Force (then songwriters for *NSync) and Kurtis Blow (now a preacher). Whodini had just performed "Funky Beat," the only video to feature Malcolm-Jamal Warner and Lon Chaney. Jalil and Ecstasy were both winded from all that running around and remembering. Neither had much to say about Cologne other than "It was a cool idea" and "You're talking twenty years ago," back when Whodini wore white suits and white leather shorts.

The first Conny Plank/Whodini collaboration was "Rap Machine," too dinky for either party to really acknowledge. "Nasty Lady," however, was a stone boot crunch, its drum machine suggesting Lurch repeatedly head-butting a door frame, his brain apparently in no hurry to push the duck button. When Whodini asks, "How many of y'all know nasty

MR. MAGIC SWAN

In 1983, a kid from Nottingham named Ivory X would dress like an "international downhill ski master" and spin on his wallet to "Magic's Wand" by Whodini, thinking the song was "Mr. Magic Swan," with no help from the vocoder. Dedicated to the recently deceased hip-hop radio pioneer Mr. Magic, the instrumental of "Magic's Wand" holds a shimmering instant of vocoder reflux—not a word, but a burp of twilight.

ladies?" it's the nasty ladies who answer, screeching on behalf of their men, assuring they'd known no better. Impressive, startling even, is how this screech carries itself across the room with all that back-raking decay. But as Samuel R. Delany once said, "There are times when all the helling and yelling won't fill the lack." So Conny Plank treats us/it to a nine-minute dub version.

Whodini's "Haunted House of Rock" should have been recorded in a castle. (On "Haunted House of Rock," you learn about a woman named Voodoo-on-a-Stick; she shows up at the party hanging on a dead man's stolen arm, her hair teased out by some hellion of voltage that cussed darkness.) This is the first song equipped with its own "Vocoder Version," and the first time I put eyeballs on the word. I bring this up to Whodini, back inside the trailer at Central Park, which prompts Jalil and Ecstasy to scrunch up their nostrils and do the "Vocoder Version" hook: "It's just what you wanted/ Something funky and haunted." I join in because there's no sense being half-assed about things. Ecstasy's twin brother Dynasty walks by, pretending not to hear.

Hashim's "Al-Naafiysh (The Soul)" (1984, Cutting Records) was the first B-boy vocoder jam to use camera shutters to emulate scratching and say, "It's time." Not to be confused with "Time is," as uttered by Good Man Brazen Face, the artificial talking head built by Friar Francis Bacon in the sixteenth century.

Back out on stage, Biz Markie needs help. He has lost his shirt and the second verse of "Just a Friend."

Ecstasy then looks at me with a trace of pity. "Man! You really like that vocoder, don't you?" I'm pretty sure that's what he said—Biz's voice box was now being piped in by the crowd, all ages. "Oh baby, youuuuuuuuuuuu-uuuuuu!!!"

"The vocoder was just something they had in the studio," shrugs Ecstasy. "Probably the engineer's idea. We didn't know what it was, really."

On stage, Biz itches the back of his head with a microphone, pretty satisfied with how it all went down.

TAKE THAT AND PARTY MACHINE

In 1981, the first rapping vocoder may have come from a "Christmas fanatic" from Nordegg, Canada, who said his only friends were farm animals. One wouldn't think twice about an electro-funk novelty like "Party Machine" had it not been recorded by Bruce Haack, the homemade synth inventor who released an album called *The Electric Lucifer*, wrote futuristic square dances for children and appeared on *Mister Rogers' Neighborhood*. That it appeared on an unreleased album called *Haackula* isn't as strange as the song being a collaboration with Russell Simmons, the party machine himself, then managing Kurtis Blow. Simmons went on to produce "The Def Jam," a vocoder 12-inch recorded by Jazzy Jay, an eponymous move to promote their label before LL Cool J did it for them. Yet the B-side, "Cold Chillin' in the Spot," received more airplay because it featured Russell Rush, burzooted out of his mind after a night of running his mouth all over town. Meanwhile, Bruce Haack returned to Christmas with the vocoder children's album *Zoot Zoot Zoot, Here Comes Santa in His New Space Suit*.

Any kid worth the pile of broken robots under his bed knew that voice. Maybe from a *Transformers* cartoon. Or Berzerk, a video game that caused two fatal heart attacks and taunted your Now-and-Later finances with a vocoder ("I hear quarters in those pockets!") just so you could catch your death from a bouncing smile named Evil Otto. Most likely it was the Cylons of *Battlestar Galactica*, happily embraced by those unimpressed with C3PO's fussy accent, too scolding, too parental—*too human*. The Cylons, with their glowing red wall-eye and silver armor, shining like a lasagna pan licked clean. We wanted the Cylons to laser their names into Lorne Green's eyebrows, even if they had to use subtitles while doing it. (The vocoder's lack of intelligibility did not suit *Battlestar*

Jackpine Savage, *Together (a participation musical concept album for all children)* (1971, Dimension 5 Records). Jackpine Savage was the alter-ego of Bruce Haack, creator of the Dermatron (a skin-sensitive oscillator) and children's synth tracks such as "The Witches' Vacation." Haack's "Mean Old Devil" is the best song about Satan to use a homemade vocoderish device named "Farad." Farad debuted on *The Electric Lucifer* (1971) and was used for the choruses on the Jackpine Savage album *Together*, released the same year. (Courtesy Edan)

Dimension 5 presents

TOGETHER
(a participation musical-concept album for all children)

created and performed
by JACKPINE SAVAGE

narration: Esther Nelson
Jackpine Savage

STEREO D151
Sonic motion is important
play on stereo equipment

Including:
MAYBE THIS SONG
TOUGH
RAIN OF EARTH
O.K. ROBOT
COLORS
FUNKY LITTLE SONG
ABRACADABRA
PUNCHING BAG
RIGHT ON
OUTERMISSION

©1971 – Dimension 5

A Cylon strolls through Forrest J. Ackerman's foyer in Los Angeles, California. The Cylons of *Battlestar Galactica* spoke through an EMS 2000 vocoder. (Photograph by author, 1998)

Galactica's prime-time slot.) When the Cylons spoke, they threatened to squeak-wipe humanity off the face of TV, in an EMS voice that said "By your command" for 2,500 pounds per unit.

+ + +

Afrika Bambaataa, who gave humanity a shot, does not recall how much his vocoder cost. He lost one to a fire and another to Germany, which was different than the one that accompanied him to DC, when Soulsonic Force opened up for Trouble Funk and got blasted off the stage by "Trouble Funk Express." The idea of losing track of one's robot brought our conversation, somehow, to the TV show *Bewitched*. "*Bewitched* had a vibe on me," Bam says. "Seeing the magic and all that

jumping in. I was always into all that, powers of wizards and teleportation. Things have definitely been flipping since 1947. The World's Fair saw the future. I'm just surprised they haven't caught up with *The Jetsons* yet."

Bam is a fan of homeland teleportation, it turns out. The ability to vanish by shrugging one's nostrils is useful to someone like Bam, who is hard to track down. Though it takes more than a wrinkle in nose for someone to get around the Bronx, it does allow him to emulate a Cylon's monotone, if not smell the neglect and poverty. Though the olfactory receptors may be our strongest mnemonic cue to the past, the future is in the sinuses, or as Bam calls it: "The Funk." We shrug our nose (and occasionally go pig-squint blind) when we *hear* something nasty, something never heard before.

Humans always scrunch their glabella when saying, "Rock, rock, Planet Rock," as if trying to birdcall the chorus, mating a loon with the Penguin. Arthur Baker, co-producer of "Planet Rock," says there is no vocoder in the song. "It's been mythicized. It's a PCM 41 with just a really slight delay. So it's basically a flange."

Though the collective hip-hop memory often begins with "Planet Rock," the song itself is grateful to a moment in 1981, when Afrika Bambaataa, Collector of Records with Artificial Voices, saw Kraftwerk play New York in support of *Computer World*. During "Numbers," which would become the 127-bpm pulse of "Planet Rock," Ralf Hutter allowed the front row to play their wonky calculator. "You know I was right up there on it!" says Bam. "Waiting to play that joker! They put it down and people come up and start hitting the stuff. It was all that veep-voodoo-doodoo—the way the record goes. You're hitting it and it's vibing with the music. It was no joke."

Afrika Bambaataa & the Cosmic Force's unreleased vocoder 12 inch "Cosmic Punk Jam," allegedly recorded in 1982. "Cosmic Punk Jam" was cosmic because it was of the unknown and unheard. It was punk because it sounded broke as lint and got bootlegged. (Courtesy Freddy Fresh)

"Planet Rock" essentially gave us Miami Bass, due to its speed, sub-frequency (a sine wave generated by the Japanese-made Roland-808 Drum Composer) and an orchestral stab. This symphonic pounce, played by co-producer John Robie, was a preset function of the Fairlight synthesizer, the prototype of which now sits in Vivian Kubrick's basement. Called ORCH-5, the sound was recorded in 1979 by computer programmer David Vorhaus, who'd sampled it from a piece composed by Stalin pawn Dmitri Shostakovich, or maybe it was Stravinsky. ("One of those 'S' composers," Vorhaus thinks.) Orchestral pit becomes crater, making deep space for a gloomy synth figure, played on the Fairlight but abducted from Kraftwerk's "Trans-Europe Express." "Planet Rock" is truly the sum of its machines: Russian stab, artificial German strings, Japanese bass—all for an (African) American song about a global utopia. *Live it up, shucks.*

I once heard a father chanting the chorus to his newborn in a stroller. "Planet Rock" can still hold the floor when backwards masked in its entirety, powered by its own myth-machine, as if retracing its steps. The forgotten ad-lib *zuh-zuh* from Pow-Wow—who once claimed the bassline had been inspired by a Danny Kaye dance routine—make sense.

"Cosmic Punk Jam," a song Bambaataa did with the Cosmic Force, had "Planet Rock" ambitions but never smelled retail. I first heard this unreleased vocoder track while immobilized by a stomach virus—on an unlabeled cassette, a dub of a dub's second generation lo-bias bag of Cheetos half-cousin, once removed from the back of a furniture store somewhere north of Boston. "Cosmic Punk Jam" was cosmic because of the unknown and unheard—an infinite eight minutes that was never allowed to be a record. It was punk because it sounded broke as lint, as if recorded in Jazzy Jay's sock drawer. Bam's sustained vocoder drone was soothing, an electric toothbrush on low batteries. "I was trying to make it sound like a bunch of voices harmonizing like the churches," Bambaataa says. "Funky and spooky. I didn't know that tape still existed. It was great for the clubs."

Cosmic Force were teenagers chanting their name into our memory over the melody of Michael McDonald's "I Keep Forgetting," ten years before Warren G hit the same doobie for "Regulate."

DOES YOUR DOG BITE?

Battlestar Galactica nerds have started Internet wars over whether the vocoder barks of Muffit—a duct-taped dog/bear—were done by a Sennheiser or an EMS.

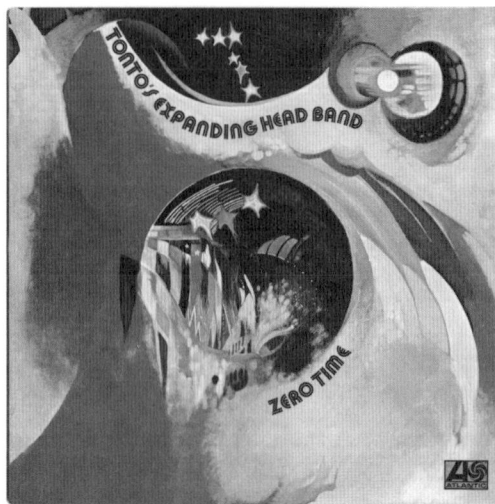

Man Parrish's self-titled debut album (1982, Importe): "Be naked and talk with a vocoder —that's my philosophy." Man Parrish listened to a lot of TONTO's Expanding Head Band. The Original New Timbral Orchestra synthesizer was built by Malcolm Cecil and Robert Margouleff and used by talk box maestro Stevie Wonder. When Cecil told me "we live in a nine dimensional universe, for sure, minimum," he could've been referring to TONTO's room-swallowing need for space. (TONTO courtesy of Jeremy Campbell)

"That song doesn't exist," Jazzy Jay says, sitting in his Brooklyn basement, his record shelf about to topple. "If you got the 'Cosmic Punk Jam' on tape, I guess it does. But don't ask me what happened to it."

TONTO JUMP ON IT

In 1976, executives at CBS Records weren't getting their promos because some kid in the mailroom was sticking them in his pants and taking them home. Back then it was good being Manny Parrish. It was good being sixteen and David Bowie's biggest fan, hanging out with Bowie's publicist, Cherry Vanilla. It was good to have purple hair and know something about computers.

Manny Parrish liked to do things big. At fourteen, he was out of the closet after seeing Bette Midler and Barry Manilow duet at Manhattan's Continental Bath House. At sixteen, he was ejected from the School for the Performing Arts for "being a hyperactive asshole." By twenty-five, he was the gayest vocoder expert to make a hip-hop ode to the Bronx, sell over a million records, make a "waist-down" cameo with indefatigable porn star Vanessa Del Rio (*Girls USA!*), road manage the Village People, and headline over Madonna at Studio 54. "A very resourceful young man," says Cherry, a proud grandmother, now working with the synth composer Vangelis Papathanassiou. Adds Parrish, "Be naked and speak through a vocoder. That's my philosophy."

Parrish felt pretty lucky to have the groomer of Ziggy Stardust as a chaperone. With hair of Muppet drummer red, Cherry Vanilla ran Tim's Fantasy Phone Service, one of the first phone sex services in Manhattan. Feats like this impressed Parrish, who was more than happy to tag along one night when Cherry went down to Electric Ladyland Studios to hear a new Bowie track. "Give me glitter," he sighs before finally meeting his glam idol. Yet while Bowie auditioned "Young Americans," Parrish went for the blinking wall of Moog across the studio, a massive synth with a co-dependent relationship with space, inner and outer. "There's Bowie, my hero, but I'm such a gear whore I want to touch the synthesizers. I'm standing in front of this monolith, completely starstruck. Like, 'Duuude, that's what Keith Emerson used.' The studio engineer says it was named 'TONTO.' I was like, 'TONTO?' Oh yeah. I smoked pot to this.'"

"We live in a nine-dimensional universe for sure, minimum," says Malcolm Cecil, TONTO's creator, on the phone from his home in England. "It was easier to take acid than pot back then."

Parrish spent afternoons popping brain cells in his midtown stoner's paradise, listening to TONTO's Expanding Head Band and Emerson, Lake & Palmer's *Brain Salad Surgery* amid the violet incense, an armadillo tank named Tarkus, "state-of-the-art speakers the size of dishwashers," and Christmas lights blinking behind frosted Plexiglass. "Space between world and beyond is like space between soul and another. Nothing and everything," said the drowning ghost in TONTO's "Riversong." "The robot said something," thinks Cecil. "Nobody's really sure. 'Current' sounded like '*urrrrrr*.' There's so much folklore from TONTO—the one about ingesting psychedelics through a headband. I usually leave it to people's imaginations and let them come up with whatever."

Since Manny Parrish couldn't afford a TONTO, he bought a dinky Radio Shack keyboard with see-through circuitry. He set up a bedroom studio and made ambient "cocktail polka porn" soundtracks, one of which was used for Joe Gage's *Heatstroke*. One night at the Anvil, a club at 14th

Street near the West Side Highway, Manny saw a guy onstage launching dildos from his rear over heads and across the room, nearly taking out Phillipe of the Village People (in Tontastic headdress), who happened to be dancing on the bar to something familiar, fuckingly familiar if you'd seen *Heatstroke*.

"The DJ was playing one of my soundtracks," Manny says. "I didn't even know they pressed it up. He said these guys from Importe Records were looking to sign me and I immediately did." The contract was a paragraph (maybe a page), and Parrish didn't see a dime but didn't care because he was having too much fun freaking out the neighbors, building synthesizers and living life with his pants around his ankles. Released under the name Man Parrish, the follow-up to "Heatstroke" was "Hip Hop, Be Bop," which became an instant electro classic at clubs like Danceteria and the Roxy, selling 2.5 million copies. The eponymous *Man Parrish* LP included "Planet Rock" co-producer John Robie on keyboards, the stratospheric Klaus Nomi ("operatic angel robot") and Parrish himself on vocoder.

FREEWAY HICKIE

"Hip Hop Be Bop" appears on the soundtrack for the videogame *Grand Theft Auto: Vice City*, introducing Man Parrish to a new generation of kids eager to shoot up Miami in a pink-finned Cadillac.

Parrish first heard the vocoder while passed out in a cab in front of his apartment, listening to Alison Steele, "The Nightbird" of WNEW. (Driver: "Hey, weren't you in *Bad Girls Dormitory*?") "She sounded so sexy. You were thinking voluptuous Vampirella, but what you got was an old mountain woman with long gray hair." Somewhere between Iron Butterfly and the Doors, the Nightbird played Kraftwerk. The driver killed the meter. Six minutes and one "Trans-Europe Express" later, Parrish remembered he actually was in *Bad Girls Dormitory* and decided he needed a vocoder. "But back then you didn't just go out and 'buy a vocoder.' Nobody knew what it was. I went to Sam Ash and they had this thing the size of a VCR under the counter. They were like, 'Take it! We can't get rid of it. Some guy from ELO dumped it on us. We don't know what the hell it is.'"

THE FLOOR BELOW

In fall 1983, Parrish reported to Studio 54 to perform at an anniversary party for Fiorucci Jeans, a Fifth Avenue store where live mannequins did the robot in the window. The line outside is a reach-around guest list, someone who knew someone who mistook themselves for somebody.

Madonna is set to go on at, say, four in the morning, and Parrish's ex-boyfriend is already drunk at the fog machine. Parrish himself is unglued. He'd spent the afternoon graveside at his mother's funeral and is now suspended twelve feet above the stage, waiting to Geronimo into a dry-ice cloud that's supposed to be Yoda pond high but now calls for a foghorn.

Parrish wears a black hooded cape by Kansai Yamamoto, a Stardust perk. Two plastic beer-helmet tubes snake up to his head. One tube pumps frozen carbon dioxide into his face, which is painted gold. The other keeps Parrish from suffocating. Down below, a troupe of *Dark Crystal* "midgets" marches across the stage in purple robes carrying lanterns—the borrowed kids of a friend. Parrish can't see a thing. "I kept thinking, 'Where's the floor? Don't land on the vocoder. Just *near* the vocoder!'"

Parrish lands on his ankle instead. The kids with lanterns don't notice. They're just happy to be up past bedtime at Studio 54 bobbing around in fake smoke. A "freaky leather two-headed lizard bird puppet" pops out of the smoke—a Skeksis—and rips off Manny's hood. The lizard bird has glass eyeballs which, according to the prop stylist, did not come cheap. Madonna's pretty into it. Purple robes are bumping into each other. Parrish hobbles over to the vocoder, an EMS-2000, his ankle throbbing to the same ambient Radio Shack pulse that inspired Del Rio to blow the cast of *Girls USA*.

Next week: Return of the Jedi party.

Print ad for Korg's VC-10 Vocoder: "Vocoded effects can be spacey. So can their prices." One of the first affordable vocoders ($1,299), the VC-10 should've been hired for the *Dark Crystal* bog burp. Allegedly used by Aerosmith on "Prelude to Joanie" and Jonzun Crew for synthetic substitution. (Courtesy Korg)

THE NIGHT-TIME MASTER BLASTER

I hear you in the shadows. I don't care about your DNA. I just want to see your fucking heart.
— Tattered man speaking to air conditioner window unit, Manhattan

Germany still calls me asking for "Freakenstein."
— James Garrett

In 1983, I heard the vocoder demolished by Run-DMC, with Michael Jordan as my witness. I was at UNC's youth basketball camp in Chapel Hill. Jordan and future NASCAR analyst Brad Daugherty were lounging poolside by the dorm, listening to Tyrone Brunson's "Sticky Situation," an a capella vocoder born from a chlorine sinus tickle. I walked by thinking, "Seventeeen seconds left against Georgetown, huh? *And* Jordan likes Tyrone Brunson." A visiting coach from New York then entered the pool area and Radio Raheem'd them with "It's Like That." My priorities shifted from getting Jordan's autograph to befriending a stranger from the Bronx who had the good sense to push the RECORD button while listening to Mister Magic's Rap Attack.

Chapel Hill was home to "Nasty Rock," a vocoder track recorded by the Garrett's Crew. "Nasty Rock" has what my knee surgeon would call "intra-articular space." It took "Word Up" out in the woods by its underwear, tore out the elastic and whipped it silly. "Nasty Rock" calls for hyperbole because it was a stretch—driven and pitched all across North Carolina's back routes, released on three different labels (Hol-Gar, Clockwork and Prelude), and "acquisitioned" by Patrick Adams, a prolific disco producer from New York. "Nasty Rock" was limber yet Ohio-tight and, unlike its electro peers, minimal to the point of almost being quiet, but still letting you in on it with ample room to glide. Hi-hats were lisping rattlesnakes, keyboards were amulets, and hand-claps boxed your ears. The vocoder went: *Do it, do it, so nasty, do it.*

"Dude, that's retarded!" said *New York Times* critic Jon Caramanica, impressed by how that gravelly larynx popped monster tires. The song was originally called "Master Rock" until James Garrett's five-year-old daughter Latisha started dancing around the studio squealing "Nasty

THINK HE SAID HER NAME WAS VOODOO-ON-A-STICK

rock! Nasty rock!" What the kid said, went. The only catch was that the songwriter John Mitchell was on the run and in arrears down in Fayetteville. To protect Mitchell's identity, the publishing was credited to Latisha's eleven-year-old brother, James L. Jr. Not too many kids at Fuquay-Varina Junior High had a vocoder radio hit in their name back in 1983, a novelty fully grasped by James L. Jr., beaming his way through the lunch line. Corndogs and Nutty Buddies on the house.

James Garrett, Sr., now runs Garrett's Amusements from an indoor flea market in Fuquay-Varina, selling Apple Jacks out of a gumball dispenser. For ten dollars you can get your picture taken and framed inside a license plate or customized clock. The walls at Garrett's Amusements are covered with these picture clocks, friends and lovers who passed through, copped some Apple Jacks, and smiled while kids ran around licking magic sugar dust off their hands. When I visited James Garrett in May of 2004, we laughed about the difficulties of clapping inside a Red #40 space vacuum. I asked if I could get a clockface photo of him and he said, "There's already a clock on the wall over there—with six James Garretts on it." When I thanked him, he said, "No problem, Dave. I like making people happy." He put his hands behind his head and smiled. "That's what time it is."

When James Garrett finally drove "Nasty Rock" to WPEG in Concord, DJ Les Norman, the Night-Time Master Blaster, had it on the air before Garrett was back on the interstate. "Les had a good heart," says Garrett. "He reached out when he didn't even know us. That's how we got to New York. That's how we opened for the Isley Brothers and the Manhattans."

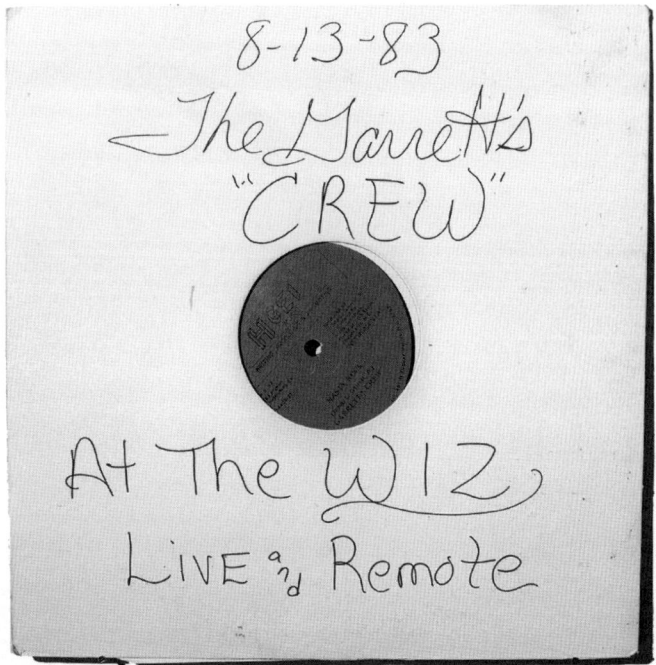

Garrett's Crew, "Nasty Rock" (1983, HGEI Music). North Carolina vocoder classic named by a five-year-old. Future synth boogie optimist Dam Funk wants to know what machine made those handclaps.

The Nasty Rock Clock: James Garrett, creator of "Nasty Rock," photographed six times inside one of his customized clocks in Fuquay-Varina, North Carolina. Garrett also recorded a vocoder track called "Freakenstein" and Glenda McCleod's fast boogie "Stranger to Love."

I remember that night in 1983 when my friend Nate called and said Les Norman had been killed. Mom burnt the meatloaf and I yelled "Fuck." I remember Nate's subdued wheeze on the other end of the line. He'd heard the news on the radio. A single bullet to an artery in the leg and the Night-Time Master Blaster bled to death in a ditch in Biddleville, North Carolina. "Nobody really knew what happened," says Fred Wellington Graham III, PEG's program director at the time. "It was really hard on the black community. Les knew everybody. He was the Night-Time Master Blaster."

+ + +

I first heard "Nasty Rock" the day I accidentally put my best friend in the hospital. I had just mowed the grass when Nate tore through on his

THINK HE SAID HER NAME WAS VOODOO-ON-A-STICK

purple Schwinn Mongoose. He cut a power slide at the front porch and kicked up a williwaw of unbagged yard hair. My older brother sneezed. I said, "How's it going?" Nate said, "I can't breathe." He handed me a tape and barfed. We looked at Nate's shoes—fruit-stripe Chuck Taylors, spattered in wasabi green. Mom's porch caught the worst of it. I said, "Nate's got asthma." My brother squinted through the gnat panic. Nate said, "Hospital."

Nate always had two things in his pocket: inhaler and tape. The inhaler hissed like bus brakes. The tape was from a Les Norman shift at WPEG. (We say, "PEG it!" when anywhere near a radio.) Despite Nate's near-fatal run-in with lawn particulates, I realized he wasn't going to just up and die on me, not with the Master Blaster on the air every night. So once back from the hospital, we listened to "Nasty Rock" while he lay in bed, shot up with epinephrine, waiting for his bronchial trees to deconstrict.

SCORPIO UPCHUCKING

The shit erupted so much it scared me.
— Scorpio on "Scorpio"

My mom and I did aerobics to this song.
— Sara Roy on "Scorpio"

While "Nasty Rock" was locally grown, the next track on Nate's tape made you forget your asthmatic friends and yell "fuck" in front of your own mother. Called "Scorpio," its vocoder could've belonged to the giant adenoid of Lord Blatherard Osmo, which grew the size of a city block and had to be neutralized with electroshock, gas and cocaine. Recorded in 1982 for Sugar Hill Records by Grandmaster Flash & the Furious Five, "Scorpio" was the eponym of Eddie Morris, the group's in-house wardrobe consultant. ("If they had fifty suits, I had seventy suits.") This song didn't begin as much as it sneezed lasers and blinked out the lights. "Ahh Scorpio!" For all that hype about electro and video games, "Scorpio" shot the arcade to pieces.

"Scorpio" is what happens when Rick James tells you to show no shame. The Furious Five, who toured with Rick, took it to heart. One night at

Stacey "Nate McMillan" Moore, photographed in Def Jam Recordings T-shirt, Wrightsville Beach, North Carolina in 1987. Nate introduced me to Grandmaster Flash's "Scorpio" after a near fatal asthma attack.

ABOVE: Grandmaster Flash & the Furious Five, "Scorpio" (Sugarhill Records). This song was inspired by a Rick James stomach ache.

PAGE 221 TOP: Furious Five's Scorpio, Melle Mel, Dynamite, and friend, circa 1984. Old school rapper gym rats, Mel and Scorpio learned to do the "Back Bump" while training at the WWE semi-pro wrestling camp in Atlanta. (Courtesy Dynamite)

Sugar Hill Studios in Englewood, New Jersey, Melle Mel and Scorpio had a mini-orgy with some fans under a piano. Mel, who signs his gym memberships as Melvin Glover, then went into the booth and started punching out robots. "If you want the truth, the truth is The Truth," Scorpio told me. "What I brought to the group was beyond style. It was my freakiness."

"Scorpio was always doing some abstract shit," says Mel. "Show no shame" became the Furious Five's universal fancy handshake leather lightning-bolt motto. Yet it was a Rick James stomach bug in Dallas that made "Scorpio" officially shameless. After the Furious Five tore through their opening set, the promoter asked if they could go back out and kill another twenty minutes while Rick tried to talk his way out of the bottle. Scorpio said they didn't have shit to do. They'd already used Grandmaster Flash's "deep bubbly space music" record, which sounded like the alien in Rick James' stomach when Scorpio described it to me. "We just did our whole show! When we was touring we never did 'Scorpio.' It was basically filler on the album. Then we went 'Ahhhh Scorpio' and the crowd lost their motherfuckin' minds."

Bless Scorpio. Bless the Night-Time Master Blaster.

+ + +

1984. My front yard has settled into October decay. Nate and I are waiting on my stepbrother Tad to give us a lift to Shazada Records in downtown Charlotte. Tad liked to stay up all night red-eyeing old Westerns, scratching his feet and drinking iced tea. He wore Kool Moe Dee sun dimmers and loved "Scorpio" as much as he loved Rush, playing it between "Witch Hunt" and "YYZ." Tad possessed a brand of not-all-thereness that could get us to Shazada in outlaw time.

A '68 Camaro finally rumbles up in gamecock burgundy, a mother's nightmare with fat tree-swing tires and twin-exhaust backtalk. You imagine this car leading an all-county chase through someone's crops, smearing aphids, corn shocks flying into the air picking off birds, nylon husks slapping at the windows. Nate shares the front seat with a pair of hedge clippers. I hop in the back and land on a homemade machine gun tangled in speaker wire. "Safety's on," Tad says. The soldered barrel is cool under my legs, the business end, mugged by an oily dishrag. The butt's wrapped in silver duct tape. Nate says, "PEG it." Tad nods, puts in a tape and stomps the gas. The speakers sneeze into the back of my head. Ah. Scorpio. I notice the volume knob, popped off in Tad's hand. Jumper cables are on the floor, grinning like baby gators. I can't seem to get control of my seatbelt, dadgummit. Tad thinks I say "Tadgunnit" and slaps the speedometer past license revoked, now making jail time. Windows vanish. Tad tries to light a cigarette with the volume. Rearview mirror, full of sun dimmers. Nate, laughing in the clear.

BELOW: Tad Adams' 1969 Camaro, photographed in Rock Hill, South Carolina, circa 1985. I highly recommend listening to "Scorpio" while taking a short cut through a cornfield in this car.

THE F-4000

When the Fearless Four imagined what rap would sound like in the year 4000, it would be like "Scorpio," only with pods and anchormen. "We loved 'Scorpio,'" says Tito, one of the group's writers. "We came right behind them with 'F-4000,' three months after. The reason it was so effective—you're able to run with somebody else's style of music. But we gonna slow it down so you can hear exactly what we're talking about. We wanted to base ours around lyrics. 'Scorpio' was cool, but it was a party joint."

Tito and I are sitting on a park bench in Harlem discussing the importance of outer space and skull masks when making an impression on a bunch of kids in a high school gym. At sixteen, Tito wore wrist-activated flamethrowers onstage. He demonstrates the motion, a sort of Spider-Man web-fluid release. "We're talkin' about levitatin' and shit! What are we gonna do? Sparks and fog? Fuck that! We had fire comin' out our hands!"

There's much to like about Harlem's Fearless Four. They battled their heroes. They followed the classic old-school model where nobody ate lunch because the entire cafeteria was making nose milk watching MC Shoe getting clowned backwards and forwards by Kool Moe Dee. They could actually sing. They rapped over a Cat Stevens electro song about dogs and doughnuts. Their 1982 hit "Rockin It" was created when a producer named Pumpkin replayed a Kraftwerk synth riff 137 times, by hand. Fearless Four are the first (and only) to speak the words "pod" and "anchorman" through the vocoder. Released in 1984 on Elektra Records and produced by Kurtis Blow, "F-4000" would be the first song rapped entirely through the vocoder and released on a major label. The F-4000 sounds like the kind of thing you order from Captain Catalog, wait four-six weeks, and rip out of the box in a flurry of amoebic Styrofoam—a product of Acme wizardry that ends up in the coyote inventor's garage next to the electric swordfish clippers and the Atlas Vaporizer. The A-side, "Problems of the World," came with a B-side resolution: Let's cryogenically freeze ourselves and skip the blight and millennial apocalypse (Earth needing an extra 2,000 years to sort itself out) and thaw out on the beaches of 4000, call ourselves "God of the Pods," and catch up on our legend and retro-jock our savoir faire.

Looking at the cover of "Problems of the World," one can't help but admire how Tito's blue Le Tigre golf shirt matched Tito's Italian boating shoes. "The Baller's dock shoe," he says. They used to call him "Gorgeous George." "I wanted to look good. I wasn't interested in looking like the asshole."

SOMETHING PUMPKIN DID

The Fearless Four's producer, Eroll "Pumpkin" Bedward, was a multi-instrumentalist from the Bronx who produced classics by Grandmaster Flash & the Furious Five, Treacherous Three and Spoonie Gee. When asked about these records, his peers often helplessly shrug and say, "I don't know. It was something Pumpkin did," as if there was nothing he couldn't do. Pumpkin was called "Pumpkin" because his smile was bigger than his head. Little is known about him other than that he was jolly, in demand, underpaid and, in a tragic footnote, died on August 24, 1988.

"I don't know what Pumpkin was hearing when he came up with some of these beats," says Larry Smith, producer of Whodini and Run-DMC. Pumpkin may not have known either. Dave Ogrin, a popular session engineer, says Pumpkin was fairly deaf. They had to design "extra-crankable" headphones to keep Pumpkin from destroying the studio's amps. He could've worn a hearing aid with a vocoder chip that transposed high frequencies—often lost on the deaf—to a lower audible range.

Released in 1983, Pumpkin's productions for the Fantasy Three, "It's Your Rock" and "Biters in the City" seemed to be test-driving new technology at a time when folks were just happy to get out of the studio without blowing up the drum machine. The Fantasy Three B-sides are instrumentals only in the nominal sense, so improbable that we nearly thank the woofer that blew away Pumpkin's eardrum. Things are heard where they are not, headphone figments of a guy that Spoonie Gee once

Fearless Four, "Problems of the World" b/w "Fearless Freestyle" and "F-4000" (1984, Elektra). Produced by Kurtis Blow and Davy DMX, "F-4000" is the first vocoder rap on a major label. Tito is pictured here in royal blue Le Tigre and "baller's dock shoes." Also pictured: DLB ("F-4000" songwriter), Great Peso and Mighty Mike C.

described to me as "never a day without a smile." Vocals are taken from Side A and spliced into "The OtherSide" (the best dub versions being paranormal), not so much voices but half-awake memories trying to get a word in bladewise. A vocoded appliance. A blurt that cannot contain itself. Phrases are snatched away as suddenly as they appear, caught speaking out of turn in an empty room.

The instrumental of "It's Your Rock" was done alone in the studio at night while the rest of us dreamed it. The track doesn't begin so much as emerge, a subway at the tunnel's mouth, a roar that never actually passes, looped four times, each haunted by its own reverb. This is the sound of what you cannot see coming, the approach of tunnel darkness itself, swallowing the track, as if Pumpkin had squished his headphones to his ears and released, either making sure he's hearing things or deciding to let the outside world in on it. Do this with cupped hands and the act of vanquishing noise is stronger than the noise itself, winter in a conch shell.

Fantasy Three, "It's Your Rock" (1983, Specific Records). Fantasy Three was produced by Pumpkin, a near-deaf drummer from the Bronx. Though Pumpkin's hearing could have benefited from Bell Labs' vocoder-based digital hearing aid, it may have placed this record in immediate danger of sounding ordinary. Said Brigadier Fitzroy Maclean, on the vocoder with Churchill in 1943: "Pumpkin, sir? I'm afraid I don't understand what you mean."

I know this part well. It was the first thing I heard after learning that my oldest brother had died of an aneurysm. I had been listening to the vocal side of "It's Your Rock" with a friend, marveling at how it had been sampled by Three 6 Mafia ("Fuck All Dem Hoes") or maybe how Pumpkin's bass line mimicked a playground chant (There's a girl from France, something something underpants, etc.). The song ended with the telephone ringing—my dad with the logistics. The posterior cerebral artery had burst at a farmhouse in west Georgia. *Your mother and I are going to Atlanta tomorrow to see the body*. I hung up and sat on the living room floor, holding my head, recalling the last conversation with my brother. (Vocoders, toad lasers, carpenter bees.) My friend then flipped

THINK HE SAID HER NAME WAS VOODOO-ON-A-STICK

the record over to the instrumental because that's what you do—the only way back to life before the phone rang. Down the hallway, the approach of tunnel darkness, the rush of blood. What we can't see coming. What we can't believe we hear. Then the beat kicks in. The song actually begins.

+ + +

"'It's Your Rock' is really superior," says Danny Krivit, resident DJ at the Roxy when the club first opened in December 1979. "It was editing at its finest; that's really what made it. When that came out, hip-hop was pretty sparse. There was not a lot going on. More than half of it was borrowing familiar songs. 'It's Your Rock' was made from editing and different sounds. It really stuck out. We had a thing called skate-in-place where we stop everybody on the floor and they would just skate where they are. That was the perfect opportunity to play Fantasy Three, a great jam but a little jagged. That's the one people went home remembering. You play it just to be different."

They woke with it in their heads the next morning as Pumpkin's snare seemed to be clanging on pipes, filtered through a basement vent. A syncopated duct tap, the phantom pings of heat in a building, groggy on a winter day.

THE VAMPIRE IN YOUR VACUUM CLEANER

That people are prone to bite: and that biters may sometimes be bitten.
— Martin Chuzzlewit

Tonsillectomies are performed with a vacuum cleaner.
— Werner Herzog

A friend once informed me that the vacuum cleaner is on the tarmac. "It's on the runway," he said. "You have to let it go. The vacuum must leave the tarmac." He's referring to a moment from the Fantasy Three's "Biters in the City," a vocoder drone on the instrumental. As with "It's Your Rock," the Biters dub was the A-side letting its demons out for air. Though electronically realized, it's far from automated—you hear Pumpkin fooling with the new gear, crashing up hi-hats while a humming lightsaber makes a few passes, just grazing. The Fantasy Three themselves weren't happy with "Biters," complaining that it was too fast for the streets. "It's a really creative record," says Larry Mack, the all-state swimmer of the group. "'Biters' was a little much for me. It was too out there." When I played "Biters" for engineer Dave Ogrin, he smiled. "A lot of that was homemade and improvised. Pumpkin and I experimented with a lot of different sounds. We didn't have digital reverbs then, so we were mic'ing hallways, bathrooms and toilets to get these weird wooshy sounds."

"Biters" only exists as vengeance, a riposte to the Crash Crew, a Bronx group who copied the arrangement of "It's Your Rock" for "On the Radio" (which became a hit for Sugar Hill Records). One can hear why "Biters" was strange enough so as to never be duplicated. Who would even try? In a time when everyone held on by the skin of their fronts, trying to mimic a hit, this song remains alone. Alive and well on the friendless voyage.

When most of the old school was in the tri-state area, figuring things out, Reggie Hobdy, the Fantasy Three's writer, lived on a military base in Alaska. When he returned to the dirty-sock snow of New York, he was calling himself "Silver Fox," after a new Audi coupe and because his old name (McCoo) reminded people of a nearsighted cartoon. Fox ended

Biter's cassette courtesy of Phil Most Chill, inspired by Fantasy Three, customized and detailed in 1983.

up mentoring LL Cool J and Kool G Rap, was the only MC to carry his own mic—a Shure EK-G—in a barber's briefcase. "The shaving kit was one of those old fashioned zip-up-the-middle, brown leather jobs," he says. Instead of lather, razor, brush and scissors, it was microphone, green rhyming dictionary, blank tapes, pistol and a few joints.

According to Tito, Silver Fox was the only MC that Kool Moe Dee feared. "Fox brought that mic with him everywhere. A lot of cats did it for fun but Fox took his trade serious." "The EK-G was my vampire," Fox adds. "The vampire slept in this old shaving kit. My shaving kit was my coffin. When it was time to battle, I had to let the vampire out the coffin and go for blood."

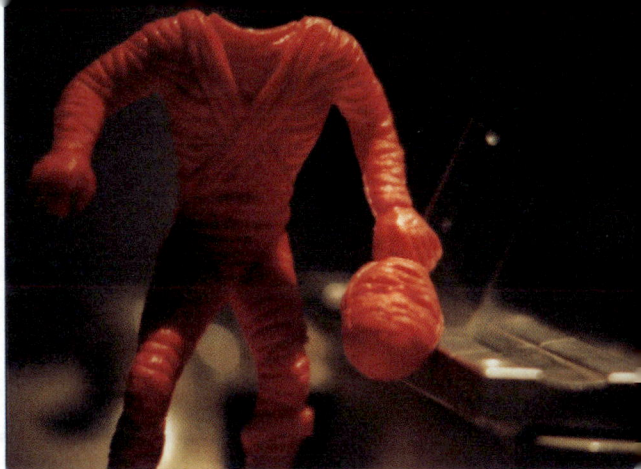

"Biters" ends with the vocoder caught boosting somewhere between a mirror and the hardware store. It could say "You are" but it would sound like "Myyylar"—a polyester resin that turns wrapping paper into a funhouse face-melt, catching our duplicates in the act of trying to be something else.

+ + +

In Philip Kaufman's 1978 remake of *Invasion of the Body Snatchers*, San Francisco has been repopulated with biters, dub versions that drift the Haight while their originals remain cocooned in strands of cotton-candy goo. Their doubles appear in New Age mud baths or pupating in lawn chairs in the back yard.

The scuffed edit block at Cutting Records studios, used by Latin Rascals and Aldo Marin to hold 2-inch recording tape for cutting and splicing remixes. Aldo Marin's edits for "It's Your Rock" were done in this studio. (Courtesy Gabriele Caroti)

It's morning. Donald Sutherland strolls in Golden Gate Park, a frizzy hatrack in a beige raincoat. A friend approaches, eyes bloodshot from sleep deprivation, stifling hysteria. A warped, ain't-right bagpipe version of "Amazing Grace" plays nearby. She whispers. (It's really me!) Sutherland, who spent the night getting cloned, opens his mouth and points. The drone escapes through his mustache, Silver Fox chased across the ice by an Inuit throat sled, tarmac to tundra, a chorus of dupes tricked out of the pipes their mother gave them. She cups her ears and screams. The camera zooms into Sutherland's tonsils, taking us into the blackness, ducking Sutherland's uvula, which should have a screaming face of its own. Biters, all of them.

TRYING TO BARF OUT THE UNIVERSE

On a park bench in Harlem, Tito and I talk pods. "Biters in the City" was the first 12 inch that refused to leave my mom's turntable, as if the spindle just couldn't let it go. When I finally managed to wobble the record away, it would always try to eat the spindle itself, stuck in the grips of torn vinyl from the exit wound. A friend helpfully described this effect as the record trying to barf out the universe. Nervous about damaging mom's turntable or the record, I'd leave it be. Just let the thing keep on, this black hit of space.

Tito goes with it. Behind us, four girls in fuzzy bomber jackets form a circle around a dry stone fountain and fire up a chorus to keep warm. Tito recognizes someone approaching. I want to see Sutherland, pointing, vacuuming. Instead it's a guy who says he knows Just-Ice.

The word *pod* still sounded pretty mysterious back in the Walkman era. "'F-4000' was a club banger," says Tito. "Back then it wasn't as saturated, so everybody got their airplay and everybody could get they shit heard. DJs would cut 'God of the pod.' And we in the club." He smiles. "And they play it and fuck with our names. Tito. God-god-god of the pod-pod." Behind us, the girls in fuzzy jackets fight the wind for a harmony.

WHATEVER YOU SAY

TORQUE OF THE TAPE

The edits on "It's Your Rock" were done by a young KTU DJ named Aldo Marin, who would later start the Electro-Freestyle label Cutting Records. Albert Cabrera of the Latin Rascals once warned about the dangers of disappearing inside the edit, mummified in two-inch recording tape—so deep inside the track that one had to literally cut their way out.

You can't talk because we've extracted all your teeth and given you a complete vocal cord resection.
— John Frankenheimer's 1966 film *Seconds*

I am listening to "F-4000" while standing next to a shipwreck diving helmet. The swatter in my hand is mint green and shaped like a tulip. The helmet was welded together by the Morse Diving Company back in 1923. It's painted gold, weighs forty-seven pounds and seems to be missing its Kraken. A fly has buzzed itself in through the third-floor window and into a loft apartment near the Holland Tunnel in downtown Tribeca. Overseeing the damage is Rammellzee, a vocoder extremist in kung fu slippers and waterproof pants. At 6' 3", Rammel prefers looming to standing. His head is squeezed inside a black do-rag with an acrylic mudflap down the nape.

To my knowledge, Rammellzee is the only one out there who has corrected ocean pipe fissures in the Gulf of Mexico and rapped on "Beat Bop," a 12-inch single recorded with gallery graffiti icon Jean-Michel Basquiat. He has led as many lives as he has voices. Rapper, diver, sinister masked man, dentist, jeweler, letter defender, quantum engineer, painter. Toy encoder, toy assassin. "Professional heretic." Self-admitted bull-shitter. Allegedly pushed Stephen Hawking's wheelchair. His childhood distrust of the Catholic Church tops a list of aversions that includes mayonnaise and the word *whatever*.

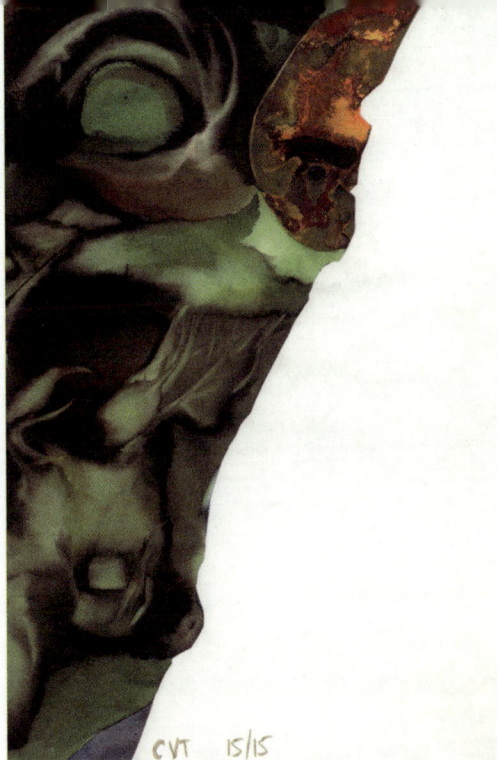

"He's a genius," says director Jim Jarmusch, who cast Rammel in his 1984 film *Stranger Than Paradise*. "The kind of guy you could talk to for twenty minutes and your whole life could change, if you could only understand him."

Rammel likes "F-4000" so much that he's convinced his name is in the song. Apparently it's up to me to make sure it's there. We're making our second pass and he's got me checking lyrics on the back sleeve. His name is nowhere to be found, so I try to fudge a match. *Anchorman with the master plan?* This will not be easy. Every vocoder track I play him is taken as a WWF challenge. "Pack Jam" fires him up. "He wasn't an engineer!" Rammel says of Jonzun. "He wasn't with the military! But he could play!"

+ + +

CVT 15/15

Untitled by Bo Tompkins, watercolor, circa 1987. This D&D lab accident of a face is what a vocoder looks like after being sucked into the Fantasy Three's vacuum cleaner.

You may have seen Rammellzee at the end of the film *Wild Style*, rapping like broken-nose revenge, waving a flintlock dueling pistol over his head. He is best known for "Beat Bop," a ten-minute track recorded with Basquiat and the rapper K-Rob back in 1983. The 12 inch now goes for hundreds of dollars, or thousands, if you want to splurge for the original Basquiat cover art. Despite its legend, Basquiat thought the record was a failure. "Jean was involved with the process," says Al Diaz, a graffiti writer who played wood blocks, bells and timbales on the track. "It wasn't like he was just doing lines and writing checks."

"Beat Bop" is an eventful walk home from school, intended to be a conversation between two people (a pimp and a kid) but sounding like an argument among six (Rammel). One going home, the other, out of his mind. "K-Rob was kind of on this good-boy trip," continues Diaz. "Saying, 'Your mind can't function,' 'Waiting at home for Mr. Right,' and then Rammel's going on about cocaine. It was some sinister shit. The session was fairly controlled. There was a lot of cocaine, but we were focused."

Jean-Michel Basquiat and Rammellzee entering Disneyland in 1982, photographed by Stephen Torton (© ADAGP, Paris). Their flight to Los Angeles was shared with Eddie Van Halen. According to Torton, who worked closely with Jean-Michel and Zee, Rammellzee was a kind of muse to Jean-Michel; a constant source of material. "Our own T.S. Eliot."

Al Diaz thinks that this "Beat Bop" session may have driven K-Rob to choose Christ as his savior, possibly because he ran into the Gangster Duck, the Evolution Griller and "The #1 Stain on the Train." Characters, right down to the letter. All this reverb and interruption is confusing. When you hear K-Rob say, "Say what? Say what?" he means it. Understandably, K-Rob does not make it home for dinner that night.

That's what ten minutes and ten seconds of "Beat Bop" will do to you. It makes you late for things. It made rap late to its own funeral. It's one of those vocoder songs that doesn't use a vocoder, or need one. K-Rob and Rammel are so in the room that you keep turning around to make sure they aren't.

I purchased "Beat Bop" during a family Christmas excursion to New York in 1984. When I got home, I let those disembodied voices inhabit the living room: the unplayed piano, the plaque on our coffee table saying "Nixon Put His Feet Here," the clay skunk I made in second grade. I had questions. What is 720Z? Who was making with the freak freak?

Nate would somehow learn all the words to "Beat Bop." This was quite a feat for a seventh-grader short on breath, considering the song's length and how most of the words aren't even words. The more we listened to it, the more we understood that we had no idea what was going on. Thirteen years old, looking at the label. *What's a Rammellzee?*

✦ ✦ ✦

"F-4000" is still at full-throttle in Rammel's apartment. Still decoding, trying to make a name from adhesive air. It must be when Fearless Four's DLB says, "soon you'll see that DLB's." Two *L*'s, two *E*'s. This must be the place. A *Z* is an *S* on vibrate, anyway. Shake hands with a cicada joy buzzer. A friend would later say, "You think you heard them saying his name because he's saying they're saying his name?"

Rammel calls "F-4000" "non-negotiable war music," which means one more pass for the peas. "That's it!" He looks back over his shoulder. "They didn't print it right on the back of the record! God of the pod of this brand of peas. That's only certain people in Afro-Futurism and that would be that brand of peas. Start with George and Bootsy. James Brown."

What about Sun Ra? "Sun Ra is definitely in one of them pods! I don't know if he's in my pod. That's where I tip my hat. I've got a lot of spaceships." He lumbers off to the kitchen for a beer. I notice the Tasmanian Devil (*sarcophilus harrisii*) pointing at me from the back of his T-shirt: "You're Next!"

I defer to the fly, still woozing around the apartment. It lands on the Verne helmet, wipes its goggles and considers its chances. "See, he likes that vocoder shit," says Rammel, nodding to the insect. "It's just a sound. There's no place to go. We need to stop using water in the shower. We should use sonics to vibrate the bugs off our bodies instead of giving them more food to war—to cause cellular dysfunction. Fearless Four! Now that's pure war music. It's introducing a crew, ready to kill. You better know why they're coming for you." I salute him with the tulip.

"F-4000" has stopped for the last time. The room is quiet.

"Please kill the fly, boss."

CHAPTER TEN

COOL, AS LONG AS NOBODY HEARS IT

A talking and singing machine will be numbered among the conquests of science.
— Sir David Brewster, *Letters on Natural Magic*, 1839

Good Fred Ellis, inventor of the Jheri Curl, at La Rutan Barbershop, 2009. Good Fred helped mentor the early LA electro hip-hop scene, providing Egyptian Lover and Uncle Jamm's Army with an office to run their label, Egyptian Empire, and distribution company, West Coast Wax. (Courtesy Brian Cross)

OPEN YOUR BOOKS TO PAGE FREAK

God only knows, but the freak-masters...
— Ray Bradbury, *Something Wicked This Way Comes*

Richard Pryor pulls up to the La Rutan barbershop in a new convertible Rolls-Royce and asks, "How the hell does this thing work?" La Rutan's owner, Good Fred Ellis, laughs himself into the front seat for a test drive. It's 1975. The Rolls is custard, Pryor's hair is Natural and the sky is generous.

Along with Al Green, Leon Isaac Kennedy and Charlie Pride, Pryor was among the regular clientele at La Rutan—French for "natural" backward —which for the past forty-six years has been cornering 54th and Western in South Central Los Angeles. Good Fred started out shaving Mohawks in Detroit in the Fifties before moving to California, where he'd later become Godfather of the Activator Curl. In the early Eighties, Fred's son Darryl and a young DJ named Rodger Clayton helped bottle Fred's homemade Jheri-curl emulsion of glycerin, water and alcohol, which was stored in 300-gallon drums in the back of La Rutan. Samples of Good Fred Oil were then test-marketed at parties held by Clayton's crew of DJs, originally known as Unique Dreams before changing their name to Uncle Jamm's Army (with George Clinton's blessing). Uncle Jamm's main attraction, Egyptian Lover, would throw sample vials of Good Fred "Hansom Dude" pomade wave accentuator into the crowd while cutting up Zapp records. Folks stood a fighting chance of getting dinged in the head while the vial trajectory was being so eloquently described by Zapp's Mini Moog, an activator bungee jump. Repeat often as necessary.

The Good Fred formula would ultimately be deconstructed by the chemists at Johnson & Johnson and mass-produced for millions of Michael Jackson dollars. Though discouraged, Fred Ellis was told by a marketing professor at UCLA to keep building his pyramid and customers would come looking for him when he reached the top. Egyptian Lover (a.k.a. Greg Broussard), LA's most wanted DJ, would find himself in a similar circumstance—specifically, in a Superman suit, apexed on a pyramid stack of fifty Cerwin-Vegas, humping the speakers and violating the sacred order of the eyeball's parking

JUST PLAIN BACKWARDS

In eighth grade, we'd impress ourselves by quoting the backwards Sir Mix-a-Lot line, *Keerfatsujehs.* We listened to Capt. Rapp's "Bad Times" (another classic from Jimmy Jam and Terry Lewis' pre-Janet phase) at the wrong speed, unaware that a 12 inch could be a 45. This went on for years until my mom pointed out the correct speed on the label.

Egyptian Lover in the chair at La Rutan Barbershop, top right, Los Angeles, 2009. La Rutan's clientele included Richard Pryor, Leon Isaac Kennedy, and Bobby Womack. (Courtesy Brian Cross)

space. This may seem excessive, but somebody must've been doing something right if George Clinton, Dr. Dre and Roger Troutman are showing up at your parties.

Good Fred would advise Egypt and Clayton, encouraging them to start their own label, Egyptian Empire Records (and distribution company West Coast Wax), as well as provide an office, across the street from La Rutan. The first record, *Breaking and Entering*, was released in 1983 as a soundtrack for a documentary that included Samoan kids spinning on their heads and a drum-machine tutorial by Egyptian Lover himself. The EP also featured Ice-T, who would later collaborate with Morris Day refugees Jimmy Jam and Terry Lewis for an electro masterpiece called "Cold Wind Madness." Only twenty-five copies of *Breaking and Entering* were pressed; one remains with Egypt, and the rest are now presumably in Teutonic custody.

On the first single, "Dial-A-Freak," Egypt tells callers to open up their books to page freak, over some pulse-dial jitter and musky synths. This was followed, in a hurry, by the vocoder monster "Egypt Egypt," which in turn was pursued by legions of miniskirt admirers dreaming of long fishnet walks by the Nile, if not Venice Beach, and heavy breathing that defied smog alerts. The radio commercials that Egypt and Uncle Jamm aired on KDAY to promote their parties were as good as if not better than the records themselves, often selling out the Sports Arena in downtown LA, where a significant number of the 10,000 heads in attendance had at some point been activated by Good Fred Ellis.

The LA Sports Arena would be the site of Run-DMC's California debut when Rodger Clayton booked them for an Uncle Jamm party in 1983, back when Run had hair. Egypt introduced the teens from Queens to their first palm tree and drove them over to Good Fred's to get their ears lowered. There, an eighty-nine-year-old regular noted Run's shelltoe tongues and said, "How come you boys all on TV with no shoelaces in your shoes? You can't afford no shoestrings?" Outside, girls in "Freak Patrol" T-shirts distributed Uncle Jamm's flyers. Behind them, on La Rutan's wall, was a mural of radiant pyramids, pre-mummy pharaohs and a guy rocking Tut's diadem on his head. That would be Egyptian Lover, who remains a Good Fred customer to this day.

TOP: Victor & the Glove Breakmixer Series: A mix of songs by the late Rich Cason, a prolific LA vocoder producer whose catalog includes "Street Freeks," "Magic Mike Theme," and "Radioactivity Rapp," which would be sampled in 2005 for Mac Mall's "Dredio" (mentioned: Café Escalon, Steve Urkel, Decepticons, *Planet of the Apes*, glasspack mufflers).

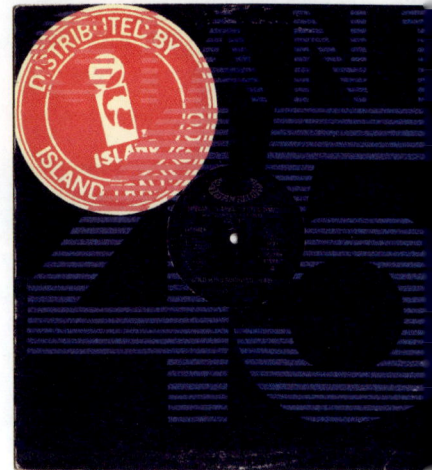

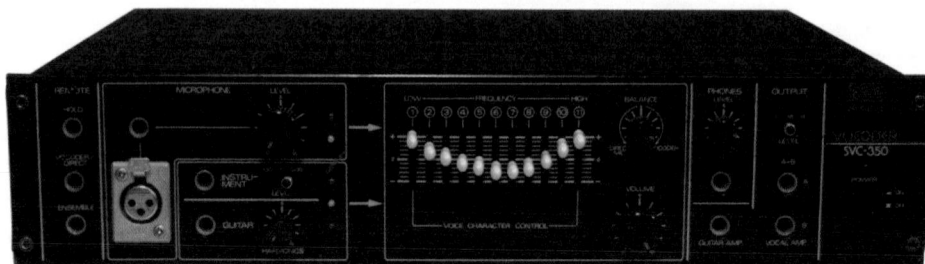

Egyptian Lover's Freak Machine: the Roland SVC-350 Vocoder, first introduced in 1979, for under a grand. The voice modulates the carrier wave provided by a synthesizer, an evolution from the radio station in Homer Dudley's mouth.

At Uncle Jamm's early parties, Egypt and his younger brother would show up in surgical gowns and say they were from Cairo. "We dressed up in doctor suits and did doctor dances. We did fake heart attacks, different gimmicks to get girls. We had the green surgical scrubs, masks and gloves. The girls liked the gloves."

The dance back then was "The Freak," invented by the Carson Freekateers and later stolen by the Lambada. "The Freak dance took Los Angeles to another level," says Egypt. "It brought so many people to the dances. Everybody was freaking from beginning to end. Guys humping girls all night long. There were serious freaks going on. It was the only dance we did. All the other dances were obsolete when the Freak came out." In LA, you'd think the word *freak* had been invented by the vocoder. Egypt says they turned everything into a freak song, often speeding up classics like Whodini's "Five Minutes of Funk." "The vocoder is what the freaks liked to freak to. 'Scorpio' changed me. When I played it, I was like, 'Oh man, this is a Freak song.' We had Freak contests. A thousand dollars to the best freaks. They used to get seriously freaky. You didn't even need a partner. It could be one guy laying on the ground, five girls dancing over him. It was a live sex show with clothes on."

This did not fly with parents who would sometimes show up to defreak their daughters. "Once this girl's momma came in wearing hair curlers. I got her name and said on the mic, 'Your momma's here.' Everybody knew who [the girl] was. They put the lights on her. She was freakin' this dude." It didn't help matters that the dance floor was muddy from

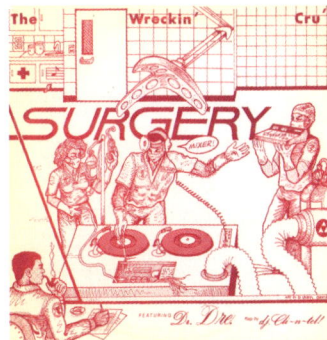

LEFT: "They used to get seriously freaky." Egyptian Lover and speaker cabinets, circa 1984.

RIGHT: Wreckin' Cru, "Surgery" featuring Dr. Dre and Cli-n-tel (1984, Kru-Cut Records). "Surgery" inspired kids to do the Freak in hospital scrubs. Don't let The Chronic fool you, Dre used to love that vocoder. ("Horny Computer"!) Dre also produced "Killer Daytons," the first song about carjacking, and the underrated Sleeze Boyz ("Dance Til You Drop"). The Kru-Cut logo looks like a starfish doing a double bicep pose on Venice Beach.

a leak in the roof, what Rodger Clayton called "a Freak-a-leak." "She was there freakin' dude in the mud," says Egypt. "The flooring had been ripped up. It was so hot and crowded in there, with sweat coming up from the floor. It was a mess. It was wet from all the humans. The walls were sweating. Sweat was dripping from the ceiling. Her momma was hitting her with a belt on the way out!" One night Egypt's dad showed up. "I was talking real nasty on the mic and I turned around and my dad was standing on the stage. And he said, 'Talk that shit, boy! Talk that shit!' I was so embarrassed. I was seventeen. I looked at my brother like, 'Why'd you bring *him* here?'"

Though LA seemed to be all fast times at 123 bpm, one of Egypt's best move would turn out to be slow, backwards and only heard if you were at the party freaking in the mud:

> I played "Planet Rock" backwards from end to beginning and my arm was sore. They'd never heard anything like that. This was 1983. It was like hearing "Planet Rock" for the first time. At the end it goes, "party people," but the words were going, "imsump imshumpyump." It was like speaking another language to the beat. I play "Planet Rock" backwards with one hand and get girls' phone numbers with the other. That was a good one.

While Good Fred's Accentuator would flourish with Ice Cube and khaki in the Comptonian future, the vocoder and the Uncle Jamm parties couldn't survive as venues grew increasingly nervous about gang insurance. Egypt remembers the shift. "The gangs would have one fight and say, 'I'll see you at the next Uncle Jamm's Army party,' and then have another fight at the next one. It got so they'd say, 'If they're coming, we ain't coming.' Ninety percent of the gangsters came to have fun. It was the ten percent who couldn't get a girl. They were the ones starting problems. There were so many women there—women outnumbered us five to one. This was at the Sports Arena. Everyone was selling dope and making money back then. Gangsters with money—no problems. But play Michael Jackson—that will make you fight. The Rolling 60s Crips would shoot up every-fucking-body. Slow songs and ballads make the gangsters fight. No room for Michael Jackson. Sorry, Mike."

INSTANT ROBOTNESS

Uncle Jamm's Army at La Rutan, including Egyptian Lover (center) and Rodger Clayton (Uncle Jamm, second from left, bottom row).

By 1982, when the vocoder was putting Los Angeles on freak notice, Kai Krause was ready to sell his Sennheiser to Neil Young. The freelance vocoder consultant drove north on the Pacific Coast Highway with his VSM-201 in his trunk, headed for Young's ranch in Half Moon Bay. Selling his machine to Young for $13,500 would be a final act of vocoder good will for Kai, who had spent much of the past five years peddling Martian voices and explosions to Hollywood. Yet instructing Stevie Wonder, Herbie Hancock and Frank Zappa on how to use the vocoder had its perks. "Almost anyone would want to hear and see it," Kai says, emailing from a castle overlooking the Rhein. "We sold one to a hospital in San Diego. They used it for linguistics."

Kai first met Dr. Fritz Sennheiser in 1977, at the Audio Engineering Society in LA. "Figure out if there's anything Hollywood can do with that thing," said the doctor, leaving Kai with a 45-pound vocoder the size of a microwave.

The Sennheiser unit was billed as "the first Entertainment Vocoder," now that it was declassified. Kai ended up writing vocoder manuals for Sennheiser's American clients, enticing them with promises of "instant robotness" while telling them to get their creatures in order: "The vocoder could make Mr. Rogers sound like Stevie Wonder or an unbelievable sore throat." Yet his demo tests went much further. The sound of football stadiums and castle winds roaring through twenty channels, in German, were almost too Grayskull for my outgoing phone message.

In the manual accompanying Herbie Hancock's 1978 album *Sunlight*, Kai definitely saw the future, calling the vocoder the "ultimate phone answering machine." "There were many odd encounters with the Sennheiser machine," says Kai. "Clients adored it, amazed how it could work, and we grinned quietly." There were Dracula screams for the ABC Movie of the Week ("Kind of like Tarzan's yell"), Icelandic Christmas choirs ("Figures they would take the holidays seriously up there, it gets dark a lot") and collaborations with Keith Emerson ("Watched lots of Benny Hill"). Yet stocking effects for *Tron* and *The Black Hole* would leave a "strange Disneyesque aftertaste." "For Disney, this meant explosions. Machine sounds, spacy blurbs of all kinds, lots of low rumbles, rocket stages, and a sheer endless set of mechanical sound effects. They used me more like a live animal: Let him make his beeps and burps, we just hold a mic to it and call it something later."

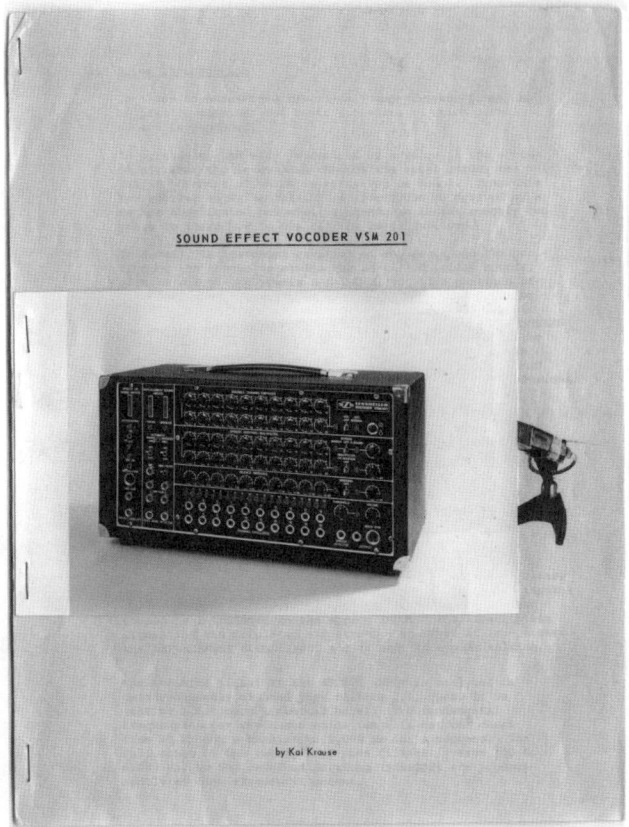

SOUND EFFECT VOCODER VSM 201

by Kai Krause

The Sennheiser VSM-201 Vocoder clientele included DARPA (Defense Advanced Research Projects Agency), Frank Zappa, the Jet Propulsions Lab in Pasadena, Devo, and Disney. While each unit cost $18,500, Kai Krause would charge $52 an hour for vocoder consulting.

Dr. Fritz Sennheiser. In 1977, Sennheiser charged Kai Krause with introducing his VSM-201 to Hollywood. "Using mere oscillators to talk through is a trivial application of the technology," says Kai. The Sennheiser vocoder was used by Kenny Loggins, Neil Young, *Star Trek*, and Cheech & Chong for a deleted alien abduction scene from *Cheech & Chong's Next Movie*.

Kai felt the machine was meant for better things than, say, an alien-virgin abduction scene in *Cheech & Chong's Next Movie*. "The entire process was highly chaotic, lots of screams and tin-foil hats. When they took me to dinner later, one of them mumbled that the whole scene had only one intent: Audition a few dozen actresses. Glad the vocoder could help."

Though the droids were often the Sennheiser's bread and butter, Kai quickly tired of it, preferring the sound of "three saxes with a frog in a blender falling down the stairs with a nun, backwards. Never mind the robots. Using mere oscillators to talk through became the most trivial of all possibilities in that sense. All that robotness was quickly explored to its edges." To cope with the tedium, Kai would lock himself in a room and trap weird noises inside his head. No clocks, no windows. He explains:

> One of the richest veins in sonic surprises for me was to hook up the Sennheiser with two radio channels, one on each input, and just turn the dials. It was like a window with hundreds of variations flying by. I would use drums to play "through" an orchestral recording, or use water drops over Gregorian chants. Extremely interesting results came from feeding two radio channels into it at once. Not a blending, nor a true morphing—but an odd cross-correlation. The pitch from song A being re-EQ'ed by the spectrum of song B…. and often you could still hear both. A Bach fugue being modulated by the Beatles' "Michelle" was absolutely eerie… you could still hear the words, faintly intelligible, but without the pitch of the song. It's a shame Sennheiser labled the inputs as "Speech" and "Replacement Sound," already expecting robot voices.

In 1982, the year *Tron* hit theaters, Kai was contacted by Neil Young's producer Joel Bernstein and hauled his entire synth rig up into the mountains. "[Neil] was kind and polite, but also a bit spaced, hard to get him to concentrate on any detail. It wasn't possible to get him or anyone else there to listen to the how-to and why of the whole set-up. In the end, I had to give up and let go. He did explain that he was a huge Kraftwerk fan and wanted to re-create that sound desperately. About a year later, I heard *Trans* and suddenly knew where it all had gone."

YELLOW MAGIC ORCHESTRA

Yellow Magic Orchestra (YMO), Japan's self-de-scribed, ironic "Techno Pop" superstars, made electro from M-80 popcorn exploding on cookie sheets. Adopted by the Tokyo school system, YMO became the soundtrack for gym exercises, lunchroom ambience and after-school eraser clapping. As video age pioneers, YMO vocodered the Tokyo Tower into space and glazed their faces with Bio-Clear, a spray-on instant mask used while touring for their 1978 album *Behind the Mask*.

I'M A LOT LIKE YOU

A severe motor disorder, a father's guilt, a commercial flop, a landmark lawsuit, cut-out bin hell, throwback redemption. Neil Young's relationship with the vocoder was complicated. More than just a guy with a Kraftwerk jones, Young recorded 1983's *Trans* for his son Ben, a quadriplegic born with cerebral palsy. As a device which in itself struggled to communicate, the Sennheiser became a tool of empathy. "It's communication but it's not getting through," said Young to his biographer, Jimmy McDonough. "And that's what my son is. I was looking for a way to change my voice. To sing through a voice that no one could recognize and it wouldn't be judged as me. [It's] my search for a way for a severely handicapped non-oral person to find some sort of interface for communication." Neither Geffen Records nor the fans got the message, resulting in Young being sued by his own label for not being himself, a contradiction in itself, or a crime—abetted by the vocoder and punishable by $3.3 million in damages. Young filed a countersuit for $21 million (worth 1,555 Sennheisers) and settled out of court. His VSM-201, however, was never heard from again.

While *Trans* was deemed too sterile, Young countered that you can feel more from someone who doesn't (or can't) show pain because it's roiling inside. Suppression of emotion is an emotion itself, and Young felt it was nobody's business. Nor should pity bribe an honest day's two-star review—many weren't aware of the muse until long after *Trans* had been discarded. It was unforgivable to Neil fans, who took it personally despite having no idea just how personal it really was. Betrayed by the vocoder. "You gotta realize you can't understand the words," said Young. "You can't understand the words—and I can't understand my son's words. So feel that." "You either loved it or you ran for your life," wrote David Fricke in *Mojo*.

The misinformation surrounding the project had people believing that Neil had actually spoken to his son through the vocoder (this was never confirmed) or that it was just a deliberate prank on pop music's blind trust in new technology. On the European *Trans* tour, Young sounded like Miss Piggy while "Transformer Man" was undermined by the interpretive phantom dancing of guitarist Nils Lofgren. (Lofgren would

later be required to wear five-pound ankle weights "so he wouldn't bust the noir vibe with his fuckin' girly spins," as one die hard Neil fan explained.) The tour culminated with Neil Young trying to strangle his bass player.

BAND PASS FILTERS

The vocoder managed not to offend fans of Queen, Pink Floyd and Blue Oyster Cult and was permitted to mooch off the novelty of synthesizers that became more commercially available in the Seventies. Genesis replaced their Mellotron with it. The Alan Parsons Project used the vocoder to ride Asimov's sideburns into the future on 1978's *I, Robot* and let it inhabit the wormy throat of "The Raven" on 1976's *Tales of Mystery and Imagination*.

ELO would run their entire production budget through the machine. Richard "Magic Fingers" Tandy, the group's vocoder specialist, calls it the "whiz woosh wash." "The vocoder was our main machine," he tells me, on the phone from London. "We used it as much as we could. We

ELO, *Out of the Blue* (1977, Columbia). This is what it looks like inside an ELO song. While some say the vocoder could destroy the atmosphere, ELO used it to become the atmosphere itself. ELO ran everything through the vocoder and had the good sense to distinguish between special effects and "very special effects."

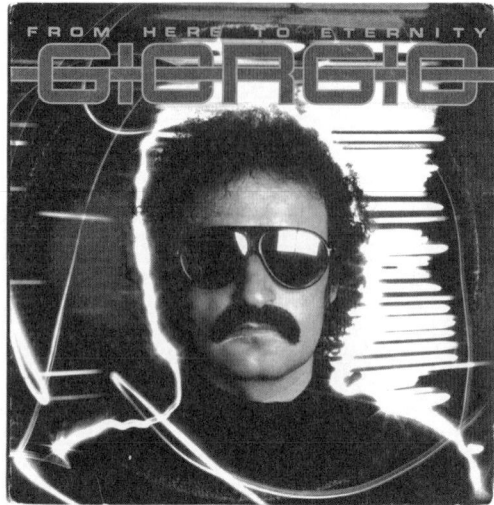

RIGHT: Giorgio Moroder, *From Here To Eternity* (1978, Casablanca Records). Giorgio Moroder was born with a vocoder installed in his name. Moroder also never returned my emails, triggering a recurrent disco nap nightmare where I'm driving an easy chair (or leather couch, something from Monty Python's furniture races) down I-85 South to Moroder's "Faster than the Speed Of Love." Speech is shaped from darkness and filtered through the mustache in the rearview mirror. (Courtesy Gabriele Caroti)

were mixing things together like sound effects of thunder and voices, drums and strings going through it. We began feeding absolutely everything through it—anything you could think of. Just to see what it sounded like. We used to have a big choir on the string tracks. Then [the machines] started playing themselves and we sat there and watched them. That was fun. Jeff would imagine things and write stories."

ELO songwriter and arranger Jeff Lynne used album credits to distinguish between special effects and "very special effects," between being butterflies and nausea. On "Yours Truly, 2095" (from the 1981 album *Time*), Lynne falls for an IBM who turns out to be a telephone wearing a jumpsuit—all set to a vocoder chorus in silver robes.

Tandy goes silent thinking about it. ("I was just expressing astonishment.") He doesn't remember where they got their EMS-2000 vocoder or how it fell into the hands of Man Parrish. It cost £2,500 when introduced in 1976. Tandy first saw it in 1977 while recording *Out of the Blue* in Munich, approximate to Giorgio Moroder's vocoder activities in disco.

One of ELO's biggest hits, "Mister Blue Sky," was a wistful Johnny Head-in-the-Air, a daydreamer naïve to the pleasures of a gray afternoon.

"The Whale" was a one-man polyphony submerged in Moog gurgles, some four dreams deep, awakened by a blinding synth and a string section that fried your curtains into frequency bands. What dismantled human speech somehow retained Jeff Lynne's character, tricking his voice into believing the world was his chorus. Before touring, ELO's backup singers gave up, realizing that the vocoder was essentially doing their job. "So they packed up their coats and left," says Tandy.

+ + +

It would take *Ultraman* to make me realize that ELO was more than another UFO on a T-shirt. At the *anime* exhibit Little Boy, the best of my time was spent on a wall of sketches by Tohl Narita, a Japanese sculptor who kept Ultraman in monsters for most of my childhood. It was an impressive lineup: a heap of Michelin bladderwrack, a blowfish meteor, Godzilla's cousin with wings, a fire-breathing sweet potato that drank gasoline, and a 20,000-ton walking artichoke.

Their origins—informants of Hiroshima, Dadaism, Buddhism, Greek mythology and various deep-space hairballs—were unknown to American kids who'd get home from school in time to see Ultraman's name appear in a churn of green swill (the credits alone were the grossest thing on TV) after a day of flossing teeth with train sets, being silly, destructive and completely irresponsible—of being kids, essentially. (In the video for their vocoder hit "Intergalactic," the Beastie Boys suited up for a *kaiju eiga* appreciation.) Staring at Little Boy's Ultraman wall, I heard a vocoder version of the Cantata Wedding March drifting from the plasma screen behind me. Scored by ELO's "Twilight," it was a B-29's view of an atomic fried egg, its blast radius rippling through Tokyo. As part of this animation short for the Japanese science fiction convention Daicon IV, the ELO sense of grandeur suited the vision, in both its epic scale of destruction and hope of regeneration through the unreal: a girl in a crimson Playboy cocktail suit, surfing above the mushroom cloud on a sword.

The most unavoidable Japanese vocoder zeitgeist would be disguised in a Canadian prison opera set in outer space. Nobody understood the hook from Styx's hit "Mr. Roboto," the most commercially successful

Herbie Hancock did the unthinkable and used the vocoder to actually improve his voice, thanks to his keyboard skills, one of the most human applications of the device. Songs like "I Thought It Was You" and "Come Running... To Me" are boogie lounge mainstays.

use of the vocoder, yet everyone remembers. As a friend said, "Just being Japanese in third grade and having to listen to fools say that Roboto shit all day" was enough to make her puke.

In 2002, I attended a Styx autograph signing at J&R Music World in downtown Manhattan to check in on Roboto's legacy. A crab fisherman from Long Island thought the song was just weird and didn't care much for it, honestly, but was glad they stuck around. His wife sang the chorus and said it was neat and something different. A policeman on duty at J&R

said Roboto reminded him too much of "Funky Town," a song by Lipps, Inc. He then did the chorus of "Funky Town," (as it appears in Mel Brooks' *History of the World, Part I*) while his friend said that Queen could have done a better job. (See "Radio Ga Ga.") A man from Brooklyn mistook Japanese for Spanish. His friend added that "Mr. Roboto" always made him think of a Puerto Rican robot shopkeeper on *Sesame Street*, chasing little kids out of his bodega with a talking broom.

WHEN THE STUFF HITS THE FAN

If we were any fresher, you'd have to slap us.
— Fresh Market billboard, Greenville, South Carolina

In 1979, Bob Mitchell, resident of Concord, Massachusetts, went on a vocoder witch-hunt. After a Herbie Hancock show in Boston, he wrote in to *Musician*, demanding a $10.51 refund. The letter was published in the July issue, under the heading "Funk-A-Dunk": "What's gotten into Herbie Hancock? Where does he think he's going with that ridiculous vocoder? That thing isn't just a waste of time, it's a complete waste of taste. I didn't pay $10.51 to hear one forty-minute set with twenty minutes of it devoted to Herbie playing Kid Scientist on the vocoder. I wrote to you hoping that you could talk some sense into him. Obviously no one else is."

Bob Mitchell wasn't any more thrilled with Herbie (singing *and* disco!) than Neil Young's people were with *Trans*. "We took a long time to get it," says Kai Krause, who coached Herbie Hancock on the Sennheiser "It's more natural-voice-oriented than most. Herbie really can't sing— he would be the first to say that. Oddly, many 'more than most' listeners never really figured out that this was purely electronic, but rather thought he 'just sings weird.'"

On the inner sleeve of *Sunlight*, there's a photo of Herbie singing through the vocoder, his mouth somewhat lopsided, struck by an invisible fist an idea, a fat "Oh shrrrrrrit!" in slow motion, leading some to believe that the vocoder had actually mutated Herbie's jaw. One imagines that Bob Mitchell wasn't happy with the Wall-E boogie of "I Thought It Was You" or "Come Running to Me." In 2000, the refrain of

Fab Five Freddy & Beside, "Change the Beat" (1984, Celluloid Records). Fab Five Freddy didn't want anyone to hear him rapping in French. "I flavorized it with how I flowed it."

Herbie ghosts would be borrowed and buried by Jay-Dee for Slum Village's 12 inch "Get Dis Money," banshees filtered through a pillow, the mattress, the box springs, the floor, heard half-asleep through a summer fan, drifting up through vents from that Dilla bottom. At a D'Angelo show that spring, it went through the rafters of Radio City Music Hall as the band (led by James Poyser and drummer Ahmir Thompson) translated Dilla's loop into a robed choir and just let the thing vamp from Herbie's mouth to vocoder to Dilla to Dilla's machine, then back to church—circuit closed. There but for the grace of band-pass filters.

+ + +

If Bob Mitchell caught Herbie Hancock's performance of "Rockit" at the 1984 Grammys, he would have seen a troupe of dancing robot pants. Robots smacking each other in the back of the head. Robots trying to get out of bed. Robots doing the Robot. Humans dressed as robots doing the Robot. Bob would've fired a beer can at the TV and retreated to a bitter night's sleep, chased to bed by Vincent Price's *Thriller* laugh as Michael Jackson won Album of the Year.

Hancock's vocoder played a minor role in this operation, a handful of gobbles to make the headset feel wanted. The torn rasp from Grandmixer D. St's turntable that night would be a different story—the word "fresh," a scrape of word, truthfully, more gasp than whisper and dry as mummy mail. The record itself was "Change the Beat," released on Celluloid Records in 1982 and credited to Beside and Fab Five Freddy, recently namedropped on Blondie's "Rapture." The word became noise and ultimately one of the most germinated sounds in all of music, its likeness propagated by the thousands, one of which was heard on a recent Verizon commercial, supporting data compression in cell phones. D. St, who later changed his name to DXT, influenced hordes of DJs and made a living from this susurration. "That's why I'm here, I guess," he says with a weary smile. "I was the first to cut that sound."

Rarely giving interviews, DXT was as much an inventor as Grandmaster Flash, known to use the vocoder with turntable pedal effects while playing the *Exorcist* theme, "Tubular Bells," on a synthesizer. (While most groups encouraged the crowd to throw zodiac signs, DXT's Infinity

Rappers chant about the synthesizer, letting the nerd into the party.) After the success of "Rockit," DXT says he kind of went "vocoder crazy," admitting to doing tons of "nutso underground mysterious demos" and running his turntables through the machine. "Whenever we'd use the turntables, rest assured you were gonna hear the vocoder somewhere around."

According to Bill Laswell, producer of "Change the Beat," "Fresh" was no more than an impulse at the end of the song, a ghost with a ravaged throat leaving a message at the beep—"This stuff is really fresh"— knowing that without it, the song really wasn't and so was released into the world as an afterthought. "Fresh" is the only thing remembered about "Change the Beat" (it's about a detective?) and so became its default title. Beside was the nom de whim of Anne Boyle, then the wife of French journalist Bernard Zekri who, along with Jean Karakos, started Celluloid Records, anticipating hip-hop as "the next wave." (An early release featured Archie Shepp and a sixteen-year-old singer from East Orange named Whitney Houston.) "It was a scene moving very fast," says Laswell. "You had Basquiat. Rammellzee, Dondi, Futura 2000. Phase 2, Bambaataa."

Habitually in the right place, Fab Five Freddy agreed to do the Beside 12 inch, in French, but with one stipulation: He didn't want anyone to hear it. "I didn't want to play myself. So we worked out the lyrics —it'd be a private detective with a hip-hop flavor. [Bernard] wrote out the story and then [Anne] would write it out in phonetics so I could say it in French. Once I got it then I would flavorize it with how I would flow it. Cool—as long as nobody hears this shit!"

"My hair spray was my record cleaner." Grandmixer D. St was the first DJ to scratch the word "fresh" from vocoded white noise, one of the most strepped rasps in all of music, more pile of dead leaves than speech. A frequent collaborator with Herbie Hancock, D. St. was also fluent in talk box.

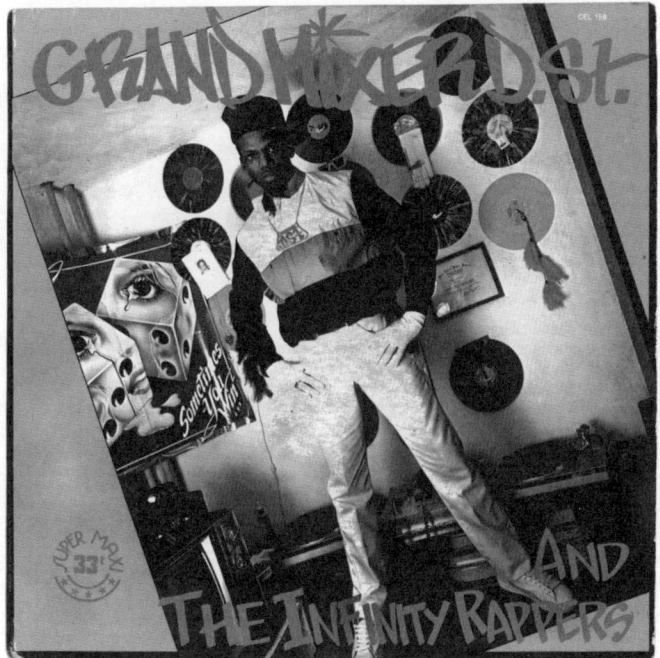

Freddy was then, in his words, "vocoderized." "It became like a sound unto itself, like an instrument or whatever. It was just a crazy ill sound. The most scratchable joint." The record Freddy wanted nobody to hear would be heard by everyone, pillaged by DJs and marketing guys, vocoded carbonation from some unvoiced hiss energy drink. Refreshing, soda speak.

The "Ah" took on a toothless life of its own. When backwards-masked, it became a reverse sigh, the "disappearance of being in the act of being." "That weird backward sound is just feedback," says DXT. "The vocoder is just waiting for sound. So any noise, any distortion, you can talk and it's gonna resonate those sounds. It's mutated by the scratch and it didn't have a melody when that part was being done."

According to Laswell, "Fresh" was the voice of his de facto manager, Roger Trilling, who happened to be in the studio in Red Hook, Brooklyn, that evening. "No one would believe it if you told them," says Laswell. "I don't think Freddy even knows that." Earlier that day, Trilling auditioned some Laswell tracks for Bruce Lundvall, then head of Elektra. "Bruce was about as country club as it gets," says Trilling. "A very Minnesota kind of character. He would put his feet up on his desk and his hands behind his head, and if he liked the song, he'd say, 'This stuff is really fresh.'" Later that night at the studio, delirious and ready to go home, Trilling would quote Lundvall through the vocoder. "[Bruce] didn't know that 'fresh' was in hip-hop currency at the time. I don't even think we thought of it that way, either." One of the most cloned hip-hop noises was but an imitation itself, mistaken for someone else in disguise, imitating the imitator on the A-side but replicated by machine. Just some late-night filler. A way out of the studio.

"I'd like to say I'm the master of all time and space," says Trilling. "But that's just me imitating the whitest of all record executives."

Roger Trilling, below, said the word "fresh" through the vocoder while imitating a white-bearded record exec from Minneapolis. Which kind of blew the author's mind.

On September 9, 1943, Bell Labs employee W.E. Widden circulated a classified memo describing the physical constants of a turntable used for SIGSALY. They were (a) moment of inertia, (b) running friction, (c) transient of speed characteristic, and (d) torque-versus-displacement characteristics both with and without feedback.

All of this translates to scratching records on hallucinogens if you're Luis Quintanilla, who spends most of his time as DJ Disk. When I last saw Disk, he had a grocery bag over his head with horns and called himself the Shigger Fragger, something he accidentally mumbled one day, unaware yet pleased to later discover he'd named himself after the act of grenading a superior officer. Disk and a DJ named Q-Bert spent most of 1995 on acid, trying to cut the vocoder sound from "Change the Beat"—fresh, ah, and every flashing color between—as fast as ball-trippingly possible. "It actually kind of worked," Disk says, on the phone from his house near Berkeley, California. "We take acid, drink OJ and eat Subway sandwiches. And then scratch at two hundred beats per minute. Non-stop for eighteen hours. Subways, two hundred bpms and acid. That's it."

Disk calls "Fresh" the perfect freak accident. In 1997, Bill Laswell would end up bequeathing the vocoder used on "Change the Beat" (a Roland SVC-350, Buy It Now! eBay! $1,200) to Disk. "It was my dream. I finally had the machine that made that sound. Who in their fucking mind would think I would ever have this? I freaked out."

Disk wouldn't let it out of his sight. That night, the vocoder sat with him and Laswell at a Korean barbecue restaurant in Manhattan. He held onto it through airport security at La Guardia. During the flight back to California, the vocoder sat next to him on the plane. Nobody was allowed to touch it. Yet the day we speak, Disk waits for the vocoder to be shipped from his studio in Los Angeles. This is the only time they've been separated. "It's on its way," he said. "I can't wait. I'm like a parent. All anxious."

The Shigger Fragger listens for the door. "*Where is it?*"

TO THE CRAZY AUNT FUTURE

During a 1983 performance at the Brooklyn Academy of Music (BAM), Laurie Anderson stood onstage running down tongues: English, Polish, Spanish, Yiddish, Swedish, lingering on the unvoiced sibilance, as if shushing a child. No vibration, just wind and teeth. A home phone towered on the screen behind her, its pinholes too threatening for conversation. Somewhere between English and Russian, the phone was replaced by a scattering of Bell telephone logos. Then a question mark haunted by the dim shape of an airliner. With Finnish, a language cheated out of sunlight, the screen goes black.

That same night, Anderson performed her 1981 hit "O Superman," the most un-Pop thing on the British pop charts, its beat literally spoken for by a syncopated *ah*, a hookless phone crying for its receiver (far more soothing than a nasally-inflamed busy signal). The index finger had moved from puckered lips to a naughty wag in a holding pattern, a gentle reprimand for a cookie thief.

Much of the song takes place on an answering machine imagined, a disembodied voice addressing a room that was less empty than just withholding presence. A future in waiting. The vocoder wasn't in space freaking freaks or doing rails at Studio 54. It was in your home when you weren't there a mother warning about the planes.

On the evening of September 11, 2001, Anderson performed "O Superman" in Chicago. The planes had come, the towers fell, and loved ones couldn't be reached. Speech compression was choked in cell phone panic. (The fear in "O Superman" would take flight in another Anderson track, "From the Air," in which the vocoder creates not speech but a loose *uh*-oh on the run.)

"O Superman" takes comfort's last stand as being the first vocoder song to just say, "Hi, Mom." Anderson would point out that the "hello" hand signal shares the same wave as "goodbye," especially to one not acquainted with earthbound oxymoron. It's up to the voice. During the performance at BAM, Anderson would use a vocoder for the William S. Burroughs tribute, "Language Is A Virus," anticipating information as a commodity. To be compressed. The screen behind Anderson posed a question that already had its answer. "Can you invade our scrambler system?"

Anderson's hit stands out in the vocoder space helmet party of the Eighties. Three of the most important vocoder songs are by women: "O Superman," Wendy Carlos' version of Beethoven's Ninth and Cher's monster hit "Believe." Cher's producers claimed the effect was a vocoder—a decoy to conceal Auto-Tune's identity. With its pitch/bitch issues, the vocoder's "frequency discriminator" (a Bell Labs term) failed to recognize higher female voices. The machine's errant pitch condition turned Eisenhower's wife, for example, into an octogeneric stranger. "Who is this, really?" Ike wondered, his question echoed in "O Superman."

DJ Disk, the Shigger Fragger, photographed in 2009 with the original Roland SVC-350 Vocoder used on "Change the Beat." Along with Mix Master Mike, Q-Bert, and Short Kut, Disk was part of the Invisibl Skratch Piklz.

As a high-ranking British officer leading a double life, Dr. Alan Turing had to inhabit more than one persona to get access to SIGSALY, Bell Labs' most veiled project, in a place where suppression was understood and embraced. During the war, Turing's ideas of artificial intelligence were supported by the military's prosthetic extensions, the fatal reach of its branches of technology, what "O Superman" called "the hand that takes." What Alan Turing would have made of these Laurie Andersons in a vocoder—arms, petrochemical, electronic and military—as if false security and comfort were indivisible. Let us embrace? Had Alan Turing not been driven to eat a cyanide apple in June 1954 after being forced into hormone therapy to "cure" his homosexuality, he may have heard "O Superman" on the radio in England, himself in need of a crazy aunt with a kind ear.

Laurie Anderson once told me her goal as an artist was to be able to jump out of her own life, the vocoder being just one way out. "I want to feel empathy and be able to go to another person's position. It's my goal as a person, as well." When we met for an interview in 2005, she was subaudible with a mug of tea, recovering from a cold. "With vocoders I like being able to be a little bit removed. It's like a French farce. You can be the governess, the crazy aunt. I didn't have to always be myself, which can be pretty tiring."

Four years prior, I'd spoken to Anderson on the phone, a cold call after receiving the number through a friend. She answered, or rather clicked over. "The vocoder software of today can't come anywhere close to the analog sound of the old ones. There's no comparison. No warmth." She politely said she was living in the future, thanks for calling. Two years later, she became the first and only vocoder to have an artist residency at NASA. Into the crazy aunt future she went.

Laurie Anderson's surprising vocoder hit "O Superman" reached Number 2 in England when it was released in 1981. Less of a mask than a vocoder duet, "O Superman" was driven by a voice sampling keyboard called the Emulator, another device of early electro, used by Art of Noise, Freeze, and Martin Dupont.

GRANDMIXER PORTABLE HAIL MACHINE

I'm terribly well known for my voice and I don't want to have that voice…because I'd still be Vincent Price.
— Vincent Price

In 1977, I sat in a small theater watching Vincent Price do an Oscar Wilde stage monologue called *Diversions and Delights*, a birthday surprise from my mother. (First stay-up-late memory: watching *House of Wax* with her when I was six, with Charles Bronson as a deaf mute in his first screen role.) Until then my only experience with Oscar Wilde was a third-grade production of "The Selfish Giant," in which I played a tree that sang Cat Stevens. Bored because Price wasn't onstage burning witches, I slept through what critics regarded as the performance of his career. Afterward I got an autograph and shook his gaunt hand. I couldn't speak, thinking of *The Tingler*, when Price injected a deaf mute—and himself—with LSD. So I made teeth and fled to the bathroom, sick with excitement. I missed the chance to ask about *The Abominable Dr. Phibes*, a film in which Price spoke through an artificial larynx that plugged into a golden phonograph on wheels. So many questions. What became of Phibes' Vincent Price mask? Did he normally leave his face hanging on the phone cradle next to his customized Wurlitzer with orange Lucite pipes? How did Phibes not short himself out when taking slugs of Moët through the speaker jack in his neck? Why didn't Phibes' robot jazz band, the Clockwork Wizards, defend his house with tommy guns (as originally planned)?

I showed Grandmixer DXT a photo of Phibes speaking through the phonograph, hoping for some insight. He leaned back and smiled. "Ahh…Dr. Phibes! We meet again." At age thirteen, DXT caught the Phibes double feature at the Melba Movie Theater in the Bronx. In 1929, Phibes had been nearly barbecued in a car crash while rushing to the hospital to see his wife Victoria dying on the operating table. Like any devoted husband, Phibes blames the surgical team, disinters the body and transfers it to a music conservatory in London. Mad with grief, Phibes consults the Bible for revenge, using the Curses of the Pharaohs to dispose of each doctor, each murder more ingenious and more absurd than the next. (One doctor gets iced by a Portable Hail Machine in the backseat of a Rolls-Royce.) According to writer John Parnum, Phibes' sense of humor was as "black as the insides of a buzzard's bowels." Tragedy and disfigurement become the motherless mothers of all invention.

"Can you make it say 'From Dr. Phibes'?" Vincent Price autograph, acquired in 1977 when the author saw his performance as Oscar Wilde in the Jeff Gay production of "Diversions and Delights."

Along with old-school vets like Afrika Bambaataa and Rammellzee, DXT regards Dr. Phibes as a vocoder prototype. Bambaataa goes so far as to call Vincent Price a vocoder. Rammellzee says Vincent Price "is good for the culture" while being impressed with Phibes' portable hail machine ("That's good engineering"). DXT was under the impression that Price was still alive:

Vincent Price, starring in the 1971 horror film *The Abominable Dr. Phibes*, speaks through a modulated artificial larynx plugged into a phonograph. "As you see and can hear, I have used my knowledge of music and acoustics to re-create my voice!" Bambaataa and D. St. consider Price/Phibes to be a vocoder prototype.

If Christopher Lee is out there still kicking and fighting Yoda…Phibes had the original voice box. He couldn't even move his mouth. It was really Dr. Vibes. But they figured it wouldn't work, so they had to make him Dr. Phibes. That old-fashioned turntable gimmick he had, with the headphone jack in his neck. He was already plugged in. He had MIDI before anybody. His whole shit was about sound. When he was planning, he was listening to music, thinking.

"I'll be goddamned if Vincent Price isn't listening to his larynx in stereo!" said one friend, who at age eleven broke into the Wurlitzer factory using a hatchet. "Dr. Phibes' organ skills were ridiculous," says DXT. "Man, Phibes was creative. I'm calling George and Bootsy now. We're going to do Dr. Phibes Redux!"

THE MAN WHO LEFT HIS FACE IN A CHAIR

Dr. Phibes wasn't the first vocoder prototype to leave his face lying around the house. In H.P. Lovecraft's 1931 story, "The Whisperer in Darkness," Henry Akeley uses a "mechanical utterance machine" to speak with unspeakable bat-squid entities while helping them shuttle human brains across the void. Stored in "fresh cylinders," the brains remain sentient during transit and have fantastic dreams. They converse with brains from other voids, in voices that Lovecraft describes as metallic, lifeless, inflectionless, expressionless and scraping and rattling with an impersonal precision that is utterly unforgettable.

Somehow resisting his instinct for extra-dimensional ick, Lovecraft compares cosmic brain shuttling to something far more domestic: taking a record over to a friend's house and playing it on their turntable. The records themselves sound like the "drone of some loathsome, gigantic insect ponderously shaped into articulate speech." Akeley arranges to have them sent overnight, perhaps the first next-day delivery of rare records to occur in an issue of *Weird Tales*. Leaving the narrator with a feeling of "blasphemous infinity," Akeley then disappears, leaving his face behind in an easy chair, his hands still clutching the armrest, his scraping whisper backwards fresh.

CHAPTER ELEVEN

EAT A PLANET AND GO ON TO THE NEXT ONE

Words (power of), I, 4, 9, 10; (familiar), I, 8; (transmutation of), II, 17; (machine),
II, 18; (the word "word"), II, 41; (gutted), III, 12

— Index, *A Night of Serious Drinking*, Rene Daumal

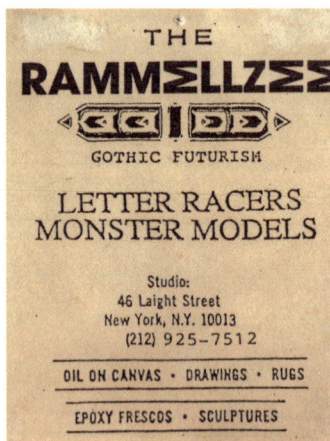

THE
RAMMELLZEE

GOTHIC FUTURISM

LETTER RACERS
MONSTER MODELS

Studio:
46 Laight Street
New York, N.Y. 10013
(212) 925-7512

OIL ON CANVAS · DRAWINGS · RUGS

EPOXY FRESCOS · SCULPTURES

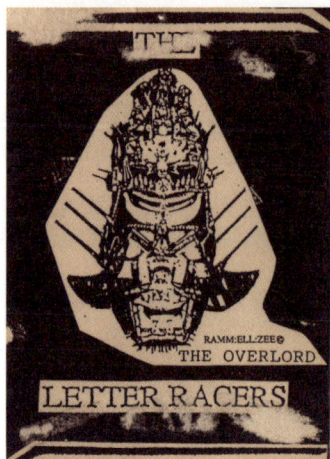

RAMM·ELL·ZEE©
THE OVERLORD

LETTER RACERS

His card. Rammellzee doesn't speak through the vocoder as much as try to suck out its soul, vibrating his diaphragm for chainsaw-tooth waves. This could have been what Sir David Brewster meant when he wrote about "the power of sound in throwing down buildings" back in 1839.

TAPPING THE TOAD HAT

Half a day into "Beat Bop," Rammellzee officially becomes Dr. Phibes long enough to screech "RPMs" for no apparent reason other than to taunt the record speed, his nose in jumper cables, the word "nose" itself to follow. He calls this style "nasal passaging." The passages themselves already had their fill of big-city excitement: aerosol fumes, markers, resins, industrial epoxies, subsurface toxins, Goofer Dust, cocaine, and unclaimed garbage.

The nose of Dr. Phibes merely took in flames and gasoline. Yet how Phibes rebuilt his sinuses was a junior concern for a film more interested in using the Pharoahs to discorporate the health care system. Rammellzee considers *The Abominable Dr. Phibes* to be a great teaching tool, a mixture of heartache, revenge and insanity that yielded brilliant inventions, including a toad helmet that crushed your skull by remote control. Rammel, the face mechanic, was impressed. "The screw-on toad helmet! How'd they do that? It's a prank. There is a way of doing that, but I would never like to have anybody do that to me. When they tighten dude up in the toad mask…you think I'd miss that? That's why I sit in this house!"

+ + +

Rammel calls home "the Battle Station," perhaps due to its ongoing conflicts with reality (astonishingly rent-free for over a decade) or maybe because visitors often find themselves under siege. If I'm not under siege at the Battle Station then I worry. Today I'm sitting on a back seat that appears to have been ejected from a minivan, surrounded by masks fashioned from garbage, grandmother jewelry and glue. A fleet of skateboards and suped-up Tonka chassis hangs from the ceiling, each an armored letter from Rammel's transuniversal alphabet, aeronautic structures of disfigured angles and points, encrypted and long estranged from the word itself, now helmed by plaster dragons, doll heads and dimetrodons, sprayed in gold. To my right is the quickest way out, a third-floor window overlooking the Holland Tunnel and the First Precinct. Outside, jackhammers blast the sidewalk, a rubble-rousing promise that New York will go on being New York, continuing its business of build

The Battle Station, with Garbage Gods in the mirror, photographed in 2003. (The giant eyeball is Chimer, the Vocal Wells God.) During my first visit to the Battle Station, I learned about the Mettroposttersizer, an electromagnetic planet-smasher that causes "The Wizard's Game of Pool," leaving the solar system in a "molten state." Also referred to as "another reason to drink beer."

Battle Station interior. Rammellzee's quantum armamentarium (left), with letter weapons hanging from ceiling. At right, a Morse Diver's helmet from 1923: 47 pounds, witness to barnacle scrubbing and narwhal jousting. (Bottom right) That tiger head was recently spotted on Rammellzee's rooftop barbecue grill, eating a purple smoke bomb.

and destroy, while my host talks church and vocoder and explains how the letter *Z* can cruise at seventy miles per hour.

PEOPLE DISAPPEAR, STAIRS DO NOT

When I first spoke with Rammellzee over the phone in 1992, he promised to cook me with Texas Pete Hot Sauce. Since then, he's called me a virus, accused me of being with the Defense Department, labeled me the worst goddamn critic he's ever met in his goddamn life, made jokes about my eyebrows, and offered to throw me from his rooftop. The photo he sent of himself was no less confusing than the good-natured threats. For one, he was nowhere to be found. Yet that's him, somewhere behind three, maybe four sets of fangs, encrypted inside an armored suit called the Gasholeer. It's as if Tetsuo's Iron Man had taken up costume jewelry and plastics and blown up a Hasbro factory. The Gasholeer weighed nearly 180 pounds and spouted flames from the wrist, heels, throat and, most impressively, two doll heads that depended from the waist, within alarming proximity of the Gasholeer's in-house stereo, which is powered by a 100-watt amp.

"The sound system consists of a Computator, which is a system of screws with wires," Rammel told writer Mark Dery. "These screws can be depressed when the keyboard gun is locked into it. The sound travels through the keyboard and screws, then through the Computator, then the belt, and on up to the four mid-range speakers…I also use an echo chamber, vocoder, and system of strobe lights. A coolant device keeps my head and chest at normal temperature."

In terms of data compression—coming from one who said, "Too much information in the room is not good policy"—Rammel should be wearing a vocoder on his person at all times. When asked if he had seen the new *Transformers* movie, he said, "I don't need to see it. I am it. Why do I need to see me?!"

+ + +

To get to the Battle Station, one could either chance the traffic flying out of the Holland Tunnel without the help of pedestrian cross mirrors

FLOWERS FOR ALGEBRA

Rammellzee's Gasholeer armor was co-designed by a toymaker named Gary Johnson. Gary was first spotted denuding a flower bed near the Holland Tunnel. "He was so white, he glowed," Rammel told me. "Just out there ripping up red flowers."

(Rammel had borrowed them for an album cover), or just take the caged crosswalk over the noise and to the firehouse-red building that sat next to Grabler Pipe Fitters. The four flights up to his loft on Laight Street seemed to favor murderous plunge over ascent, discouraging poachers as well as Afrika Bambaataa one time, apparently winded by the third flight where things took a crooked extra-dimensional lurch. Once I reached the top, Rammel confirmed this ("Yes, boss, the stairs do shrink") and then assured me they wouldn't disappear. "People disappear, stairs do not."

I was then led into some mad tea party situation, only the tea was beer, the hatter wore a do-rag and the dormouse was Swiss. A team of graffiti writers from Zurich sat hunched around a plank on cinder blocks while the TV behind them showed a ghoulish version of Tweety Bird chasing Sylvester around a laboratory. (The bird weighed at least 400 pounds; the cat was in pieces.) The Swiss had flown over to challenge Rammellzee to a drag race with flying letters on zip wires. There would be death metal, gambling and kitchen rocket science. Sketchbooks and trash talk were in full circulation. There was an argument about who was going to take whose letter, or in some cases already had, and which letters were armed with swiveling harpoons. The air was thick with weed and nonsense. It was barely noon.

Later that day I stood in the rain at the 1993 Rocksteady Zulu Nation Anniversary up at 98th and Amsterdam, near Harlem. A park full of rappers awaited the Brand Nubian reformation, despite the sky cracking up above them. The Cold Crush Brothers came with umbrellas. Brooklyn rapper O.C. performed "Time's Up" in a deluge. A crew of Japanese B-boys hydroplaned over tennis courts. Mikah 9 blistered the "Deep Cover" instrumental with a lightning-friendly plate in his head.

Going soggy, I tried to reason with the morning's events at the Battle Station. The ghoul bird, the guys from Zurich, and the letters tortured beyond recognition. I remembered at one point Rammel glaring across the table and muttering, "When you start thinking too hard, the culture dies." I looked away and found refuge under the plank, in a cinderblock hollow. There stood the silent witness: an empty bottle of Texas Pete.

ANT BANKS

When Brian Eno first arrived in New York, he saw a midget writing Chinese on a bank window and knew he was in the most wonderful medieval city in the world. During an interview with Todd Haynes at CUNY in 2005, Eno would say that technology had done little interesting for the human voice beyond the vocoder.

TRYING NOT TO GET KILLED

A publicist once told me a story about meeting Rammellzee at an art opening. "This guy said he liked a nice ankle. Then he introduced himself to me as an equation. I realized who it was and thought, 'Oh god. I know who you are, and I'm not ready to have this conversation. Not the equation conversation.'"

Not surprisingly, Rammellzee will not declassify his name. Real names are for next of kin. As an aerosol writer you want everyone to know your name, but nobody can know who you really are. Rammellzee's father was a transit detective, so home was no safer than sneaking around beneath the city at night, especially when the yard keys went missing. "I got home covered in paint and soot and my father would beat my ass!" He caught a memorable whupping the morning he came in from the Mott Avenue Station, last stop on the A in Queens, where he'd written "EG"— Evolution Griller, his first tag using a Zippo flip-top marker. "In school, we'd convert those old lighters into markers. We'd slice erasers into really thin strips, take the Zippo out, put the strips in and flood the motherfuckers with purple super-marker ink." Pretty resourceful, using an eraser to create an identity that your own MTA kin calls defacement.

"Nobody in my family likes what I do. [His brother is a tank repairman in Iraq.] They damn sure don't understand how I got to New York and how I got to stay, and how I got to go overseas and how I got to meet people like Bambaataa, Dondi and Kurtis Blow. They don't understand that. They hear them. They understand them. But they don't understand me."

Born in 1960, Rammel had a fairly regular childhood growing up on the eleventh floor of Carlton Manor Projects in Far Rockaway. "I don't know what I was doing. Eating bugs, chasing a basketball, tripping over chains, running around in the streets trying not to get killed." He stubbed his toe on a cement turtle, threw eggs at buses, pissed in Dixie Cups and dropped them on kids below. He watched *Dark Shadows* with his mother. He played what he called "Hide and Go Seek and Beat Your Ass" and disappeared under a church. "You come out of the basement pipes and the trees and them sons of bitches started a whole new game. And they'd still beat your ass! Kids just want to hurt things."

A FAN'S NOTES

Three-year-old sings into electric fan to alter voice, Los Angeles, 1974.

Rammel guesses he was around eight when he first spoke into an electric fan and had his voice returned to him four years deeper from the future, laughing, a prolonged "ah" neatly clipped into a pulse of "ha," somewhere between "O Superman" and Three 6 Mafia's "Stay Fly." Engineers call it "vortical shredding." Talking to fans is as much a part of growing up as interrogating ants with a magnifying glass. A notary public from Apex, North Carolina, used to throw Little Orphan Annie into her fan, making "Tomorrow" sound like Ethel Merman on crystal meth. ("Crystal Methylmerman," she said.) A condenser fan analyst at Delphi-Harrison Thermal Systems claims to have spoken to rare helicopters. Another, a vintage-poster embalmer, got into fans because she wanted to talk like Cookie Puss, an ice cream cake from outer space.

DENTAL PLAN OF THE UNSTOPPABLE

I once tried holding a conversation with Rammel's fan—a GE Blizzard Oscillator—and discovered not a vocoder effect but a chronic dental condition called bruxism. My jaw was popping, a side effect from clenching my teeth while asleep. According to my dentist, my teeth had been grinding away the day's stress through my dreams, one of which included Rammellzee hot-wiring my dad's Honda and systematically doughnutting all the yards in Mecklenberg County, thwacking mailboxes with a tennis racquet while my mother sat in the front seat, kind of bored. "It's like hailing Helen Keller a cab and dying in it," she said. The dentist prescribed a mouth guard.

My host, it turns out, is qualified to build the mouth guard himself. At fifteen—sometime before a foiled robbery attempt on a chemical bank, yet after proposing to City Hall that he could stop graffiti by camouflaging the transit system—Rammellzee studied to be a dental technician. While enrolled at the Clara Barton School for Health Professionals in Brooklyn, he learned to build molds and dentures while mingling with aspiring hygienists. "We used the teeth of dead people to practice," he says. "Calcium is one of the hardest things you got. The teeth are the last to go."

He tells me this while rummaging through the teeth drawer, which also holds do-rags and mix tapes. Scraps of cloth, silk and acrylic whisper through the air, followed by a Ziploc bag full of watches and a cassette of Bambaataa DJing somewhere in Europe in 1982. "I know those goddamn teeth are in here somewhere!"

A decay enthusiast, Rammellzee would share a subway tunnel with some of New York's oldest—and most infamous—dental remains in 1978, when a graffiti vet named Iz Da Wiz took him under the old Chambers Street station near City Hall. Once an African graveyard dating back two centuries, the site wouldn't officially be disinterred until 1991, during a gas pipe repair near the Tweed Courthouse. INK 176, a graffiti writer who joined them, remembers rumors of skeletons being excavated as early as the mid-Seventies. "Chambers Street has so many layers of train stations underneath," says INK. "They've got 'em hiding. I said, 'It's going to be spooky down here with a bunch of ghosts and shit.' Rammel always wandered off."

Rammellzee, then just an apprentice, had never been to the Chambers Street ghost yards. "Iz was the only person who had the keys," he says. "The old keys. The snake line was supposed to be there. The trains were sleeping. There's an inconspicuous staircase and you walk down that and down the track. Tunnels below the tunnels. We got up on top of the trains and looked up at coffins, arms hanging from the ceiling. Skulls. It was a graveyard for black people buried from slavery. There's your next monster picture." One can see why he started referring to himself as a Gothic Futurist, staring into empty tunnels and hollow sockets, or why he titled a painting "Floor Plan of the Unstoppable," a steel train plowing through the ossified past, encrypting the memory of New Amsterdam's first builders, stone to the bone, while above City Hall gargoyles stretched their shadows and watched.

On the catalog cover for an exhibition at the Galleria Lidia Carrieri in Rome, held in 1986, is a photo of the gargoyle himself, hunched in the archway of a church wearing a ski hat and kung fu slippers, only two pairs of lizard glasses on his forehead. "Gothic makes sense," Rammel would tell me. "Gothic makes debt. Gothic makes death—if you know math and structure. Gothic is the point of reference."

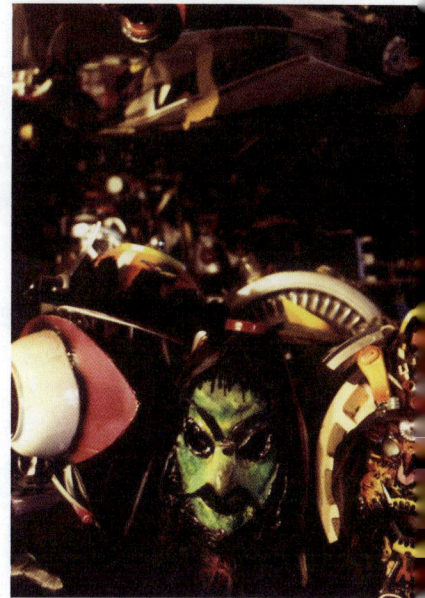

A tactical model of Barshaw Gangstarr, "the dragon duck" (also one of the Garbage Gods). His hands are reminiscent of Gary "Big Hands" Johnson of the San Diego Chargers (1975-84).

BEER IS MATH

The Gothic future lives in Walter M. Miller, Jr.'s 1959 science fiction classic *A Canticle for Leibowitz*, a book with Rammellzee's interests at heart: monks, bygone ciphers and the apocalypse. In 3124, history has been deleted by a nuclear holocaust. Conducting their own vocoded analysis and synthesis, monks try to reconstruct a lost tongue in the basement of a desert abbey in Utah. A Czechoslovakian play about robots is mistaken as evidence that man first showed up at the beginning of the twentieth century. The numbers fare no better than the word. Leibowitz, the nuclear physicist, is sainted, and the monks are doomed to repeat the aftermath in a blind flashback. The end of the word. Ever the suffix man, Rammellzee might call this "friction formation of electromagnetic knowledge." He claims, "Remanipulated strictly from a subject Equation Formation Latin, [it] warns any misuse without the representation and reformation of the alphabet structure formator will lead you into apocalyptic wars."

Is there safety in integers? Rammellzee:

> The integer is a nation by itself. The function leads you on into the future, without it you have no control. To wipe out a language and make a new one is hard work. The hours are long. The idea is to read this stuff, for humans to have something to read, not just blow them away. We have our history. We know what we've done to ourselves. Now we want to know how much time we have so we can make sure we can live past ourselves. You have to know we built these words, monks, church, whatever you want to deal with. Whatever gavel you want, first bet, last bet— we make them.

"I'm a gargoyle in argyle socks." Rammellzee, squatting in a church doorway in Rome, 1986, favoring Kung Fu slippers over his red Sebago's painted silver. Cover for his exhibit catalog from Galleria Lidia Carrieri, Rome. The equation is Ramm x's Ocean=Elevation. (Sigmas=Summation Operator.)

While these conversations often end up in apocalypse and malt liquor through a straw, one gets the feeling that my host had been maimed by a spelling bee at an early age, fueling a bitter distrust of Old English and the Overstructure—finished, done or just no more. "I don't drink for nothing," he grumbles. "I'm scared too. Man drinks for reason. Fear is math. It goes further and further and faster and faster. Mathematics dictates to all of us. One day, a physicist will hit us so bad with equations. Never listen to poets who are astrophysicists. You may not like what you find."

VOLTRON'S ELBOW

Rammellzee found it safer to listen for garbage trucks. Like the monks of St. Leibowitz, he has been refiguring language from the leftovers of an apocalyptic wasteland: the curbs of Chinatown in Manhattan, before the morning trash pickup. "I still have a lot of garbage. It's a lot harder to find garbage these days. From bums to rich people to rich bums, everybody wants to keep things now." In "Beat Bop," Rammel may have taken K-Rob's moralizing—"You may as well work at the sanitation"— as a challenge, fashioning indecipherable letters from unwanted trinkets, Tonka mini-monster wheels, doorknobs, a fake candle stolen from the chandelier of an Italian restaurant, nozzles, Voltron's elbow. These are his building blocks, his broken language. Something from nothing.

He hands me half a dragon and says it's part of the letter *A*. A curve of plastic, once an electric fan guard, serves as a *K* or an *R*. Not sure. It's a tough read. "Why throw it out?" he asks, admiring a loose doll head, a fake lash wink to automatons. "Don't it look good?" Despite the recent dearth of yo-yos (his favorite), the garbage has been good to Rammel. He calls himself "the Garbage God." One man's rubbish is another man's theory. A quantum crackpot on a recycling binge? Re-fuse? Rammel dubbed his letter systems "Ikonoklast Panzerism," symbol destroyer, inspired by Rommel, the German tank general who greeted the desert sunrise with a blinding wall of engine noise, his larynx plugged into his radio, while in a basement in Algiers, the vocoder guarded the spoken letter from code-breakers so Winston Churchill could tell his spy to shut up and could cry like James Brown: "Good God!"

In Walter M. Miller's sci-fi classic *Canticle for Leibowitz*, monks in the year 3124 try to reconstruct speech that perished in a nuclear holocaust. (The word "lizard" means *fallout*.) "To wipe out a language and make a new one is hard work," says Rammellzee. "The hours are long."

THAT WOULD BE A TANK

"Rammellzee armed the letter so it could defend itself, actually," Dondi would explain, when the late graffiti legend was interviewed by *Style Wars* director Henry Chalfant. "He says the Christians put a Catholic symbol on the letter and the only way to destroy a symbol is with a symbol." Dondi points out the hinges and barbed missiles on Rammel's armored *Z*. "This would be a tank."

Al Diaz first met Rammel in Jean-Michel Basquiat's loft on Crosby Street. "There were all these graffiti dust-head parasites satelliting around Jean. But Rammel—he had this theory about Ikonoklast Panzerism. He was sort of a delusional paranoid but he was micro. He had the details—it's all figured out."

"We wrote on the fastest-moving, biggest goddamn underground gallery in the world," Rammel told me back in 1993. "The idea was to make the letter move without the train. In order for hell to freeze over the letters must race." I ask what letters he prefers and he immediately says the *s* and the *R*. "The *R* can mutate easily. It can become a *K* or *B*. The *S* can become an *L*, and, boy you better be good at math to do that. There are no pictograms here. What I draw and design is architecturally built. And will fly. I race for thunder."

In 1988, long after the trains had been sent to the ghost yards for an acid bath, Rammel would cite Dondi's Sabbath masterpiece, "Children of the Grave," in an an eight-minute screed called "Lecture." That's Rammel on the cover, a pile-up of bee-stung Geordi La Forge shades on his brow, some without lenses. Released on Island Records, *Missionaries Moving* may have sold enough copies to replace the wicker chair torn up for the cover art. Back in high school, I showed this to some friends—"He's the one wearing traffic mirrors on his pants"—and played them "Lecture." While we decided who was going to steal beer that night, Rammel talked about a voice that shot lasers in the catacombs and called the vocoder a "Tower of Panzerism."

For "Lecture," Gettovetts producer Bill Laswell looped a recording of the Tokyo Bullet Express. Podium became platform and Rammel arrived

Part of "Tower of the Apparitors," for "Theater of War's Linguistics" (left). Unfinished letter racer (right), possibly *S*, with drag coefficient still at large. Traxx (bottom right), "bounty hunter of diction mutants," equipped with "brain broiler."

with a purple suitcase full of watches he designed at the Fashion Institute of Technology (attended, briefly), none of which could tell time from a hole in a worm. (One watch has a nine-millimeter slug expended into its face.) The beat chugs off, vanishing into a horn blurring three stops away, just before he says, "Sneeze with me." That's "Lecture." Definitely not a first-date song, too medieval for the Golden Age of Rap, and curtains for the A&R department of Island Records.

"Rammel did that in one take without anything written down," says Laswell. "It's powerful if you hear it. It's coming from the other side. I have no idea what he's saying and I'm quite sure he doesn't either. But that's irrelevant. But the vocoder is way beyond music. That's the hippest take on the vocoder, I guess. Hippest, esoteric, unexplainable. The monks are in there. That's an important thing."

Gyume Tibetan monks vibrate at 60 hertz, at *mdzo* levels, a yak low trapped inside a bazooka amp. The technique is *ngarskad*, "roaring voice of the god of death." Glottologists know the vibrating gravel as the "vocal fry," those parched good-morning croaks, scroll-dry. The vocal fry finds an electronic parable in the artificial larynx used by Pope John Paul II after his tracheotomy, a device originally innovated by Homer Dudley, who believed his vocoder emulated chanting monks.

Real vocoder music is to subliminalize or consciously control or war," says Rammel, vocal flaps no less cooked. "When I use it, I launch missiles. They want to dance and entertain. I want to war. I'm in the church or the catacomb; these guys are onstage. I'm in a basement; they're on a stage."

Gettovetts, *Missionaries Moving* (1988, Island Records). Rammellzee with Shock Dell and Delta II. This album tanked. Includes the vocoder song "Go Down! Now Take Your Balls!" The traffic mirrors were acquired from a crosswalk near the NYPD's First Precinct.

THE GANGSTER DUCK DOES VIENNA

In 1984, Rammel first encountered the vocoder in a basement in Vienna, rapping about the price of art in a city where the Nazis acquired it for free. According to Rammel, the equipment—a Roland SVC vocoder and DMX drum machine—had been stolen as well. With him was Phase 2, a spray-can art icon who invented bubble letters. "Phase is sittin' in the corner laughin' at me and I went ahead and played that shit. He didn't even know I was an MC at that time."

When I asked what it sounded like, he said, "Keyboards that sounded like a fan playing backwards. You push your voice out or you suck in. Sucking it in was better because it gave more power. Instead of the mic projecting, you was the one projecting, sucking the energy out of it. This gave a very deep sound. When you want to push out, you want to go castrated tenor."

With Phase doodling cave echo on the DMX, Rammel talked about "crimes of the gods." "This is a subway war. I kept saying, 'We will see. We will see.' Talking about how much art would sell. Because we were there for art, not really for music. And Phase was talkin' a lot of shit so I talk some shit back." He named the track "Gangster Chronicles." Under headphones, the vocoder seems to be chasing him around that basement, just half a quack of a shadow behind. There's a nod to the year 4000, something about food-chain rhythms, and a "devil bomb after dark"?

"It's supposed to [sound like a bunch of different voices]. One finger is ten people. Five fingers gave you an orchestra. The echo causes it to be catacombic, church-like. It's hard to be eighty-eight people."

TIME-SUSTAINED DIAPHRAGM

I came here to jam with my diaphragm.
— Class A Felony

Rammellzee's feelings about the vocoder run gut-deep. "It's a very special weapon. Not too many people can take it. You have to have the discipline to enjoy yourself. If you don't enjoy yourself against that weapon then that weapon will attack you and ensure that you are hurt. It can hurt you in your bones, in your joints and muscles. You have to push, even though you're breathing in. It's like you're pumping an engine and it's been in there cookin', fireplace debris and shit. To power such a machine is to become the weapon yourself. Lots of people don't want to be weapons. But I've got the guts." In spring 2003, in lower Manhattan's Harvest Studios, Rammellzee nearly lost his guts to the vocoder, rattling his diaphragm so hard he vomited bile in the hallway. He called the song "Pogo" and the vocoder "the gun and the gut." "That was upsetting," he says. "That was a little too deep. But the beat called for it. I felt good afterwards. The garbage damn sure came up. Time-sustained diaphragm. Garbage up, garbage out. Eat a planet and go on to the next one."

You have to admire the man's dedication. "You have to hold the note," he follows, "and know how to vibrate. That's some sore-throat shit. And if you don't like sore throats, get out of the game. Get out of the vocoder. If you want to keep your voice, suck in half the time. You're a machine-man and that is vibration material. It's all work."

QUAQUALUNG LIVES

You don't have to vibrate yourself inside out to get a decent vocoder sound, but I'm not going to argue with someone who installed flamethrowers in his sneakers. Apparently Rammellzee learned to punish his diaphragm like a monk while working for his uncle at Marine Moisture Control (MMC). Once a supplier of battleship decks during World War II, MMC now specializes in petrochemical hazard removal and transport. According to Rammel, he was dispatched to an oil rig in the Gulf, where he repaired fissures in pipes that dispensed oxygen to pressurized rooms beneath the coast.

As a diver, he became acquainted with the bends, the narcosis, euphoria and bad judgment caused by decompression. This can be avoided by inhaling an elixir of oxygen and helium, which has less density than air. Pushing against a gas of low density, vocal cords encounter less resistance and vibrate more rapidly, in higher frequencies. Bell Labs' Manfred Schroeder calls it "restoration of the Donald Duck." While at Marine Moisture Control, Rammel ingested his share of the noble gas, cartooning his pitch while scrubbing barnacles and sea slugs, admiring the "crazy stuff floating by." Yet he learned the Gangster Duck style not from frogman helium but Jahmel, a rapper he'd met at a Far Rockaway Police Athletic League center, where they would change voices and get-ups to trick the cops. ("I owe my life on the mic to that dude.")

I'm both fascinated and baffled by the idea of this guy spending time beneath the sea. Rammellzee has always been on good terms with water, having grown up near Far Rockaway Beach, where he once hauled some knucklehead kids out of the rip tide, victims of "baloney sandwich cramps." Yet it's sometimes difficult to separate the man from the morphology, if not his imagination—as if sub-aquatic compression were a side effect of trying to go sober, surviving the excess of being an international downtown gallery star in the Eighties. This could be a salvage operation.

Rammel says his teeth chatter and that his eyes still hurt. He is often guarded about his previous life as a diver, though occasionally I'll get a message saying, "Catch me now, before I go back underwater." Or he'll just redact the conversation altogether: "Off record! Off shore!"

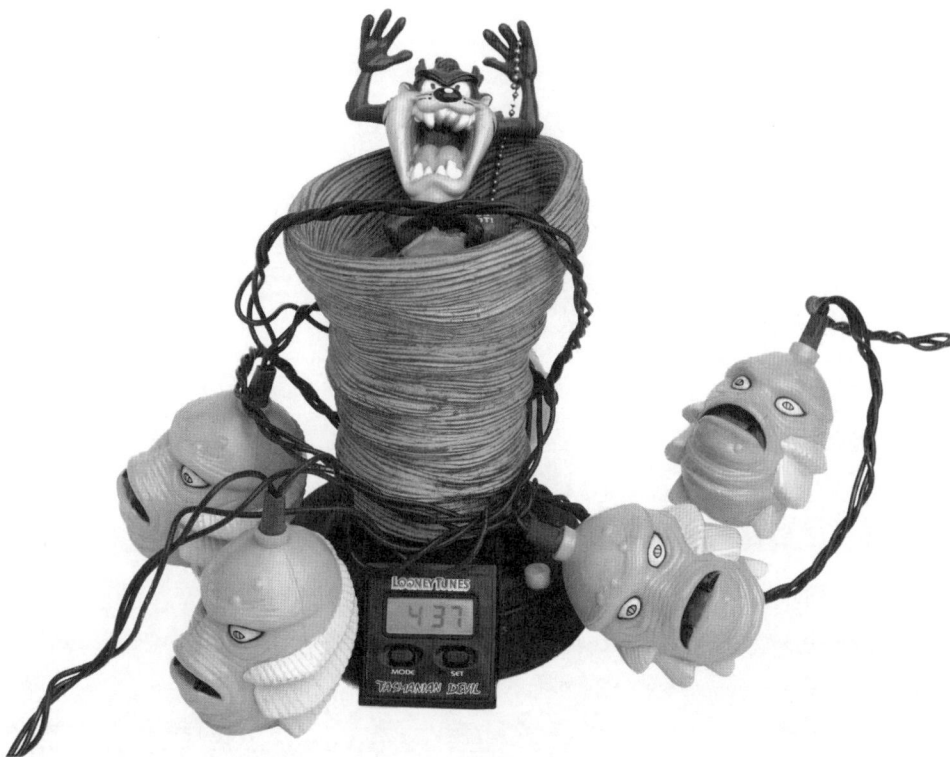

GEORGE AND BOOTSY AT THE BATTLE STATION

It's good to bring offerings when visiting Rammellzee. A joint, a beer, an idea, a Willie Stargell autograph, my mother's Tasmanian Devil alarm clock. Something to take the edge off. One Halloween, I brought a Gill Man head—seasick green and with lagoon dimples. Rammel looked at it ("Hello, friend!") and planted it in the fulcrum of a nautical steering wheel, in the corner near the toy train with the blue head of Cookie Monster poking from its window.

Another time, I sacrificed my friend Matt, an authority on zombies and compost, who grew up blowing away anthills with shotguns. Matt and Rammellzee would discuss hot glue guns over arugula and cans of

Author's Tasmanian Devil alarm clock and *Creature From the Black Lagoon* light set. The Gill Man is one of the best Florida exports next to Speakerhead's 1989 album *Booty Shakin' Breakout*.

"Rammellzee is a special piece of magic galaxy dust," said Bootsy Collins. (Left to Right) Rammellzee, George Clinton, Bootsy Collins. Photographed at the Battle Station, circa 1987. (Courtesy Rammellzee)

Natural Ice. When it came to evacuation procedures in the face of industrial adhesives, they agreed that riding a bicycle out the window was best, though Rammel knew he wouldn't make the moon. ("I got rocks in my ass like a dinosaur!") After reaching an impasse about which came first, the word or the void, they thumb-wrestled to Black Sabbath. *Everyone's happy when the wizard walks by.* "I always take people up there," says Bill Laswell. "Anybody I meet who may be able to influence or support Rammellzee. I took Killah Priest there recently. They connected, but it blew him out. Priest was gone."

One of Laswell's better feats of social engineering was bringing Bootsy Collins and George Clinton to the Battle Station. "I told George I was taking him to meet someone deeper than he was. George didn't know who he was. Rammel had on the [Gasholeer] suit because it was a big deal. He shot the rockets. As soon as George walked inside he goes 'Voop!' and the rocket fell on the ground ('hssssst!') and shot into Rammellzee's kitchen and blew up. George looked into the kitchen and was just like, 'My man!'" "Rammellzee is on purpose," Bootsy Collins would tell me. "He is a special piece of magic galaxy dust. The Magic Scripulator."

"I was demonstrating pyrotechnics off the wrist," says Rammel. "I wanted flames and all I got was smoke. Very upsetting. They're exciting people. They kept me up late." In 1988, the year Jean-Michel Basquiat died of a heroin overdose, Rammellzee met William S. Burroughs in Belgium. The exterminator was curious after reading a Rammellzee screed from Rotterdam's prestigious Museum Boijmans Van Beuningen, which included works by Dondi, Futura 2000, SEEN, Lee Quinones and Zephyr: "Hyperbola to parabola to death. Just like a seashell. Hmm. Motion is bad. It's five on a dime, can you spin it, raise it to nine? I am a gargoyle in argyle socks. Yes, I love syntax because it's natural, because it floats. It's like a mountain turning into a molehill. It has to rain for thousands and thousands of years. What is old is old. What is new is very rare." "They finally met in Belgium," says Laswell, who arranged it. "I think Rammellzee was bumming pot off of him and [Burroughs] said something like, 'How does it feel to be dead and still here?' It was like an incredible, minimal exchange." According to Rammel, they talked about where the species was going. "You meet brilliant people briefly," Rammel grumbles. "And all we wanted to do was smoke marijuana."

RIP CORD REX

We are the centuries. We are the chin-choppers and the golly-whoppers, and soon we shall discuss the amputation of your head. We are your singing garbage men...chanting rhymes that some think odd.
— Walter M. Miller, Jr., *A Canticle for Leibowi*

"I can put the mask on and I don't have to worry about it being a song sung by a crazy guy, or some girl, or a lizard or some welder, a duck, a race driver, an eraser." The first mask he built, called the Rammellzee, has as many jaws as it does sunglasses, a mad welder's realization of a sawtoothed speech wave. Two jaws protract like H.R. Giger's Alien. Another has four-sided fangs, a starfish wearing a retainer. Next jaw: comb teeth. The lowest jaw has a goatee bristling with spikes. It detaches into a fist of iron knuckles, sanctioned by some medieval wrestling federation. The leather handle is cut from boxing headgear. Rammel has trouble reattaching it. The glue is parched. "Everything is falling apart," he says. "But I like the dust. The dust is gothic, word."

Many things end in "word" around here. Word—hip-hop's affirmation of truth. The word here is "stound": a moment in time, also a sharp pain and a thrill. Stound is nearly impossible to use. In print, it's a typo. To the ear, it's amazement misheard. "What a great word," Laurie Anderson would tell me. "Everything is in that word. When you see a word in a film you don't say it. It comes to your eye in such a different way if you turn off the sound. It's a silent literary world. By sound, the word 'stound' is totally different from seeing it."

If word is bond, then Rammellzee is sniffing the glue that holds it together. The smell is the truth. Sometimes the truth stinks. Sometimes you can't be in the same room with the truth. The neighbors complain. The fire department arrives and issues fines, glue fines. Still, the glue must go on—just about everything, it turns out.

One mask has a strand of dice drooling from its mouth. Another has a race track for a hat, saturnizing his head. Somewhere, an umbrella is missing its nose, a hair clip goes hungry and a chest of drawers walks around blind. A bicycle seat painted white is a goat's face. Or it looks like a goat's face. You have to be careful around here. Start looking into things and things start shooting back. A stereo speaker just tries to fit in, its woofer crying for help.

All bets are on. In a world where golf tees are incisors, where Garbler Pipe Fitters could be a front for bootleg synthetic larynges, and men can be equations, word can

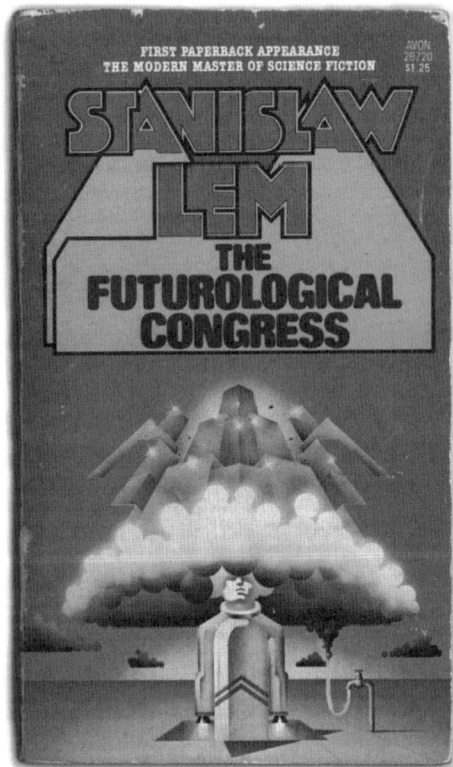

FIRST PAPERBACK APPEARANCE
THE MODERN MASTER OF SCIENCE FICTION

AVON
28720
$1.25

STANISLAW LEM

THE FUTUROLOGICAL CONGRESS

be whatever. "Wordplay is a gamble," says whatever's arch-enemy. "You think I ain't playing with you right now. I am surgical with you. I will make sure everything counts."

+ + +

I hear the clatter of loose cassettes behind me. Rammel is now raiding an old trunk in his fireplace, looking for the "F-4000." "I got that tape somewhere! I just wanted to play the vocoder because it's a beautiful machine given to civilians. I have mythology. Let me do drag race stories. This is inside jets." He turns from the fireplace. "A-ha! I bet the F-4000 is in there!"

He is pointing at Rip Cord Rex, a mask with a tapedeck built into the top of his skull. Once equipped with "Syncro Dubbing," the tapedeck is now part of a spare mouth. The silver nitrous tubes are eyebrows. I try the Cushion Eject, hoping that Rip Cord Rex's brain will quietly release the "F-4000." Instead I find a Polaroid of Rip Cord Rex in a Kimono, wielding an orange leafblower under a strobe light. I am told that he likes to steal engines.

DAMN YOU, IMPERSONAL FORCE

I'm a face carpenter.
— Mobb Deep (misheard)

During my last trip to the Battle Station, the building was in scaffolds and slated for demolition. My host was uncharacteristically somber. "They're going to gut it," he says. "It will be empty—a tooth with a cavity." After twenty-two years, Rammellzee, Rip Cord Rex and all hell else will have to ship out. He's being accused of squatting but calls it "hop-scotching" which sounds better. When I ask how long he's got, he says, "Later... Later we'll find out what later is. I don't know what later is." For now he's relocating to an apartment in Battery Park City, sharing a building with New York City Police Chief Raymond Kelly on the western tip of Manhattan, on a centuries-old plot of garbage and landfill. He'll have access to 800 rich people's trash and has already been through most of it.

Outside his window, jackhammers continue arguing with concrete. Polyethylene pipes are stacked on the sidewalk next to a trench, waist deep. "They're building some big drainage system out there and they're putting up these phony-ass poles. They're ruining my view." Rammellzee closes the window. "I'm going to hate leaving this place. But the dust stays."

The Morse diver's helmet is acting pretty stoic about the whole thing. Rammel thumbs back to the masks and the wooden trunks on wheels where most of his arsenal—the entire alphabet—is now packed. "Don't let that motherfucker come to life. The Battle Station is closing. I'm packed in boxes." (Quick to clarify.) "Coffins."

One assumes there's a vocoder in one of those coffins. "You don't worry about vocoder sounds. If one of your vocal cords went out, we'll bring you a new throat. We don't want to pack you away. These things are going to come to pass. We have no sense of passion for you to stay the way you are. You will breathe spray paint. You will die under the water. You will know your letters are going to race when they don't belong to you. You will listen to Rammellzee. You will do as you're told or you will be crushed."

He picks up the tulip fly-swatter.

"I have to go back underwater. We're turning buildings into spaceships but we're not telling you."

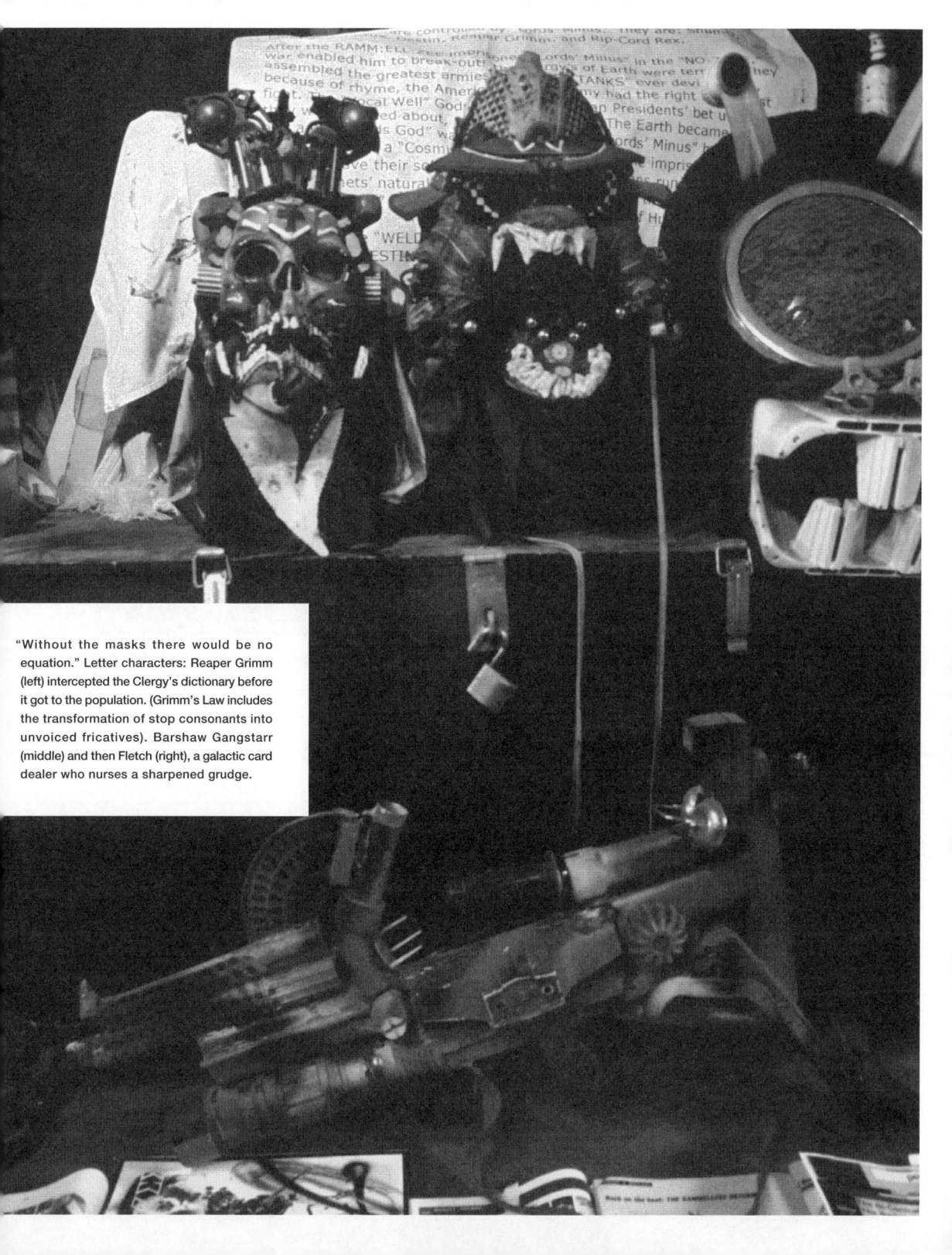

"Without the masks there would be no equation." Letter characters: Reaper Grimm (left) intercepted the Clergy's dictionary before it got to the population. (Grimm's Law includes the transformation of stop consonants into unvoiced fricatives). Barshaw Gangstarr (middle) and then Fletch (right), a galactic card dealer who nurses a sharpened grudge.

CHAPTER TWELVE

DECOMPRESSION

They say amazing things to the tune of their time has come.

— David Allen, in the car, Concord, Massachusetts

CROSSTALK CAN SNEAK

Ralph Miller says the letter is a noise, not a sound. I first met the retired crypto-engineer on March 20, 2003, the morning after "Shock and Awe." According to CNN, the desert is green and the US has been spitting Tomahawk missiles into Iraq for the past twenty-four hours. Ralph is profoundly opposed to the war. His wife, Peggy, sits on the couch with a newspaper folded in her lap, the news on mute. "The most precise machine of destruction in history" moves in silence. Ralph's not sure why we're in Iraq nor why I'm in his apartment in a retirement community in Concord, Massachusetts, asking about the vocoder. Any confusion on his part has less to do with being 96 than my showing him a photo of Michael Jonzun wearing an orange space suit. "I guess they use the vocoder for entertainment now," he shrugs. "That's funny business."

To him, "Pack Jam" would be speech compression. "The vocoder is your mouth," he'd once told me. Having spent World War II correcting pitch malfunctions for SIGSALY, Ralph Miller has, in a sense, heard it all before. He cannot be expected to cotton to the T-Pain sound. Auto-Tune's philandering pitch scale might generate nightmares of headless Eisenhower chipmunks singing. Generals can sound like robots; just keep the vermin out of it.

At the end of the war, Ralph designed a mobile eight-channel vocoder version of SIGSALY (called "Junior X") that fit inside a van, but was never deployed. By the early Fifties, Ralph was carrying his underwear in a steel briefcase and periodically disappearing down to Guantanamo Bay to work on acoustical surveillance for nuclear submarines. Later, he returned to Washington and exorcised his pitch demons at an anniversary party for Alexander Graham Bell. "I got up in front of Constitution Hall and sang 'Mary Had a Little Lamb' through the vocoder—in three different pitches. I went from a woman's soprano to a male tenor and bass. Believe it or not, I'm no singer." Ralph's wife snorts. "I heard about it the morning after. Of course he'd come home and I'd hear something about it."

We finish up in the dining hall downstairs, which is ghost-chaired this late in the day. A woman in the corner staring into her soup. Shadows eavesdrop on the suggestion of afternoon sun. Ralph works on the chicken, chuckling about the vocoder's insubordinate pitch. His wife has probably had enough of this by now. It's time for me to catch the train back anyway. Before leaving, I shake Ralph's hand and thank him for his time. "Something to remember," he says. "Crosstalk can sneak in between the pulse."

DR. PHIBES GOES RECORD SHOPPING

A week after my first visit with Ralph Miller, I'm back at Grandmixer DXT's apartment up in Harlem. More muted war highlights in green darkness. More precision bombing, more fuzzy resolution. We'd been talking about John Lindh, the "American Taliban" who defected from California to Afghanistan in 2001. As every mouse-click from Lindh's past came under scrutiny, it was revealed that he'd conducted an online Talk Box inquiry in 1997. Lindh's post read:

Can anybody tell me exactly what a talk box is, how it works, and how it's different from a vocoder? I've heard that they're dangerous in some way, but I'm willing to risk bodily harm in order to get my voice to sound like Roger Troutman.

We consider the acoustic possibilities of talk-boxing a call to prayer from a cave in the Hindu Kush Mountains.

"Pretty bugged, huh?" says DXT.

DXT then does an impression of Dr. Phibes shopping for Talk Box records. "You know, they caught Phibes in the record store buying Billy Preston records." He starts talking through his nose: "Doooo youeewwwe haaaave Billllly Pwwwweeston? TONNNNTO's Exxxpannndinnng Heeead Band? Howww aboouut Rrrroger Trrrroutmannnnn? Morrrre Boouunce to theee Ooouunce." (Roger Troutman, wherever you are, we tip our toad helmets to you.) DXT laughs. "All of that sounds like torture."

Bell Labs vocoder engineer Ralph LaRue Miller at age thirty-two. (Courtesy Ralph Miller)

I mention what Ralph Miller had said to me about the sneak pulse. DXT looks at me like I should know. "'Crosstalk can sneak in between the pulse,' huh? You know what he's talking about, don't you? This stuff is really fresh."

This stuff is really fresh? "Yeah. This stuff. Is really fresh. The vocoder was pulses. Crosstalk can occur as feedback. 'This stuff is really frrrresh' is feedback. It's signal leakage. He was holding your wrist, right? The pulse. Feedback is the crosstalk. From one mad scientist to another, you tell him I know exactly what he's talking about."

THIS STUFF IS REALLY SCHRAFFT'S

This is graveyard stuff.
— FDR

The Museum of Cryptology in Fort Meade, Maryland, was once a motel dinner theater. In 1994, the NSA converted the Colony 7 Motor Inn into a museum due to concerns that guests had been conducting surveillance. Rooms used for "logistics," to spy on the spies, have been leveled, and the swimming pool is now tarped and fenced. A replica of the German ENIGMA machine broken by Alan Turing is on display in the motel lobby. Part of the dining room now holds a replica of the wooden presidential seal that Leon Theremin used to bug the US Embassy in Moscow.

The SIGSALY decoy stands over in Schrafft's Cocktail Lounge, a massive wooden vocoder façade, once unspoken now unreal. After the war, the equipment was either cannibalized by other projects or destroyed and chucked into the Chesapeake Bay, waiting to be salvaged by some decompressed gangster duck. The vocoder that sang "Barnacle Bill" could now be serving as a synthetic reef. Meanwhile, the last oscillator sits in storage behind a repurposed motel in Fort Meade.

Across from the wooden turntables, a golden dummy SIGGRUV rests on crushed blue velvet. The 16-inch disk next to it is a real record, rumored to have been taken from a Lutheran Hour Sunday Service in Kansas City, Missouri, now playing the role of SIGGRUV.

Frank Gentges on the HY-2 vocoder, NSA Museum of Cryptology, 2009. "Intelligence is people who sit quietly in little rooms, listening."

I'm at the museum with Frank Gentges, retired vocoder engineer for the Navy. Frank has a droll, owlish disposition and could pass for a crypto-Santa. He once defined intelligence as people sitting quietly in little rooms, listening.

After Dave Coulter passed away in 2004, Frank became the sole principal of Metavox, Inc., a laboratory in Great Falls, Virginia, located next to an indoor Go-Kart track. He is now working on an ultrasonic dental scooper—to penetrate dry wall for hostage simulation training—and a device that teaches you how to read with the left brain while distracting the right brain with music. There was something else about a hotel that's going to be launched into outer space, but I didn't catch it all.

Frank acknowledges the SIGSALY exhibit with a curt sniff and moves on to Vietnam, where everything is real. "Now, this is a heavy, dude," he

Gentges dismantles the HY-2 vocoder, a speech digitizer deployed during the Vietnam War, at the Museum of Cryptology. Gentges and his late partner Dave Coulter designed vocoders independent of the NSA, causing some consternation.

says, pointing at the HY-2, the main vocoder used in Saigon. The formant vocoders that Frank and his friend Dave Coulter designed for the Navy are now moth-balled in a classified NSA warehouse, along with the speech-synth EVA. I ask what my chances are of seeing any of it, and Frank asks if I remember the scene at the end of *Raiders of the Lost Ark*—the Nazi face-melt. "They won't even tell you where the warehouse is."

We move from Vietnam to an encased display of office phones—the STU-II and STU-III—both of which are a Pentagon standard. The display includes a photograph of George W. Bush receiving a call at the Emma Booker Elementary School in Sarasota, Florida, on the morning of September 11, 2001.

Does the STU-III still have some vocoder in it? "You're getting into an electro-political situation here. It's a vocoder, but they can't call it that. Vocoders have a bad reputation because nobody wanted to listen to a damn robot. Some people's ears are built different than the rest of us. We call them Vocoder Haters. It's maybe ten percent of the population."

Frank still calls a vocoder a vocoder. Last Halloween, he aimed his massive theater speaker out toward the lake behind his house and articulated some dungeon-rack moans through a vocoder. Scared the neighborhood to death. "Kids thought the lake was haunted."

OPPOSITE PAGE: Frank Gentges listens to dead air while getting reacquainted with the HY-2 vocoder. Gentges would occasionally respond to sensitive questions by saying, "I can answer that using zero sentences."

He is now addressing a wall of phones, an interactive exhibit where one can listen to Secure Voice clips throughout history. We run through the loop several times, facing each other on the phone. I'm excited to hear that the KO-6 sounds like the F-4000. Frank is disappointed with the HY-2, a problem with the transformation from voiced to unvoiced. I hang up and he says:

"Quick! Pick up! Pick up!" So I pick up.

"Shhh!" he whispers. "Listen. I can make that voice better."

As Frank Gentges tells me this, I notice that his hand is covering the receiver.

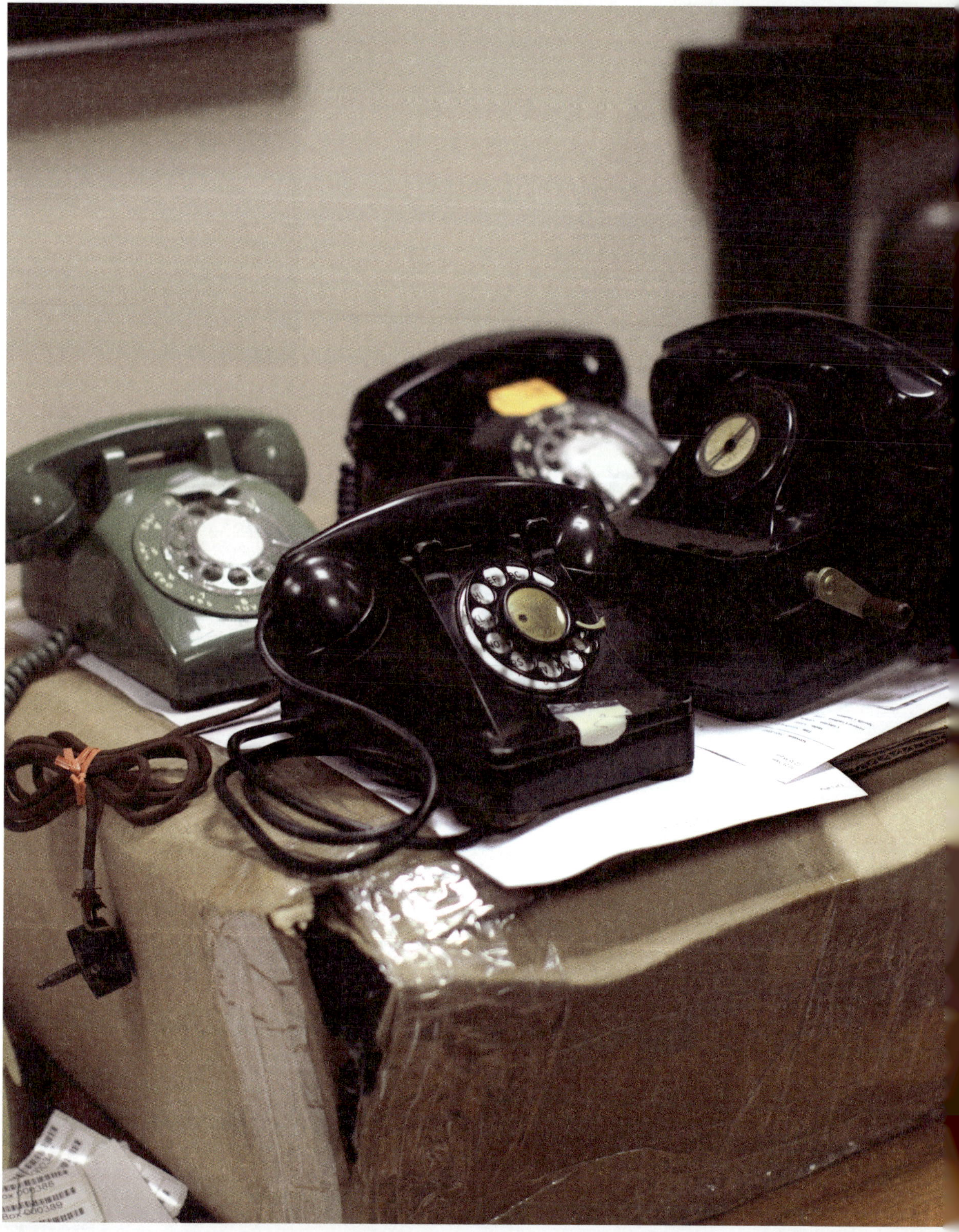

EPILOGUE:

I WAS LIKE

You couldn't fool your mother on the foolingest day of your life
if you had an electrified fooling machine.
— Homer Simpson

In the spring of 2005, I visit my niece's fifth-grade class in upstate New York. Since she's eleven years old, hers is a world where speech is highly destructible and better off for it. The word *like* has become a speaking mechanism itself, a mimetic filter. (Nothing is what it is.) This chatty substitute, its "likeness," is often compressed through cell phones as a digital replica of the vocal tract, a binary of buzz and hiss.

Today we're going to play Telephone and build a scrambler out of twenty-two kid brains. I number each student and ask them to write what they hear, or what they think they hear, so the words can be traced through the homophonic wash. Attention spans are somewhere between Mars and dinosaurs. The controls are shaky when the objective is gibberish.

Number 4 wears ladybug sandals. Number 7 chews on a clipboard. There's a picture of a meteor above the head of Number 11 who happens to have a pencil up his nose. Number 13 has a calculator on his watch. Number 5 is in a Colonial hairnet and Number 6 looks like she just rollerskated through the Phantom Tollbooth. Number 22 is new and genuinely not suspicious. My niece, Berenice, is Number 1 with tangled mermaid hair and a purple giraffe shirt. Her dad once tried to change her brain with a TV remote and she told him to walk away from his weirdness, slowly. She thinks the vocoder in "Pack Jam" sounds like Golem (Precious Golem, not the Yiddish man-of-clay Golem).

At a dinner the weekend before, I consulted some friends on how to record the experiment without the class knowing. Suggestions ranged from hiding a minidisk player inside a banana pudding to wiring myself in a bear suit. "If you walk in there wearing a bear suit, they're going to jump on you," said my friend who wanted to bug a stuffed penguin. "It takes them eight hours to write a sentence," said another. "When do they realize things happen when they're not looking? Little kids can't whisper!"

When the big day comes, the class insists on being allowed to "call Operator" once and have the phrase repeated. I start them off easy with "This stuff is really fresh." It scuttles from ear to ear, a new invention in each smile. Even when kids are thinking, they make noise. The rasp of paper, erasers tapping teeth, tongues walking on roofs, popping double-time tocks, faces cracking up into fingers grazed by stray ink. A purple formula for Space Rock fizz.

7 calls Operator. 10 apparently thinks his clipboard is a trumpet. The pencil has now completely disappeared into 11's nose. 6 says, "Don't sneeze!" 9 calls Operator. 8 goes back to 9, forgets "stuff" and just says "fresh." 15 thinks she heard him. 17's antenna is up. Security leak in a thought balloon. Now half the class is mouthing "stuff" and "fresh" to one another. Teacher says, Shush. The code is broken. "Even if you know what it is, write down what you hear," says 22, sticking to the program. Good ol' 22. We like 22. I collect the scraps of paper and read the results. This stuff is very fresh. This stuff is very red. This stuff is really sad. In fact, 14 through 21 all think this stuff is really sad. Then it's 22 to the rescue with "diss snuff" and "flesh."

Ladybug Sandals thinks this stuff is really easy. 15 asks if she's supposed to spell out the sputters. Now they're into it, ready for Round Two. I whisper to my niece. Crosstalk can sneak in between the—"Operator!!" Oh, good grief.

Pulse. She looks at me. *Are you serious?* Just go with it. *Whatever!*

This time the switchboard goes Lite Brite. "Shhhh!" "I bet that's not what he said." "That's what I heard." "Like it's not supposed to make sense!" "Well, maybe it does." "It's *soooo* random!"

I scan the bookshelf, trying not to spy. *Time Warp Trio, A Light in the Attic, Bitefinger Baby, The War with Grandpa*. I check back with the circuit. They're now flashing messages on the backs of their clipboards, mostly anti–Red Sox propaganda. 22, bless his bed-head, still takes the game seriously. His message reads, "Shhhhhhhhhh. Don't say a word!" after a drawing of a three-eyed rabbit.

Crosstalk has finally passed through, more or less, and the class is excited to show off their results.

Cross dog can sneak in between the posts. Cross Dog and Sneak Bear between the bone. Sneakers ding between the mount. Snickers smuck beet ween ya mouth. Sniffy sweep Taco Bell.

A snicker from the Margin of Error. 11 stands up and goes Ralph Wiggum: "I got Mystery Man!" Somewhere between 8 and 12, I hear the words "alligator music." I see my research funding getting cut off, plunging down the embankment in a poof of flames. The Taco Bell business is dropped and, mercifully, someone at the bottom of the order, maybe 20, sets things right: "Pea see sweet cherry bells." Then 22, our best closer: "DDT Cherry Bales." The back of his paper says, "Dude, where's my tornado?" His teacher wonders how she's going to turn her class back into a class.

Afterward, they throw their hands in the air. "What's your book about?" *It's about the vocoder.* "What's your book about?" *A machine invented by the phone company that makes you talk like a robot.* "Huh??" *Your grandpa's sore throat?* "Will it be for children?" *It's got frogs and robots.*

Later that night, my niece listens to the end of "Change the Beat," eyebrows up, seaweed tangled in headphones. "Who are these people? Why did they say that?!"

I have no idea.

Word is bear.

APPENDIX

FUTURE BEAT ALLIANCE

Author's Future Beat Alliance certificate, arrived by mail from Tommy Boy Records, September 1984.

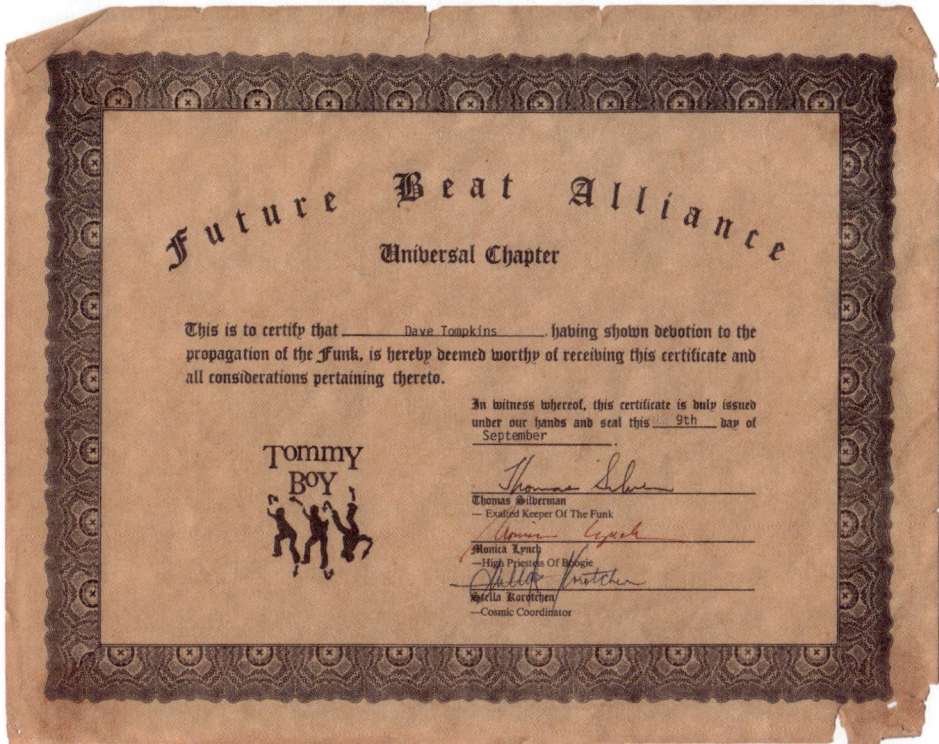

Future Beat Alliance

Universal Chapter

This is to certify that _____ Dave Tompkins _____ having shown devotion to the propagation of the Funk, is hereby deemed worthy of receiving this certificate and all considerations pertaining thereto.

In witness whereof, this certificate is duly issued under our hands and seal this __9th__ day of September _____ .

TOMMY BOY

Thomas Silverman
Thomas Silverman
— Exalted Keeper Of The Funk

Monica Lynch
Monica Lynch
— High Priestess Of Boogie

Stella Korotchen
Stella Korotchen
— Cosmic Coordinator

IT'S NOT THE END OF THE WORLD

Some Final Thoughts on Auto-Tune

In 1963, the Nuclear Limited Test Ban Treaty between the Soviet Union, Britain and the United States prohibited the detonation of nuclear weapons in "the general atmosphere." Outer space and underwater were off limits as well. Though subterranean testing was permitted, distinguishing between an earthquake and a warhead exploding underground was a problem. Bell Labs would resolve the dilemma with the Cepstrum (the "C" is hard), aka "Quefrency," a method for gauging reflections from the earth's core. With the Quefrency geophysicists could differentiate between nuking a buried Pac-Man cartridge in the desert and the Golden Gate Bridge doing a sine wave. Bell Labs would use a computerized model of Cepstrum frequency peaks to determine a pitch frequency for Manfred Schroeder's Voice-Excited Vocoder. Instead of magma reflections, engineers could measure the glottal puffs of air between speech—or pitch "periods." According to Bell, the Voice-Excited Vocoder would be the first speaking machine to sound human, thanks to a boost from the Cold War arms race.

The Cepstrum's main principle, autocorrelation, uses sound to measure seismo-acoustic reflections for mapping oil prospects. Autocorrelation would beget Auto-Tune, a pitch corrective implant invented in 1996 by former Exxon engineer Andy Hildebrand, and now sold by his company Antares. Similar to how Homer Dudley envisioned the vocoder, Auto-Tune can airbrush a defective singer—not by swapping vocal tracts, a trick Bell Labs would call "Digital Decapitation"—but by putting notes in their proper place. Auto-Tune knows where the vocal pitch is located at all times. Hildebrand says the vocoder "has no such knowledge" of a singer's pitch, an ignorance that favors the tin can in the freak pants, especially if he or she can play keyboards.

Auto-Tune is better known for its imperfection, a quality more human than robotic. (Robotic is the world in which everyone sings perfectly without even knowing it.) Set the retune function to zero and the pitch seems to be scaled instantaneously rather than a natural slide between notes, resulting in hyperactive birdcall tremolo, a jagged melisma.

In a sense, Exxon could be held accountable for the reinvention of Cher, who proved that believing in life after love after age fifty was a simple matter of geophysics, artificial enhancement and abused technology. As a 13-year-old from Yemen once told me: "The people singing the songs aren't really singing the songs." So the adolescent listener reconstructs the voice with his own off-key pipes.

Auto-Tune can't sit still any more than afterschool hormones. Maybe it appeals to kids because they're undergoing a transformation of their own, their voices modulating all over the pitch scale, their speech ambushed by puberty. At times, the frog won't let go.

Auto-Tune is the jitters—that teenage love hysteria, where the highs and lows are no less drastic than the dips and spikes of pitch-scale melodrama. (My favorite T-Pain song is "Calm the F**k Down.") That first heartbreak is the end of the world. It's not robotic. It is fickle and aflutter and it seems to be happening all at once. Retune to set zero. That parental back-pat—"one day you're going to meet someone *really* special"—means nothing. The present is histrionics. The moment, all over the place.

As the voice of pop radio, Auto-Tune is there for the confusing identity siege that is junior high. Faheem Rasheed Najm is T-Pain. T-Pain is Auto-Tune. Auto-Tune is a vocoder. (T-Pain said so.) I Am T-Pain is an App. You are T-Pain. T-Pain is a brand. No sooner did Jay-Z call for Auto-Tune's head after seeing Wendy's use it to sell a Frosty, than Apple made the I Am T-Pain app available for $2.99. As demonstrated on the Champion DJ track, "Baako," babies can now be Auto-Tuned before reaching intelligibility.

A client recently asked Andy Hildebrand if the world's problems could be represented as notes on a grid, could the right Auto-Tune algorithm wrangle them "in-tune." On the popular YouTube clip "Auto-Tuning the News," someone already attempted reducing nuclear weapons in a pop song and failed. So it's back to set zero. Return to the magma that heard it all before and sent it back. *Here, you take it.*

HOW TO RECOGNIZE A PEACHTREE FREAK

I've included here a supplementary list of 80 vocoder songs not mentioned in the book—mostly disco, electrofunk, boogie and laser lust. Atlanta's Geno Jordan is first, in honor of the giant Peachoid water tower just off 85-South in Gaffney, South Carolina. The vocoder versions of "In-A-Gadda-Da-Vida" and "Maniac" are not included. Apologies to Jodeci, Mogwai, and Daft Punk.

You're A Peachtree Freak On PEACHTREE STREET — GENO JORDAN — Velvetone Records

1 | GENO JORDAN
YOU'RE A PEACHTREE FREAK ON PEACHTREE STREET (PART III)
(Velvetone)

2 | NEWCLEUS
COMPUTER AGE
(4-track/13-minute version, unreleased)

3 | MAC MALL, MAC DRE & E-40
DREDIO
(Thizz Entertainment)

4 | PHIL COLLINS
IN THE AIR TONIGHT
(Virgin)

5 | MAN PARRISH
MAN-MADE (JAM PONY EXPRESS VERSION)
(Jam Pony)

6 | P BATTERS
BACK DROP (INSTRUMENTAL)
(Gladiator Entertainment)

7 | B+
B BEAT CLASSIC
(West End)

8 | JAZAQ
ALL SYSTEMS GO
(Enjoy)

9 | COLD CRUSH BROTHERS
COLD CRUSH (IT'S US)
(Profile)

10 | CON FUNK SHUN
HIDE AND FREAK
(Polygram)

11 | PETER BAUMANN
THIS DAY
(Virgin)

12 | OUTKAST
SYNTHESIZERS
(La Face)

13 | ABOVE THE LAW
BLACK SUPERMAN
(Ruthless)

14 | PHIL LYNOTT
YELLOW PEARL
(Phonogram)

15 | BBQ BAND
IMAGINATION
(Capitol)

16 | ZEUS B. HELD
EUROPIUM
(Strand)

17 | ROYAL CASH
RADIOACTIVITY
(Sutra)

18 | ADD N TO (X)
KING WASP
(Satellite)

19 | DIETER MOEBIUS AND CONNY PLANK
MISS CACADOU
(Sky)

20 | STEEL MIND
BAD PASSION (DUB)
(Delirium)

21 | ARMENTA
I WANT TO BE WITH YOU (INSTRUMENTAL) (Savoir Faire)

22 | Q
VOICE OF Q
(Philly World)

23 | SYNERGY
PROJECT 5
(Time Traxx)

24 | DXJ & THE BASSOLIANS
BASSOLIAN ATTACK
(Joey Boy)

25 | ESCAPE FROM NEW YORK
SLOW BEAT
(Profile)

26 | THE TOURIST
HOOKED ON YOU (INSTRUMENTAL)
(Reelin and Rockin)

27 | CAPRICORN
CAPRICORN (INSTRUMENTAL)
(Emergency)

28 | TELEX
MOSKOW-DISKOW
(Sire)

29 | THE BROTHERS SUPREME
WE CAN'T BE HELD BACK
(Street Talk)

30 | WUF TICKET
THE KEY (DUB VERSION)
(Prelude)

31 | PHIL COLLINS
I'M NOT MOVING (IDJUT BOYS REMIX)
(Box Office)

32 | MC A.D.E.
HOW MUCH CAN YOU TAKE?
(4-Sight)

33 | HERBIE HANCOCK
TELL EVERYBODY
(Columbia)

34 | G-FORCE
FEEL THE FORCE (INSTRUMENTAL)
(SMI)

35 | THE B BOYS
GIRLS (INSTRUMENTAL)
(Vintertainment)

36 | ANDRE CYMONE
GET IT GIRL
(Columbia)

37 | PEPPERMINT LOUNGE
PERFECT HIGH
(World of Music)

38 | BOSE
SLOW JAM
(Rockwell)

39 | AFRIKA BAMBAATAA
BAMBAATAA'S THEME
(Tommy Boy)

40 | DAYTON
MEET THE MAN
(Monk One Edit) (Capitol)

41 | KEITH SWEAT
**HOW DEEP IS YOUR LOVE
[UNMADE DUB VERSION]** (Elektra)

42 | TOM TOM CLUB
SPOOKS (INSTRUMENTAL)
(Sire)

43 | X-REF
DREAM SIX-0
(Citinite)

44 | IAN BODDY
THE SENTINEL
(New Media)

65 | RODNEY STEPP
BREAK-OUT
(Chique)

66 | PRETTY TONY
JAM THE BOX
(Music Specialist)

67 | MAGIC TRICK
CHECK US OUT
(Orla)

68 | VELOCITY
UNEMPLOYMENT (INSTRUMENTAL)
(Velocity)

69 | BOARDS OF CANADA
**IN A BEAUTIFUL PLACE OUT IN
THE COUNTRY** (Warp)

70 | RICHARDO VILLALOBOS
EASY LEE
(Playhouse)

71 | PYRAMID PLUS
COMIN' AT YA
(Lifeworld)

72 | N.W.A.
PANIC ZONE
(Ruthless)

73 | NIGHTLESS
CRAZY NIGHTS (INSTRUMENTAL)
(Jago)

74 | TOUCHÉ
WRAP IT UP
(Emergency)

75 | CASCO
CYBERNETIC LOVE (INSTRUMENTAL)
(House of Music)

76 | FREESTYLE
PARTY HAS BEGUN
(Music Specialists)

77 | DAZZ BAND
JOY STICK
(Motown)

78 | CABARET VOLTAIRE
COLOURS (CLUB MIX)
(Mute)

79 | NACHO PATROL
**STRATUS CHANT / FUTURISTIC ABBIS
ABBEBAV** (Kindred Spirits)

80 | COSMIC TOUCH
NOTHING EVER CHANGES
DOUG E. FRESH
NUTHIN
(Serious Gold/Reality)

BIBLIOGRAPHY

Indestructible Speech is based on interviews with Ralph Miller, Robert Price, Donald Mehl, Sidney Metzger, Mahlon Doyle, and William Bennett, Jr., as well as those currently archived in the David Kahn Collection at the NSA. I am grateful to Dorothy "Meg" Madsen for sharing SIGSALY anecdotes from her unpublished book *A World War II Memoir*. Information concerning the Sonovox's role in wartime propaganda was sourced from the Jacob Smith essay "Tearing Speech To Pieces."

Ray Bradbury's memories of the World's Fair are based on author interviews and Sam Weller's biography *The Bradbury Chronicles*.

Albuquerque Journal. "Science Speaks Up." December 22, 1940, p20.

Alchemists of Sound. BBC Radiophonic Workshop. Documentary. BBC.

Army Security Agency: European Axis Signal Intelligence In World War II as Revealed by TICOM Investigations and by Other Prisoner of War Interrogations and Captured Material, Principally German. May 1, 1946. Declassified by NSA: June 1, 2009. Army Security Agency, Washington DC. 2009: pp. 37–44.

Ashton, Nigel John. *Kennedy, Macmillan, and the Cold War: The Irony of Interdependence*. Palgrave-Macmillan, 2002.

The Audio Cyclopedia. Howard W. Sams & Co., Inc. Indiana. 1959.

Bell Laboratories. "The New Artificial Larynx." Transactions of the American Academy of Ophthalmology and Otolaryngology. July-August. 1959, p. 548.

Bell Telephone Quarterly. "Presentation to 1939 World's Fair." Bell Telephone Laboratory, 1939.

Bennett, W.R. "Secret Telephony as a Historical Example of Spread-Spectrum Communications." *Spread-Spectrum Communications*. Eds. Charles E. Cook and Fred W. Ellersick. IEE Press, 1983, pp. 50–56.

Berger, Meyer. "First Big Week At The Fair." *New York Times*. May 7, 1939.
— "At the Fair," July 10, 1939
— July 27, 1939
— May 30, 1940

Binder, Otto. *What We Really Know About Flying Saucers*. Fawcett Publications, Inc. 1967.

Birch, J.M, and N.R. Getzin. Voice Coding and Intelligibility Testing for a Satellite-Based Air Traffic Control System. April 1971. Prepared for the Goddard Space Flight Center, Greenbelt, Maryland. Unpublished.

Boak, David G. "A History of US Communications Security." The David G. Boak Lectures. National Security Agency. 1973.

Boone J.V., and R.R. Peterson. "The Start of the Digital Revolution: SIGSALY—Secure Digital Voice Communications in World War II." NSA. July 2000.

Bradbury, Ray. *The Martian Chronicles*. Bantam. New York, 1950.

Bradbury, Ray. "The Murderer." *Golden Apples of the Sun*. Bantam. 1953.

Bradbury, Ray. *Something Wicked This Way Comes*. Avon, 1962.

Brewster, Sir David. *Letters On Natural Magic*. Harper and Brothers. New York, 1839.

Briscoe Desmond, and Roy Curtis-Bramwell. *The BBC Radiophonic Workshop: The First 25 Years*. British Broadcasting Corporation, 1983: 89, 33, 141.

Campbell, Joseph P., Jr. and Richard A. Dean. "A History of Secure Voice Coding." *Digital Signal Processing*. July 1993.

Campion, Chris. "The Rammellzee. Bi-Conicals of the Rammellzee." *The Observer*. February 22, 2004.

Capek, Karel. *War With the Newts*. Berkeley Publishing Corporation. New York. 1937.

Christian Science Monitor. "Talking Soapsuds on Air? Blame It on the Sonovox." September 2, 1941, p.4. (Via Jacob Smith.)

Christiansen H.M., Schweizer L., Sethy A., Hoffenreich F. "New Correlation Vocoder." *The Journal of the Acoustical Society of America*. 1966, p.614-620.

Cohen, John. *Human Robots in Myth and Science*. A.S. Barnes and Company. South Brunswick and New York, 1967.

Dahl, Roald. *Over To You*. Penguin Books. Middlesex, England. 1945.

Daumal, René. *A Night of Serious Drinking*. Shambhala, 1979. p.121.

David, Jr., Edward E. "Ears for Computers." *Scientific American*. February 1955

Davies, Lawrence E. "Machine that Talks and Sings Has Tryout; Electrical Voder Will Speak At Fair Here." *New York Times*. January 6, 1939, p.1.

"Detailed Feuerstein Technical Project Report: Technical Interrogation of Feuerstein Employees Dr. Fritz Sennheiser, Wolfgang Martini and Dr. Martin Zappe." A TICOM Publication. 2009.

"Detailed Feuerstein Technical Project Report: Artificial Speech and Encoding." A TICOM Publication. 2009.

Dickinson, Kay. "Believe? Vocoders, digitized female identity and camp." *Popular Music*.

Dickson, Gordon R. "Computers Don't Argue." *Analogue*. 1965.

Dobbs, Michael. *One Minute To Midnight*. Knopf, New York, 2008.

Dolar, Mladen. *A Voice and Nothing More*. MIT Press. Cambridge, Massachusetts. 2006.

Dudley, Homer. "The Carrier Nature of Speech." *The Bell System Technical Journal*. October 1940, pp. 495-515.

Dudley, Homer. Lab notebook. AT&T Archives.

Dudley, Homer. "Fundamentals of Speech Synthesis." Journal of the Audio Engineering Society. October 1955, pp. 170–185.

Dudley, Homer. "System for the Artificial Production of Vocal or Other Sounds." US Patent 2,121,142. Filed April 7, 1937. Granted June 21, 1938.

Dudley, Homer. "System for the Artificial Production of Vocal or Other Sounds." US Patent 2,243,089. Filed May 13, 1939. Granted May 27, 1941.

Dudley, Homer. "System for the Artificial Production of Vocal or Other Sounds." US Patent 2,339, 465. Filed July 10, 1942. Granted January 18, 1944.

Dudley, Homer, Riesz, R.R., Watkins S.S.A. "A Synthetic Speaker." Bell Telephone System Technical Publications. August 3, 1939, pp.1-26.

Ellison, Harlan. *I Have No Mouth and I Must Scream*. Pyramid, 1974.

Fagen, M.D. Ed. *A History of Engineering & Science in the Bell System: National Service in War and Peace*. Bell Telephone Laboratories, Inc. New York. 1978.

Fant, Gunnar. *Acoustic Theory of Speech Production with Calculations Based on X-Ray Studies of Russian Articulations*. Mouton, 1970.

"Final Report on the Technical Exploitation of the Feuerstein Laboratory (Director: Dr. Oskar Vierling) carried out by a Special Team under TICOM auspices." A TICOM Publication. 2009.

Firestone, F.A. "An Artificial Larynx for Speaking and Choral Singing for One Person." *The Journal of the Acoustical Society of America*. January 1940, pp. 357–361.

Foreign Relations of the United States: Diplomatic Papers 1945. Volume III. European Advisory Commission; Austria; Germany. House Document No. 777, Vol. III. 79th Congress, 2nd Session. United States Government Printing Office. Washington. 1968.

Frere-Jones, Sasha. "The Gerbil's Revenge." *The New Yorker*. June 9, 2008.

Friedlaender, Salomo. "Goethe spricht in den Phonographen." Das Nachthemd am Wegweiser und andere hochst merkwurdige Geschichten des Dr. Salomo Friedlaender. 1916. Berlin.

Gardner, Warren, and Harold, Harris. "Aids for Laryngectomees." *Archives of Laryngology*. Vol. 73. February 1961.

Gelernter, David. *1939: The Lost World of the Fair*. The Free Press. New York. 1995, p.98.

Gerard, Philip. *Secret Soldiers*. Dutton. New York. 2002.

Gifford, Denis. *A Pictorial History of Horror Films*. Hamlyn, 1973.

Goode, Richard. "The development of an improved artificial larynx." Transactions of the American Academy of Ophthalmology and Otolaryngology. April 1969.

Graves, James. "On the Causes of Failure of Deep Sea Cables." *Journal of the Society of Telegraph Engineers and Electricians*, No. 51. 1884. Via: Covey, Jacob. Beasts! Fantagraphics. 2008.

Greene, Carol. *The New True Book of Robots*. Scholastic Library, 1983.

Harryhausen, Ray and Tony Dalton. *An Animated Life*. Billboard. 2003.

Heinlein, Robert. *Between Planets*. Ace, 1951.

Hodges, Andrew. *The Enigma*. First Touchstone Edition. Simon & Schuster, Inc. 1984, pp.251–252, 452.

Hopewell Herald. "Versatile Daddy of Pedro the Voder. Goldarnedest Thing You Ever Heard." February 28, 1940. p.3.

Juster, Norton. *The Phantom Tollbooth*. Alfred A. Knopf. 1961.

Kahn, David. "Cryptology and the origin of spread spectrum." *IEE Spectrum*. September 1984, pp.70–80.

Kahn, David. *The Codebreakers*. The Macmillan Company. Toronto, Ontario. 1967.

Kahn, David. *Hitler's Spies*. Da Capo, 1978.

Kahn, David. SIGSALY Collection, NSA.

Karpf, Anne. *The Human Voice*. Bloomsbury. 2006.

Kittler, Friedrich A. *Gramophone, Film, Typewriter*. Ed. Timothy Lenoir and Hans Ulrich Gumbrecht. Stanford University Press. Stanford, California, 1999.

Krause, Kai. "Sound Effect Vocoder VSM 201." Sennheiser. 1979.

Lanza, Joseph. *Elevator Music: A Surreal History of Muzak, Easy-Listening and Other Moodsong*. St. Martin's, 2004.

Lem, Stanislaw. *The Futurological Congress*. Avon, 1974.

London Times. "The Speaking Automaton." August 12, 1846. (Via Patrick Feaster)

Lovecraft, H.P. *The Dunwich Horror and Other Weird Tales*. Armed Services Edition. Est. by the Council of Books on Wartime, New York. Arkham House, Sauk City, 1943.

Lovecraft, H.P. "The Whisperer in Darkness." *Weird Tales*. 1931.

Lowry, Louis D. "Artificial larynges: a review and development of a prototype self-contained intra-oral artificial larynx." *The Laryngoscope*. August 1981. pp.1332–1355.

Maclean, Fitzroy. *Eastern Approaches*. Little, Brown & Company. New York. 1949.

Maloney, Russell. "Pedro Marches On." *The New Yorker*. December 25, 1943, p.12.

Nebeker, Frederik. "Manfred Schroeder Interview." IEE History Center. University of Rutgers. August 2, 1994.

Major, Eugene. "Mission Possible: Keeping Wartime Secrets." *Encore*. Spring 1988, pp.14-15.

Matheson, Richard. "'Tis The Season To Be Jelly." *The Magazine of Fantasy and Science Fiction*. Mercury Press, Inc., 1963.

Mathes, R.C. "Vocoder: 1939-1945." Bell Labs Vocoder Bible." A bound collection of memorandum given to Ralph Miller.

Mehl, Donald E. *Top Secret Communications of World War II*. 2002. Self-published. Raymore, Missouri.

Meyer-Eppler, Werner. Synthetische Sprache. Im SWF, Baden-Baden. (Typoskript und Klangtonband.) 1954.

Miller, Walter M., Jr. *A Canticle For Leibowitz*. Lippincott. 1959.

Mitchell, D. "Notes on the History of Speech Privacy Systems." Bell Telephone Laboratories. Inter-Departmental Memorandum. June 3, 1970.

McDonough, Jimmy. *Shakey*. First Anchor. 2002.

Montefiore, Simon Sebag. *Stalin: The Court of the Red Tsar*. Vintage Books. New York. 2003, pp. 329, 453, 527.

Nebraska State Journal. "Newly Invented Talking Machine Creates Speech." January 6, 1939.

New York Times. "Machine Tears Speech to Pieces And Remakes It in Varied Forms." May 17, 1939.
— "Machine That Talks and Sings Has Tryout." January 6, 1939.
— "Many Try to Get Free Long-Distance Call—Robot Sings." May 13, 1940.
— "A Perfect Back-Talker." July 2, 1939.
— "Phone Men Called Welfare Pioneers." September 23, 1939.—"Preview Is Given at Phone Exhibit." April 28, 1939.
— "Robot Device Developed by Bell Telephone Which 'Reads Out Loud' as Aid to the Blind." March 15, 1947.
— "The Wall that Talks Like A Man." August 13, 1939.
— "Voder Talks for Experts." April 20, 1941.

Newscom. "Voder-Vocoder." ITT Communications Systems, Inc. May 1963, pp. 6–7.

Newsweek. "Talking Cows" Vol. 20. July 20, 1942.

O' Neill, John J. "The Voder Learns To Sing." *Washington Post*. February 22, 1942.

Panin, Dimitri. *The Notebooks of Sologdin*. Harcourt Brace, 1973. p. 264, 267.

Perkins, Frederic Beecher. *Devil-Puzzlers and Other Stories*. G.P Putnam's Sons. New York. 1877.

Porter, Bruce, and Marvin Dunn. *The Miami Riot of 1980*. Lexington Books. Lexington, Massachusetts. 1984.

Potter, Ralph K. "Secret Telephony." US Patent 3,967,067. Filed: September 24, 1941. Granted: June 29, 1976.

Price, Robert. "Further Notes and Anecdotes on Spread-Spectrum Origins." *Spread-Spectrum Communications*. Eds. Charles E. Cook and Fred W. Ellersick. IEE Press, 1983, pp. 37–49.

Price, Robert. Personal correspondences. The David Kahn Collection. NSA.

Pynchon, Thomas. *Gravity's Rainbow*. Viking Press. 1973.

Robinson, Florett. "Roe-but or Rah-but." *New York Times*. July 23, 1934.

Roctober. Robot Rock & Roll Issue #30. Spring 2001.

Rokus, Josef W. *The Professionals: The History of the Phu Lam, Vietnam Army Communications Base*. Xlibris. February 2002.

Ronell, Avital. *The Telephone Book: Technology, Schizophrenia, Electric Speech*. University of Nebraska Press. 1989.

Scammell, Michael. *Solzhenitsyn: A Biography*. Norton. 1984.

Scholtz, R.A. "The Origins of Spread-Spectrum Communications." *Spread-Spectrum Communications*. Eds. Charles E. Cook and Fred W. Ellersick. IEE Press, 1983, pp. 2-33.

Scholtz, R.A. "Notes on Spread-Spectrum History." *Spread-Spectrum Communications*. Eds. Charles E. Cook and Fred W. Ellersick. IEE Press, 1983, pp. 34–36.

Schroeder, Manfred. *Computer Speech: Recognition, Compression, Synthesis*. Springer Series in Information Sciences. 1999.

SIGSALY 805th Signal Co. Selected Correspondence, Reports and Orders. Feb. 1942-Nov.1946. NSA.

SIGSALY Detachment Histories, Freedom-Algiers. NSA.

SIGSALY Technical Manual: RC-251 TI, NSA.

SIGSALY Technical Manual: RC-220 TI, NSA.

Silverberg, Robert. *Songs of Summer and Other Stories*. Harper, 1955.

Smith, Jacob. "Tearing Speech To Pieces." *MSMI*. Autumn 2008.

Solzhenitsyn, Alexander. *The First Circle*. Harper & Row, Publishers. New York. 1968, p.ix, 50,137.

Starr, Richard. "E-Mails from a Traitor." *The Weekly Standard*. December 9, 2001.

Sugrue, Thomas J. *The Origins of Urban Crisis*. Princeton University Press. 1996.

Sturgeon, Theodore. "The Pod in the Barrier." *Galaxy*. September 1957.

Tchobanou, Mikhail K. and Nikolay N. Udalov. "Vladimir Kotelnikov and Moscow Power Engineering Institute— Sampling Theorem, Radar Systems." Moscow Power Engineering Institute. Moscow, Russia.

Thackeray, William Makepeace. "The Speaking Machine." *Punch*. 1846. (Via Patrick Feaster)

Ungeheurer, Elena. *Wie die elektronische Musik erfunden wurde*. Schott. New York. 1992.

"Telephone link between the Prime Minister and the U.S. President 1961–63." British National Archives.

Weller, Sam. *The Bradbury Chronicles*. William Morrow. New York. 2005.

Wells, H.G. *World Set Free*. Macmillan, 1914.

Williams, Edgar. "D-Day countdown recalled by one who helped it happen." *Philadelphia Inquirer*. June 6, 1988.

Williams, P-Frank. "California Loved." *New Times LA*. August 1-7, 2002.

Williams, Greer. "The Graphic Laboratory of Popular Science." *Chicago Tribune*. July 21, 1940, p. G8.

Yoder, Robert M. "How to Talk Like a Cow from Boston." *Saturday Evening Post*. June 5, 1943. p.11.

ART BIBLIOGRAPHY

All illustrations by Kevin Christy

7   Bombs provided by Dave Hogan. Photograph by Michael Waring

11   Korg VC-10 Vocoder provided by Jason Merenda. Photograph by Michael Waring

AXIS OF EAVESDROPPERS

16   Courtesy National Archives, SIGSALY, Record Group 111/ via Mahlon Doyle

19   Courtesy NSA

21   Cutmaster DC (Courtesy Chris LaSalle and Dave Funkenklein);
Copyright 1983, Capitol Records;
Copyright 1982, Tears of Fire Records;
Afrika Bambaataa (Photo by Paul Natkin/WireImage)

25   Courtesy National Archives, SIGSALY, Record Group 111/ via Mahlon Doyle

NEARLY ENOUGH LIKE THAT WHICH GAVE THEM BIRTH

33   Courtesy AT&T Archives and History Center

35   Courtesy AT&T Archives and History Center

36   Courtesy AT&T Archives and History Center

37   Courtesy AT&T Archives and History Center

38   Courtesy AT&T Archives and History Center; color images by David Black with permission of AT&T Shannon Labs.

39   Photograph by David Black

40   Courtesy AT&T Archives and History Center

41   Photograph by David Black

42   Courtesy of the Audio Engineering Society

43   Courtesy AT&T Archives and History Center

44   Photography by Michael Waring (Courtesy Ralph Miller)

45   Photography by Michael Waring (Courtesy Ralph Miller)

47   Courtesy Patrick Feaster (Euphonia)

48   Copyright 1951, Ace Books

51   Courtesy AT&T Archives and History Center

INDESTRUCTIBLE SPEECH

54   Photograph by Michael Waring (Courtesy Ralph Miller)

56   Courtesy AT&T Archives and History Center

57   Courtesy National Archives, SIGSALY, Record Group 111/via Mahlon Doyle

58   Photograph by Dan Winters

59   Alan Turing (By kind permission of the Provost and Fellows, King's College, Cambridge)

60   Courtesy National Archives, SIGSALY, Record Group 111/via Mahlon Doyle

61   Photograph by David Black

62   Courtesy National Archives, SIGSALY, Record Group 111/via Mahlon Doyle

63   Courtesy National Archives, SIGSALY, Record Group 111/ via Mahlon Doyle

65   Courtesy *Scientific American*

66   Winston Churchill © Bettmann/CORBIS

67 Fitzroy Maclean (AP Photo/files)

69 Courtesy National Archives, SIGSALY, Record Group 111/via Mahlon Doyle

70 Courtesy Don Mehl and NSA

71 Courtesy National Archives, SIGSALY, Record Group 111/ via Mahlon Doyle

72 Photography by David Black

73 Courtesy National Archives, SIGSALY, Record Group 111/ via Mahlon Doyle

VOCODER KOMMISSAR

77 Joseph Stalin (AP Photo)

78 Alexander Solzhenitsyn © Nobelstiftelsen

83 Photograph by Michael Waring

AS IT IS, ON MARS

86 Copyright 1950, Bantam Books

88 Courtesy BBC

91 Courtesy EMS

COLOR OUT OF SPACE

96 Courtesy Pandisc Music Corp. Copyright 1985 Pandisc Music Corp

97 Photograph by Michael Waring (Courtesy Michael Jonzun)

98 Courtesy Michael Jonzun

99 Copyright 1982, Boston International

100 Copyright 1988, Pandisc Music Corp.

101 Courtesy Michael Jonzun

103 Courtesy Bill Sebastian

106 Courtesy Michael Jonzun

107 Copyright 1980, Emergency Records

108 Copyright 1985, Critique Records; Copyright 1983, Tommy Boy Records

110 Courtesy Tommy Boy Records

111 Courtesy Michael Jonzun and Dennis Ackerman

112 Copyright 1974, Pyramid Books

113 Courtesy Tommy Boy Records (Hua Hsu collection)

114 Courtesy Alan Nahigan

116 Photography by David Black

117 Photograph by David Black

118 Photography by David Black

119 Photograph by David Black

120 Photography by David Black

121 Photograph by David Black

THE SACRED THUNDER CROAK

124 Courtesy AT&T Archives and History Center

126 Reproduced, with permission, from *Transactions of the American Academy of Ophthalmology and Otolaryngology*, "New Artificial Larynx," Volume 63, American Academy of Ophthalmology, 1959

127 Courtesy Audio Engineering Society

128 Image courtesy the Ralph Rinzler Folklife Archives and Collections, Smithsonian Institution

129 Reprinted with permission from F.A. Firestone "An Artificial Larynx for Speaking and Choral Singing for One Person." *The Journal of the Acoustical Society of America*. January, 1940, pp. 357–361. Copyright *The Journal of the Acoustical Society of America*, 1940, Acoustical Society of America

130 Copyright 1976, East Anglican Productions

131 Copyright 1941, Capitol Records

133 Reprinted with permission from F.A. Firestone "An Artificial Larynx for Speaking and Choral Singing for One Person." *The Journal of the Acoustical Society of America.* January,1940, pp. 357–361. Copyright *The Journal of the Acoustical Society of America*, 1940, Acoustical Society of America

138 Photograph by Paul Eagle

143 Copyright 1983, Capitol Records

144 Copyright 1984, Slaughter Sound Music, High Altitude Records

146 Courtesy Vincent Calloway

147 Courtesy Vincent Calloway

INTERDICTION

152 Courtesy NSA

153 Photograph by NBCU Photo Bank via AP Images

155 Courtesy AT&T Archives and History Center

156 Courtesy Frank Gentges and Dave Coulter

157 Courtesy Frank Gentges and Dave Coulter

158 Courtesy Archives, Museum of Science and Industry, Chicago

160 Courtesy Wendy Carlos

161 Courtesy AT&T Archives and History Center

162 Copyright 1967, Odyssey Records (Courtesy Patrick James Longo)

163 Photography by Michael Waring

164 Photograph by David Black

167 Photography by David Black

VIETNAM, VERBOT AND CLEAR

171 Courtesy AT&T Archives and History Center

172 Photograph by David Black

173 Photography by David Black

174 Richard Nixon Bettmann/CORBIS

175 Copyright 1963, Lancer Books

176 Copyright 1983, Fantasy Records (Courtesy Dave Hogan)

179 Copyright, 1985, Express Records

180 Courtesy Forrest J. Ackerman

181 Copyright 1983, Fantasy Records

182 Copyright 1978, Tom N Jerry Records

183 Courtesy Siemens Corporate Archives, Munich

185 Courtesy Federal Screw Works

186 Copyright 1976, EMI-Electrola

187 Copyright 1983, Open Library

188 Photography by Michael Waring

189 Copyright 1966, Fontana Records (Courtesy Allen Goodman)

190 Courtesy Siemens Corporate Archives, Munich

193 Reprinted with permission of Fritz Sennheiser

194 Courtesy Klaus Kopacz

195 Akademie der Künste, Berlin, Werner Meyer-Eppler Archive, no. 277

197 Courtesy Florian Schneider and Sebastian Niessen

198 Courtesy EMS-Germany

199 Courtesy EMS-Germany

201 Copyright 1981, EMI-Electrola (Courtesy Gabriele Caroti)

THINK HE SAID HER NAME WAS VOODOO-ON-A-STICK

COOL, AS LONG AS NOBODY HEARS IT

EAT A PLANET AND GO ON TO THE NEXT ONE

274 Copyright 1988, Island Records

277 Photograph by Michael Waring (Tasmanian Devil alarm
clock and *Creature from the Black Lagoon* light set
provided by author)

278 Courtesy Rammellzee

280 Copyright 1971, Avon Books

283 Photograph by Michael Waring

DECOMPRESSION

287 Courtesy Ralph Miller

288 Photography by David Black

289 Photography by David Black

290 Photograph by David Black

291 Photography by David Black

EPILOGUE: I WAS LIKE

292 Photograph by David Black

APPENDIX

301 Tommy Boy Records (provided by author)

304 Copyright 1982, Velvetone Records

INDEX

ACKNOWLEDGEMENTS

Been Real

This book would not have been possible without the contributions and inspiration of the following individuals who passed away before it was completed: John Hughes (for the vocoder mixes and "Pack Jam" support); Forrest J. Ackerman (Gill Man appreciation and letting me photograph the Cylon in his house), William Bennett, Jr. (for sharing anecdotes about his father and Homer Dudley), Malcolm Clarke of the BBC Radiophonic Workshop (Bradburp), Mr. Magic (super-super blast-blast), Rich Cason ("Street Freaks"), Madeleine L' Engel (Tesser).

LCT, aka Gmumbo Jumbo ("Dave, that program is on—the one about the planets crashing into each other and plants living underground on methane gas with the universe and all that stuff you wanted for your book, right?"); CVT (thanks for always coming through and for the Egyptian Lover cassette, Christmas '85); Aiken "See you in seven flips of the puppet's face" Tompkins; Bo; BLT; John Crutchfield (for German translations); Uncle Dick Crutchfield (for eavesdropping on Russian tank commanders cursing their mothers); Lillian Crutchfield; Charles "Pee Wee" Crutchfield (for spying on Soviet jamming stations and swallowing the film in a plane over Moscow); Jacqueline "Pee Wee" Crutchfield ("All you have is your teeth"); the Extra T's; Sommers-Tompkins posse.

James Hughes, for always being a friend and editor, and for hearing out my schemes while this thing mutated like Blatherard Osmo's giant adenoid.

Tina Ibañez, Brett Kilroe and Tracy Boychuk the incredibly patient design wizards at Runner Collective.

JC Gabel and Sybil Perez for getting the word out and support.

Kevin Christy (illustrations), Michael Waring and David Black (photography), Brian Cross (Egyptian Lover photos—looking forward to *Keep In Time: The 808*).

I am grateful to super codebreaker David Kahn for his generosity in sharing his archives. Thank you for saying I was no flibbertigibbet.

Melville House and Kelly Burdick.

Wax Poetics, for originally publishing the Roger Troutman story (Issue 35); Ed Park and *The Believer* for publishing "The Actual History of Synthetic Larynges" (Issue 45).

Stacey "Nate McMillan" Moore for introducing me to "Scorpio."

Pete Relic, for the idea (from the squirrel with the swamp-faced gas mask to the grave of the astro chimp); Hua Hsu, for always being so close to the edit and listening to seven years of vocoder-related freakouts; the filmmaker Betty M. Park; the graphic novelist June Kim; Joseph Patel; Chairman Mao; Jeff Chang (for the Fab Five Freddy interview and portions of the Egyptian Lover interview with Mike Nardone—and support from the beginning); Jon Caramanica (loves "Nasty Rock"); Sasha Frere-Jones and his advocacy for Maurice Starr's "Electric Funky Drummer"; Gabriele "PhG" Caroti; Lily M. Kane ("What's the traps on the halved mouse course?"); Donald Mehl; the O-Dub; Frog; Jessica Wang (broken Transformers, mad support); Piotr Orlov; Kate Glicksberg; Jay Babcock (visit to the Ackermansion); Commander AYS (whatever Just-Ice says at the end of "Cold Getting Dumb"); Henry Paul Hughes.

Monk One; Toshio and the worm-controlled synthesizer; Max Mathews at Bell Labs, Peter Shapiro; Andre Torres and Brian DiGenti at *Wax Poetics*; Rik Davis and Rondo Hatton; Brian Coleman (the drive to see the OVC); Dante; Manfred Schroeder for the title; Ak-B; George Kupcziak at AT&T archives; Ralph LaRue Miller; Barbara Miller; Dodie Miller; David Allen; Rene Stein, grandmaster librarian of the NSA; Veronica at Minimal Wave.

Steinski; Roger Troutman; Afrika Bambaataa; Siemens Archives; Kai Krause; Wendy Carlos; Jared JBX Boxx at Big City; Kathryn Frazier; Robert Price (IEEE); Sacha, Gabe, and Brent at *ego trip*; Eliot Wilson; Russell Fernandez at Princeton Architectural Press; Dave Griffiths and Sara Roy; Kevin DeBernardi; Rammellzee; Grandmixer DXT; Makoto Nagatomo; Michael Jonzun; Silver Fox; Josh Davis; Matt Africa.

Jeremy Rendina; Jacob Smith; Eva Prinz; Holger Czukay; Jason Merenda (supplying the Korg); Kohji Maruyama; Jun Oki; Pat Spring; Dave Hogan (bomb provider); Tom Silverman; Lawrence Young; Paul "Thanks for the Horns and Ideas" C; Patty McKasty; P Brothers (Ivory and Paul S); Bill Sebastian and the OVC; George Mahood; Kym Shingaling Fuller; Torsten Schmidt; Uh-Young; A-1; Lost & Found; Alison Moore; JFK Library.

Noz and Cocaine Blunts; Kiwa Iyobe; Miami; Frank Gentges at Metavox; *Urb*; James Tai; Andy Beta; Edan; "Pack Jam"; Zentner; Doc Strange; Duane Harriot; Turntable Lab; Bekka; Maggotron; Speakerhead; Melville Klein (NSA); Jon Kirby; Jim Dier; Josh Dunn; *The Wire*; The Column; the guy who wrote into *The Wire* and said I was Vanilla Ice; "Being Boiled"; Steve K; Kevin Rafter; Ahmir Thompson; Alex Vaughn; Matt Anderson; Mooney; Tim Ross (Tuba Frenzy); Ray Bradbury; Travis Konkle; Marty Key; Tommy "Here on God's Business" Wright; Elena Ungeheuer; Eric Deal; PCBs; CWP; Hunter "Uncle Wiggily" Alexander; Chris Corwin; Josh Brown; Bernie "Lasers" Nabors; P-Thugg; Howard Huang; Kelly McCraven; Man Parrish; Lester Troutman; Eothen Alopatt; "Planet Caravan"; Mike Nardone; April K.

On the Go; *Grand Royal*; *The Bomb*; *Rap Pages*; Andrew Male; Richard Pleuger; *The Hellstrom Chronicle*; Reggie Dennis; Egyptian Lover and "Planet Rock" backwards; IEEE; Robin Wood; Roland; Christie Z. Pabon at Tools of War; Haskins Speech Laboratories; Sampo; Dan Seltzer; Jeremy Campbell; Matt Radune; Norbert Ryska at Heinz Nixdorf; Klaus Schmeh; Dr. Rudolph Staritz; Florian Schneider; Sebastian Niessen; Bell Telephone Laboratory; Department of Oscillations and Signals Generation at the Moscow Power Institute; the *Dark Crystal* bog burp; bronchitis; the dream about the talking dragon fireplace that used the vocoder from Cosmic Touch's "Nothing Ever Changes" in a cabin in Brevard, NC, where I first played Telephone and lost my hatchet.